IMPLEMENTING STRATEGY

IMPLEMENTING STRATEGY

Lawrence G. Hrebiniak
The Wharton School
University of Pennsylvania

William F. Joyce
Amos Tuck School
Dartmouth College

Macmillan Publishing Company
New York
Collier Macmillan Publishers
London

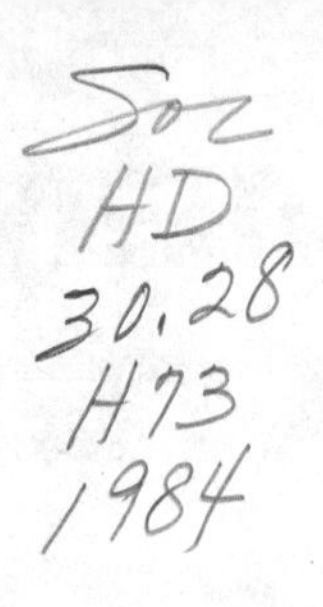

Printed in the United States of America

Macmillan Publishing Company
866 Third Avenue, New York, New York 10022

Collier Macmillan Canada, Inc.

Library of Congress Cataloging in Publication Data

Hrebiniak, Lawrence G.
Implementing strategy.

Includes index.
1. Corporate planning. 2. Management.
I. Joyce, William F. II. Title.
HD30.28H73 1984 658.4′012 83-852
ISBN 0-02-357540-9 (Paperback Edition)
ISBN 0-02-357290-6 (Hardcover Edition)
Printing: 1 2 3 4 5 6 7 8 Year: 4 5 6 7 8 9 0 1

ISBN 0-02-357540-9

DEDICATION

To Donna and Justin,
Linda and Jeff

PREFACE

This is a book about the implementation of strategy. Its purpose is to explain how critical planning, organizational design, and human resource decisions result in the successful attainment of long-term strategic aims and plans. With this end in mind, our writing was constantly affected by four guiding principles, beliefs, or criteria of effectiveness.

First, we attempted to be *eclectic* or *integrative* in our approach. Material on implementing strategy is not found in the theories and empirical research of a single field or discipline. Works in areas commonly differentiated and labeled as strategic management, organizational behavior, and organization theory clearly are pertinent and central to a sound discussion of implementation activities. Recognizing the contributions of these diverse areas, our attempt was to distill, derive, and integrate concepts and facts that are important to the successful implementation of strategy. Special emphasis was placed not only on the individual elements of our model but also on the links between them in an effort to bring together previously separate, even disparate, literature pertinent to the present task.

The second guiding principle was that we wished to develop a model of implementation that is not only integrative but also *clear, logical,* and *useful.* Our intention was not to obfuscate or create new jargon. Our wish was to present an approach whose underlying logic and utility would appeal to academics and practitioners alike. While the model clearly is rooted in and derived from the conceptual and empirical work of our academic colleagues, the goal was to explain strategy implementation in such a way that *actual* important design, planning, and human resource decisions could be made more effectively. A related purpose was to present an approach to *applied organizational change* that is suggested by the relations among the key elements of our implementation model.

Third, we were guided by a need to integrate the *short and long term* when discussing implementation activities. Recent criticisms of American management include the accusation of myopic, short-term thinking to the neglect of the long term. The organization and management literature shows a curious mix of attention to different time frames, with much of the work on strategy formulation focusing on the long run and work in organizational behavior focusing primarily on micro issues in the nearer term. The present approach attempts to show how short-run activities are, in fact, central to the attainment of strategic aims. Our conceptual framework argues for the reduction or translation of long-term strategies into planning and design issues that are relevant and manageable in the short term. Short-run decisions do *not* necessarily represent a managerial myopia that militates against strategic plans and outcomes. As we try to show, purposive planning and design decisions, coupled with the appropriate use of incentives and controls, are crucial to melding the short and the long term in implementation activities.

Fourth, we were guided by a need to *clarify relationships between strategy and structure* across several strategic levels of organization. Much of the literature has tended to treat strategy-structure relationships as an "either-or" question: "Does strategy cause structure, or does structure cause strategy?" We believe that this issue is more complex than this simple question indicates; consequently, we felt a need to address these relationships directly and carefully in the development of the basic implementation model.

Evaluation of the extent to which our work conforms to or follows these guidelines is, of course, left up to the reader. We simply wish to inform him or her of the beliefs and biases that guided the painstaking development of our model of strategy implementation. Surely, holes still exist in our model; we hope, however, that the present work fills in more gaps than it leaves open.

In pursuit of our goals, we clearly were affected by the work of a number of individuals to whom we owe a major intellectual debt. The ideas and insights of such people as Alfred Chandler, Ernest Dale, Jay Galbraith, Paul Lawrence, Charles Lindbloom, James March, Raymond Miles, Henry Mintzberg, Charles Snow, George Steiner, and James Thompson pervade our work more than is indicated by the formal references. We also would like to thank the following people whose comments on earlier versions of this manuscript, or whose work in specific topic areas, proved extremely valuable: Jay Bourgeois, Don Hambrick, Roger Harrison, Charles Hofer, Peter Lorange, Don Michael, Bob Miles, Hasan Ozbekhan, Jeff Pfeffer, Bob Pitts, Brian Quinn, Max Richards, Richard Rumelt, Dan Schendel, and John Slocum. Of course, we alone are responsible for our interpretation of what (we think) they were saying or implying.

The bulk of the manuscript was typed by Susan McMullen, Carol Morrison, Margaret Reagan, and Gwen Tolbert. For their effort, diligence, and good work, we thank them. We also appreciate their good humor, which makes any job—including the significant labor associated with writing and rewriting—much more bearable.

Finally, we would like to thank our wives and sons for their usual fine support and encouragement. Both our families are small, but close, supportive, and satisfying. Home provides a climate perfect for professional or academic activities as well as social or family fun; we are grateful for such nice places and such nice people.

L. G. H.
W. F. J.

CONTENTS

1

INTRODUCTION: STRATEGY IMPLEMENTATION MODEL

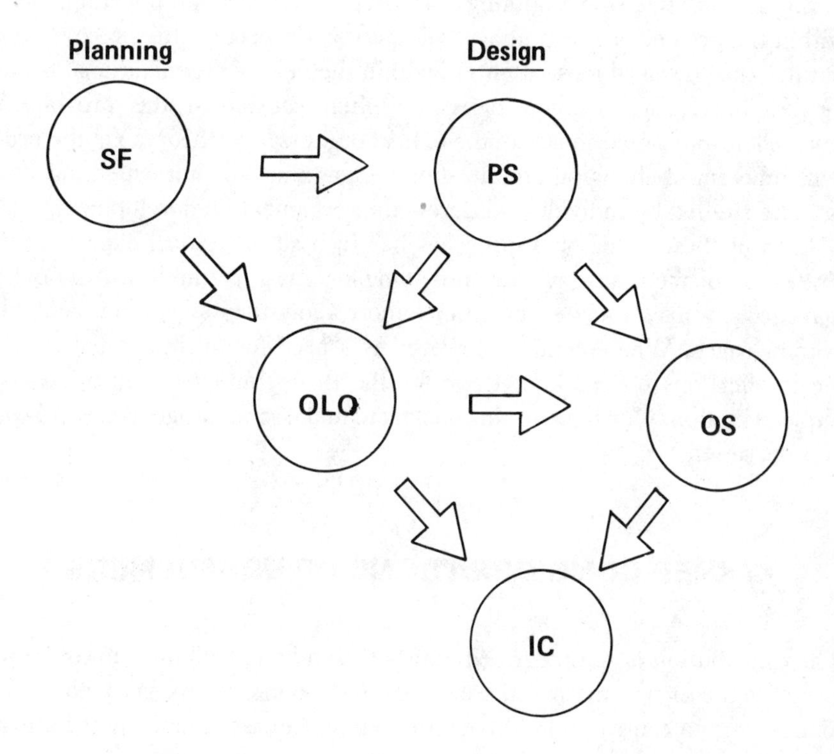

The methods and problems of strategy implementation have received less attention than have those of strategy formulation. This is peculiar because both practical and academic experience indicates that decisions made in implementing strategy have a substantial impact on organizational performance. There appears to be no unified, logical, normative approach for implementing strategy. The purpose of this book is to provide such an approach.

We believe, however, that much more has been written about strategy implementation than is apparent from a survey of titles of books and articles in academic and professional journals. The problem is not that we know too little about strategy implementation but that what we do know is fragmented among several "fields" of organization and management study. The result has been several, somewhat one-sided, views of the implementation process with little constructive integration of the many important perspectives on the topic. For example, strategic planning has been researched and written about within the area of business policy, yet a critical aspect of this process—goal setting—has received most attention within the field of organizational behavior. Similarly, organization design is often considered the province of researchers and practitioners in the field of organization theory. Yet the problems inherent in changing organization design, and thus implementing strategy, are studied by individuals interested in organization development.

Each of these fields or approaches has focused on critical aspects of the strategy implementation process, providing key insights into how it should be managed. In this sense, we know much more about the topic than is generally acknowledged. What remains, however, is a need for an integrated view of the implications of this knowledge for the theory and practice of strategy implementation. Our hope in this book is to make some progress toward such an integration.

THREE CONSIDERATIONS OF USEFULNESS

The contribution of an integrated approach can be judged in terms of its relevance to the theory and practice of strategy implementation. We believe that, to make such a contribution, three criteria must be met. These are the criteria of *logic, action,* and *contingent prescription.*

Logic. Managers confronting implementation problems face an almost bewildering array of possible activities. Decisions must be made concerning which of many strategic and organizational variables should be changed, in what order, and within what time frame. But all implementation activities are not equally salient under differing conditions, and differential costs, both human and financial, are incurred in their application. Faced with this complexity, and equipped with only limited information handling and decision-making capabilities, managers need a cognitively manageable implementation model or approach. Such a model must represent a *logical* delineation of major categories of implementation activities and the relationships among them, thereby reducing a previously intractable problem to one of limited proportions and allowing informed decision in the face of previously unmanageable complexity. But a logical model offers a second, perhaps even more important, advantage.

To be successful, managers must anticipate the consequences of alternative implementation activities, not only in the face of complexity, but often with little previous experience to guide them. We can partially compensate for this need to be omniscient through the use of a logical model that allows us to *deduce* consequences of implementation activities. By understanding a cognitively manageable and logically connected set of variables, we can then deduce a considerably larger set of consequences and particular outcomes of specific implementation activities. These specific outcomes and predictions should be quite useful because they (1) allow insight into problems with which the manager may have had no previous direct experience and (2) are founded upon the collective experience of many managers and academics (the logical model) gained across many industries and in many organizations. This "collective wisdom" should facilitate informed choice and more effective implementation.

Action. Strategy implementation takes place in the real world of management. It is concerned not only with questions of "why" but also of "how." Managers are rewarded for "doing" as well as "knowing," and this places the constraint of *usefulness* on any approach to implementing strategy.

At the same time, these constraints make development of an implementation model more difficult. Many apparently important variables are relatively inaccessible to observation and, more important, to manipulation. For example, one of the most studied effectiveness measures in organizations has been worker satisfaction. Yet it is very difficult to see, feel, or hear another person's satisfaction, or to know accurately that it has been affected by some measurable amount. How can this variable be changed?

The answer is problematic, both for practice and theory. For an approach to implementing strategy to be useful to both academicians and managers, it must emphasize variables that, first of all, are *manipulable* and, failing this, are at least relatively *objective.* Effective managerial action presupposes that key variables are under the manager's control; without this, there is nothing to manage. Other nonmanipulable variables are important because they place constraints on such action. We recognize these constraints and present an approach to implementing strategy that has a direct relation to managerial action and decision making.

Contingent Prescription. Some time ago, Simon noted that the principles of management were like proverbs; you could always find one to support what you wanted to do.[1] Recent developments in the field of organization design and theory have supported the limited utility of principles proposing a "one best way" to manage, suggesting in their place a "contingency view" in which different organization designs or approaches are believed useful in different situations. This contingency position has come to dominate management theory and practice.

Critics of the principles of management, however, have overlooked one of their significant strengths: the principles told us what to do. A useful contingency approach to strategy implementation must have this same characteristic. It must indicate both our choices *and* the criteria for choosing. It is not enough to know that "it all depends"; we need to know what it depends on, *and* what to do about it. We call this the need for "contingent" prescription.

In this book, we adhere to the criteria of logic, action, and contingent prescription. While not always referring to the criteria specifically, throughout this book an attempt is made to satisfy the demands imposed by them. The purpose is to integrate what is known about the process of implementing strategy within a useful model that meets the needs of both managers and academicians.

KEY QUESTIONS AND PRINCIPLES IN IMPLEMENTING STRATEGY

With these criteria in mind, we shall shortly propose a model for implementing strategy. The important characteristics of the model arise from answers to two key questions: (1) What decisions and actions can be taken by managers who are implementing strategy? and (2) How can these decisions be organized to meet the criteria of logic, action, and contingent prescription? When answering these questions and making decisions based on the analysis of variables or factors central to the implementation process, we believe that managers are guided by two critical principles. These are the *principle of intended rationality* and the *principle of minimum intervention.*

The Principle of Intended Rationality

In recent years there has been considerable interest in theories of limited rationality in decision making. Simon,[2] March and Simon,[3] and March[4] have argued that the classical economic theory of rational decision making does not adequately attend to the limited information handling capacity of decision makers. The classical model assumes that decision makers have knowledge of all alternatives, the consequences of all alternatives, and a consistent preference ordering and decision rule that allows choice from among them. Bounded rationality requires modification of this rational choice model, as discussed by March:

> *Because of such limits, the decision process that is used differs in some significant ways from the decision process anticipated by a more classical formulation. Decision making is seen as problem solving, search, and incremental trial and error. Described as "muddling through" by Lindblom, as "feedback-react" procedures by Cyert and March, and as "cybernetic" by Steinbruner, incremental, limited rationality is usually contrasted with long-run planning, forecasts, and commitments. The intelligence of organizational action is seen as lying not in the capability to know everything in advance but in the ability to make marginal improvements by monitoring problems and searching for solutions. Thus theories of limited rationality are essentially theories of search or attention: What alternatives are considered? What information is used?*[5]

We believe that recognition of bounded rationality and the limited actions of the classical economic decision model are essential to a theory of strategy implementation. The criterion of logic recognizes such limitations explicitly, when we argue that a logical, deductive model is required to reduce the complexity of implementation activities to cognitively manageable proportions. The major consequence of limited rationality is to require that large strategic problems be "factored" into smaller, more manageable proportions for implementation. This process delimits the "candidates" for attention, allowing more rational decision given limited decision capacity.

The limited rationality of decision makers has been previously recognized in both the strategy and organizational literatures. As an example, Hofer and Schendel argue that strategy formulation should occur at both a corporate or portfolio level, as well as at a more local business level, presumably to allow managers to focus their limited attention on a restricted set of strategic problems appropriate at those levels. They note that because top managers "have neither the time nor the capacity (limited attention) to understand and usefully compare"[6] competitors for resources, a two-stage allocation process is used. In the first stage, capital is allocated by the corporate level to particular businesses; in the second stage, responsibility for further capital spending is delegated to the business level. This is because the business level "has the detailed knowledge of markets, products, and technology necessary to make such evaluations."[7] Similarly, in organization design, Thompson[8] has recognized the concept of bounded rationality and the need for the allocation of attention in arguing that organizations must establish structural units within which rationality can be a reasonable criterion. As he notes:

> *We would expect the complexity of the structure, the number and variety of units, to reflect the complexity of the environment . . . the more difficult the environment, the more important it is to assign a small portion of it to one unit.*

Complexity leads the organization to establish structural units to deal with relatively homogeneous segments of its environment, and to then further subdivide these units based upon their capacity to undertake the necessary surveillance and information processing activities demanded by these homogeneous segments. These illustrations show how large implementation problems are reduced in size using methods of strategic planning and organization design, respectively.

Clearly, one of the most relevant and insightful discussions of the intimate relationship between intended rationality and strategy formulation and implementation has been provided by Quinn in his concept of "logical incrementalism." Following intensive study of a number of U.S. and European industrial organizations, he has concluded that because of both cognitive and process limits (the timing imperatives influencing awareness, consensus, and efficiency during strategic change) on rationality "top executives typically deal with the logic of each subsystem of strategy formulation *largely on its own merits* and usually with a *different set of people*" [emphasis ours].[9] In his view:

> *The most effective strategies of major enterprises tend to emerge step by step from an iterative process in which the organization probes the future, experiments, and learns from a series of* partial *(incremental) commitments rather than through global formulations of total strategies. Good managers are aware of this process, and they consciously intervene in it.*[10] [Italics ours]

A model of strategy implementation must therefore directly address problems of allocation of attention stemming from limited information processing capability. The model that we present shortly includes the need to selectively attend to implementation problems through appropriate planning and organizing actions. These actions delimit both the scope and the time frame of decisions to make them more manageable. But we must be careful not to become so enamored of theories of limited rationality that we propose theories of nonrationality and arationality in their place. In this book, a model of *intended* rationality is adopted as an organizing principle for implementation activities. Specifically, *the principle of intended rationality* proposes that

> *Individuals are limited in their ability to develop alternatives and their consequences, and to make unequivocal choices based upon such analyses and preferences. Typically, they employ logical and individually rational processes for decision within these constraints. Faced with complexity, individuals act to factor large problems into incrementally and cognitively manageable proportions. Given the realities of resource allocation decisions and organizational control systems, managers will seek to achieve utilitarian outcomes to the extent that these are valued and reinforced.*

While an implementation model must recognize the limited rationality of decision makers, it must not ignore the predominantly utilitarian nature of organizations and the consequent need to reconcile individual and organizational rationality.

Much more will be said regarding the factors that affect implementation decisions in the pages that follow. Our contention is that managers *intend* to be rational when formulating and implementing strategy, but that rationality is bounded by limited cognitive and information processing capacities. Within limitations, the intention of managers is to (1) focus on utilitarian outcomes in strategic planning, (2) design organizations to minimize costs of coordination and optimize efficiency and effectiveness, and (3) develop incentives and controls that motivate and reinforce acceptable performance. Other factors (e.g., amount of slack resources) may determine the intensity with which rationality is pursued, but the basic pursuit, in our opinion, is central and pervasive in most organizations. Individual values and perceptions affect the process of formulating and implementing strategy, and individual behavior based on perceptions of rewards and costs may *not* always coincide or be consistent with organizational rationality and the attainment of superordinate organizational goals. The political or self-aggrandizing nature of individual behavior potentially can militate against and detract from desired organizational outcomes.

The point is that these facts actually support the existence of rationality in organizations. Individuals behave in such a way as to maximize personal rewards and minimize costs and negative feedback. Clearly, most behavior in utilitarian organizations is individually rational. The need, then, when implementing strategy is to try to ensure that desirable outcomes at the individual level are consistent with and support positive outcomes at the organizational level. Much of what is developed in later chapters on objective setting, incentives, and controls recognizes this reality. Our approach is premised on a twofold belief that (1) key elements of the implementation process are guided by the principle of intended rationality and (2) individual and organizational rationality can be reconciled in the implementation of strategy.

The principle of intended rationality implies that any approach to implementing strategy must confront two problems. First, the limited rationality of decision makers requires that large strategic problems be factored into more local and manageable proportions to reduce the *complexity* of implementation activites. Second, long-term strategic objectives must be factored into shorter-term operating objectives, and control mechanisms must be established to ensure *consistency* of individual and organizational rationality in pursuing these objectives.

A useful approach to strategy implementation also addresses a third issue: the *efficient* utilization of human, financial, and strategic resources. The next organizing concept, the principle of minimum intervention, addresses such issues directly.

The Principle of Minimum Intervention

This principle has its roots in many areas of organizational science and management practice and is implicit in the discussions of organization design by Lawrence and Lorsch,[11] Galbraith,[12] and Thompson[13]; of strategy formulation by Chandler[14] and, more explicitly, of organization development by Harrison.[15] There is a general confluence in all this work that indicates that managers who are intendedly rational attempt to implement strategy within constraints of economic efficiency, choosing those courses of action that solve their problems with minimum costs to the organization.

This position is clear in Galbraith's[16] approach to organization design in which he argues implicitly that the traditional bureaucratic structural mechanisms be utilized as initial solutions to design problems. Only when these basic structures become overloaded by complex information processing requirements should more complex and, thus, more costly techniques be used.

Similarly, in the strategy literature, Chandler[17] argues that organizations do not change their structures when implementing strategy until they are forced to do so by operating inefficiencies. The resulting adjustment represents the minimum action needed to return to a state of efficient operation and increased economic performance.

Harrison[18] has made these points quite explicitly in the organization development literature noting that, as the depth of intervention increases, not only do costs increase but so do the risks of unintended consequences for individuals. This concept can be expanded to argue that the principle of minimum intervention has a humanistic as well as a rational side; managers should implement strategy with minimum disruption of the individual's tasks, habits, and lives. In large systems in need of complex implementation efforts, however, such disruptions may be likely, placing human as well as logical constraints on the size and efficiency of implemention.

These considerations may be stated more generally in the following form:

In implementing strategy managers should change only what is necessary and sufficient to produce an enduring solution to the strategic problem being addressed.

The point is that, faced with a problem, the organization should respond in such a way to solve it, but not at unnecessary financial or human cost. To confront a strategic problem by restructuring the entire organization when, in fact, it is possible to achieve acceptable results with a less far-reaching and pervasive approach (e.g., changes in incentives or controls) makes little sense. Violation of the principle of minimum intervention only results in unnecessary change and potentially negative impact on individuals responsible for the strategy implementation process.

Discussion throughout this book refers to and relies on these basic guiding principles as we develop our model of strategy implementation and present examples of key decisions derived from the approach. It now is necessary to provide a brief overview of that model and introduce the material that will be covered in depth in subsequent chapters.

STRATEGY IMPLEMENTATION: PLANNING AND DESIGN DECISIONS

The two basic activities in implementing strategy are *planning* and *organizational design*. Although each of these has implications for the other, they have often been discussed separately, as if successful strategy implementation could be accomplished through either. This view has emphasized linkages and variables *within* each process or set of activities to the detriment of relationships between them. Some researchers, for example, have productively focused on such issues as the implications of corporate-level strategy for the development of business-level strategies specifying how the firm will compete in each of several, possibly related, businesses. Others have emphasized the implications of structural differentiation for achieving integration and coordination of effort toward some desired organizational end. Planners and orga-

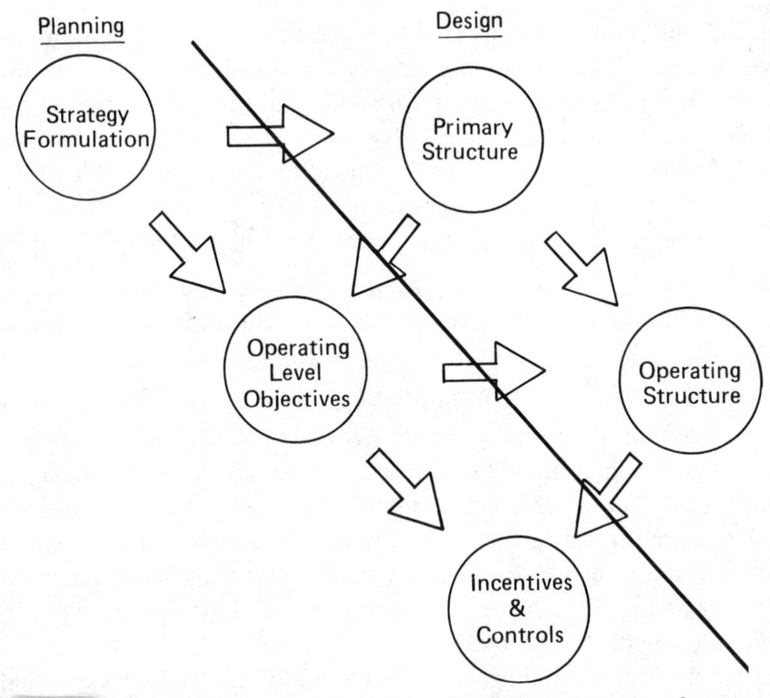

Figure 1-1. Key planning and design decisions in the implementation of strategy.

nizational designers, that is, have tended to confine their thinking about strategy implementation to their own presumably separate fields. In contrast, we believe that both planning and organization design are vital; both are *interdependent* and must be considered when implementing strategy.

The following sections outline the major elements of the strategy implementation process. We emphasize *two* sets of decisions: one set is presented under the heading of *planning* decisions and the other under the heading of *organizational design* decisions. As March and Simon[19] aptly note, the literature on organizations "has been said over and over in a variety of languages"; consequently, some of what we have chosen to call planning could possibly be included as aspects of organization design, and vice versa. The differences in terminology notwithstanding, our hope is to present a logical and useful approach to the central decisions or choices involved in implementing strategy. These are shown in Figure 1-1.

Strategy Formulation. The process of formulating corporate strategy or plans for the entire organization is the beginning for implementation actions. Strategy formulation includes the setting of long-term objectives and the requisite plans for their achievement. Top managers make decisions about resource allocations, what businesses to pursue, what types of products and services to offer within these businesses, what clients to serve, with whom to compete, and what types of technology to operate. In making these decisions, numerous activities are important. For example, the organization assesses its own strengths and weaknesses relative to its environment, its relative share of the different markets or businesses it is in, and the probable reactions and impacts of competitors, regulatory agencies, and interest groups. In these decisions, economic rationality is often paramount, but when economic advantage is slight, or the outcomes of different choices are vague, managerial values become important in strategic decision making. Because strategy formulation is fundamental to implementation by providing that which is to be accomplished or implemented, it is considered in greater detail in Chapter 2.

Primary Structural Choices. Strategy formulation represents the starting point for the implementation actions in Figure 1-1. Because a strategy applies to the entire organization, it must be broken down into smaller elements and, ultimately, short-range objectives. This causes a problem because complex strategies imply complex and interdependent objectives, and planning processes alone are insufficient to ensure consistency and unity of direction. Also, decision makers have limited information handling capabilities, as noted earlier.[20] It is impossible for all managers to work simultaneously with a complex strategy and to comprehend adequately the interdependencies and diverse information involved.

Faced with such a situation, managers take action to reduce the scope of their plans to manageable proportions. In implementing strategy, this requires that managers first make choices about organization design or the structural units within which efficiency and greater rationality are a reasonable expectation. Thompson argues that structure is the fundamental vehicle by which organizations achieve bounded rationality,[21] and we refer to such decisions as primary structural choices in Figure 1-1.

Primary structure denotes the *major operating units of the entire organization.* At this level of the implementation model, we argue that strategy formulation affects the creation or alteration of these primary units or elements. A strategy of diversification that results in the acquisition of another organization and its inclusion as a separate operating unit represents one example of the creation of primary structure. Primary structure, then, deals with the differentiation of the organization into its major components or parts. To facilitate the attainment of complex strategic objectives and plans, these objectives and plans must be reduced to smaller, more manageable proportions.

Decisions about primary structure create the operating units that are most appropriate for this reduction process and, consequently, for the successful implementation of strategy.

We are arguing here that primary structure follows strategy, mainly because the strategic decisions of the type noted earlier are made at a point in time prior to the creation or alteration of the structural units that serve to implement the chosen plans. Structure also follows strategy, at least in part, because further attempts at establishing operating objectives and plans would be futile without the bounded rationality afforded within an appropriately chosen structural configuration. To set operating objectives that relate logically to longer-term strategic ends and plans, it first is necessary to differentiate the organization into smaller parts that contribute to the overall effort.

The choice of a primary structure clearly involves decisions about major organizing modes. Depending upon strategy and the costs involved, firms choose from among functional, geographic, or multidivisional structures, or even a hybrid representing a combination of basic forms. Similarly, strategic choices about product market position involve decisions concerning the customers or clients to serve, major competitors, and what regulation to expect. These decisions determine at what points the organization depends upon or is vulnerable to changes in its environment. Rationality demands that managers take action to control elements of these environments to allow economic efficiency in the face of ambiguous or shifting competitive situations. In such circumstances, for example, managers may choose to acquire critical suppliers, thereby minimizing the threats to performance from uncertain relationships with them.

Numerous other examples abound in the organization and strategy literature, but they all make the same point: primary structure in part depends upon and follows from strategy. The dominant direction of influence at this level is from strategy to structure. Strategic decisions regarding products and services (e.g., increasing emphasis on commodity-type products) influence organizational structure (e.g., a functional organization or a technical division to achieve economies of scale). This and other issues are treated in greater depth in Chapter 3.

Establishing Operating-Level Objectives. This is the third major component of the implementation model in Figure 1-1. Operating-level objectives *are the strategic and short-term objectives of the major differentiated units of the organization.* Simply stated, objectives must now be set consistent with the choice or definition of structure. Integration of the operating objectives of major subunits with corporate strategic aims and plans is now possible because of the prior determination of primary structure. In a sense, then, planning at the operating level follows from and is delimited by structure. As Chapter 4 indicates, the formulation of operating unit or business strategy, given the existence of primary structure, reflects the constraints and opportunities in the prevailing situation.

This step represents the point in the planning process at which strategic objectives are developed for the operating units and are then translated into specific, short-term measures of performance. Focusing first on strategic objectives, it is helpful to picture the long-time existence of autonomous divisions or businesses that comprise the primary structure of the organization. Strategy formulation includes portfolio analysis and related issues of resource allocation at the corporate level. But strategy formulation also occurs at the divisional or business level. In the case of *existing* businesses or divisions, strategy formulation at the corporate and subunit levels may occur virtually simultaneously, but the former is clearly more global, whereas the latter reflects more limited local concerns. Strategy formulation at the corporate level includes assessment of, and resource allocations for, separate businesses or divisions; formulation at operating levels focuses more limitedly on a single business' or division's concerns, including its market strategy and intraunit allocation of resources. The approach to strategy development at both the organizational and local levels is expanded upon when discussing the formulation model of Chapter 2 and operating-level objectives in Chapter 4.

The process of setting operating-level objectives also includes the translation of long-term strategic aims into specific short-term objectives for the operating units. Rather than trying to focus on the entire implementation process, managers at this stage are concerned with more local problems and objectives. Specific action plans are developed to implement portions of the strategy determined in the formulation process. Structure now constrains strategy implementation because managers focus on strategic issues relating only to their segments of the business, and these segments are determined by choices of the primary structure. Complex strategic issues cannot be easily elaborated into consistent, operational objectives and action plans without first establishing a zone of discretion within which managers can take action and commit resources. Primary structure establishes these boundaries and, once identified, reduces the information that must be processed during the establishment of operating objectives by reducing the number of inputs and outputs that must be considered.[22] The determination of local operating-level objectives, therefore, is critical to the implementation of strategy, and, accordingly, they are treated in depth in Chapter 4.

It is clear, too, from the preceding discussion that operating-level objectives depend upon previous choices of primary structure as well as upon the basic strategy position of the entire organization. But the operating objectives obviously require local structure and processes for implementation as well. The next component of our model—operating structure—is created as a response to specific operating objectives originating from the first three strategy implementation activities. Thus, again, structure follows strategy and the planning process.

Operating Structure. Most of the theory and practice in the area of organizational design is devoted to operating structure, which refers to *the structure and, to some degree, related processes (e.g., coordination) within the major units that represent the primary structure of the organization.* Operating structure is the fourth component of the implementation process shown in Figure 1-1. At this stage, managers must make decisions about the specific structure of the major components of the organization. In a sense, it is possible now to talk about organization "designs" rather than a single design; different divisions or businesses within the organization can face different situations and, thus, have different operating structures. The choice of operating structure depends in part upon choices made at the three previous stages of implementation process, and the designer has many approaches to help at this point of implementation.

Decisions about operating structures fall into two broad categories: structural *differentiation,* or how to divide labor and departmentalize to achieve operating objectives; and *integration,* namely, the methods to be used to coordinate the various activities that have been segmented by differentiation decisions. Davis and Lawrence[23] and others argue that organizations are created to solve problems and to carry out tasks that one person acting alone cannot accomplish. When more than one person comes together to accomplish a task, criteria of efficiency dictate that work be divided to allow each person to become more expert at smaller portions of the task. This ultimately poses a problem because, once having divided the labor, it remains to coordinate the activities of workers toward the completion of the "whole" task.

Lawrence and Lorsch[24] have provided extremely useful discussions and much needed research concerning these dual problems of differentiation and integration. We would add to their position by noting that, while differentiation always precedes and often is antagonistic to integration, it is also clear that differentiation decisions, when defining operating structure, are usually made while simultaneously considering feasible integrating mechanisms. Thus, concerns with differentiation and integration are not always sequential, although the actual techniques to achieve the latter follow the former.

Others have also argued that operating organizations are created to help managers make decisions and solve problems and that integrating structures are dependent upon the level of information processing or decision-making requirements.[25] These and other approaches all focus on strategy implementation issues. Key design or contingency variables such as uncertainty and information processing needs are related to strategic choice. Decisions about environments or domain and technology determine uncertainty and information processing needs; these then are responded to in terms of primary structure, the development of operating objectives, and operating structures. Because of the importance of operating structures to the implementation of strategy, a great deal of attention is devoted to this topic in Chapters 5 and 6.

The picture of implementing strategy, however, is not yet complete, because the creation of structure is not sufficient to ensure that individuals will adapt their own goals to those of the organization. Some strategy of obtaining individual and organizational goal congruence is required; great care in the formulation of strategy and development of operating structure and objectives can be negated by a lack of commitment or involvement among individuals charged with their implementation. Similarly, given individual rationality, it is unwise to allow individuals to benefit at the expense of or detriment to desired organizational outcomes. In essence, what is required, then, is the careful development of an *incentive and control plan,* the fifth component of our model in Figure 1-1.

Incentive and Controls. Lorange and others propose that the planning process should contain a component dealing with the control of performance with respect to operating objectives.[26] Individual and group rewards become an important aspect of strategy implementation because they control performance with respect to these desired ends. But incentive plans must be consistent with more than the operating objectives. The primary means of implementing operating-level objectives is the operating structure, whereas the primary means of controlling progress toward these objectives is the incentive plan. All three must be consistent with one another, with the dominant direction of influence from objectives to structure and then to incentives. Thus, the incentive plan must reinforce the structure and related management processes. Thorndike's *law of effect* definitely is most salient here: behavior that is reinforced tends to be repeated.[27] This simple but powerful idea indicates the critical role of incentive planning for strategy formulation. The development of reward systems must support strategy implementation, thereby forming the fifth primary component of the implementation process. In this case, reward or incentive plans follow structure, and the cycle of planning decisions–design decisions continues within the implementation process.

Chapter 7 deals extensively with the role of incentives and controls in the implementation of strategy. To motivate behavior that is consistent with short-term and strategic objectives, it is vital to develop rewards and controls that take into account and integrate the short-run operation of the organization and its needs for long-run survival. People in utilitarian organizations are individually rational; successful implementation of strategy requires that individual motivations do not militate against the achievement of organizational rationality and the attainment of desired organizational outcomes. Similarly, control systems must guarantee the consistency and appropriateness of behavior or performance against objectives, but not at the expense of the innovation, creativity, and organizational learning that are so crucial for adaptability and long-term viability. Chapter 7 discusses these critical issues in detail.

Change Management. The final component of the implementation process is change management, and it is a component whose importance should not be underestimated. All the previous components of the model deal with implementation, representing a logical chain of action choices that, as we describe them, are sequentially dependent upon one another. However, despite the fact that each of these addresses implementation, it is still necessary to confront more directly the critical problems inherent in changing strategic and operating objectives and primary and operating structures. Managers must make decisions about the "journalistic" questions of a strategy implementation: the who, what, where, and when of changing. The final portion of the model develops criteria for such changes as well as a specific approach to complex strategy implementation involving the simultaneous manipulation of several components of the model.

So far we have outlined a series of strategy implementation actions, but we still face a difficult problem. With some knowledge of action alternatives, we are prepared to begin an implementation, but we must choose a starting point. Should all implementations or organizational changes begin with formulation, following through all of the other components discussed here? Such a procedure would be quite costly and perhaps unnecessary. But if we do not "begin at the beginning," where is a logical starting point? In our opinion, strategic problems rarely come packaged as a design problem, a reward problem, and so on. Managers must match implementation practices with problems in implementing strategy. Chapter 8 is devoted exclusively to the topic of change, but the next section outlines four principal varieties of strategic change and presents organizing principles for their selection and application as a brief introduction to this critical topic.

STRATEGY IMPLEMENTATION AND ORGANIZATIONAL CHANGE

The basic components of the strategy implementation model introduced in the previous section and expanded upon in this discussion are derived from two sources: first, the three criteria of usefulness: action, logic, and contingent prescription; and, second, the principle of intended rationality. By conceiving of managers as individually rational but as subject to constraints of limited information processing capabilities, our model and the linkages among its components were derived to represent a logical elaboration of the implementation process. Each step in the process is contingent upon previous steps, and each represents an action aimed at factoring the complex implementation problem into a number of discrete, progressively more local, and manageable tasks. While it is true that everything depends upon everything else in strategy implementation, it is also true that there is a dominant direction to this dependence deriving from the principle of intended rationality.

As we move on to discuss approaches to implementing strategy, one fact that follows from the criterion of contingent prescription is that *not all elements of the basic model will be relevant in all situations.* Consequently, we need ways of choosing or deciding the factors that are relevant in any given situation. Because the costs of strategy implementation increase with the size of the problem, this suggests the criterion of choosing, which we defined as the principle of minimum intervention.

The principle of minimum intervention provides a criterion for choosing where to begin an intervention. As the size of the strategic problem increases, we work backward in the basic model of Figure 1-1 from the incentive and control component, through the various action steps, toward formulation itself. Small strategic problems may require only an adjustment in incentive plans, whereas larger problems may require changes in operating structures and, consequently, in all components of the model that follow this segment. In all cases, the principle is the same: change only those portions of the system that must be changed to produce an enduring solution to the strategic problem.

In Figure 1-2, the principle of minimum intervention is shown to affect the number of components of the basic model that should be considered in implementing strategy. But application of this principle leads us to a second problem that now must be addressed. After having decided which of the implementation components must be considered, we must decide how they will be implemented; that is, whether they will be *implemented sequentially,*

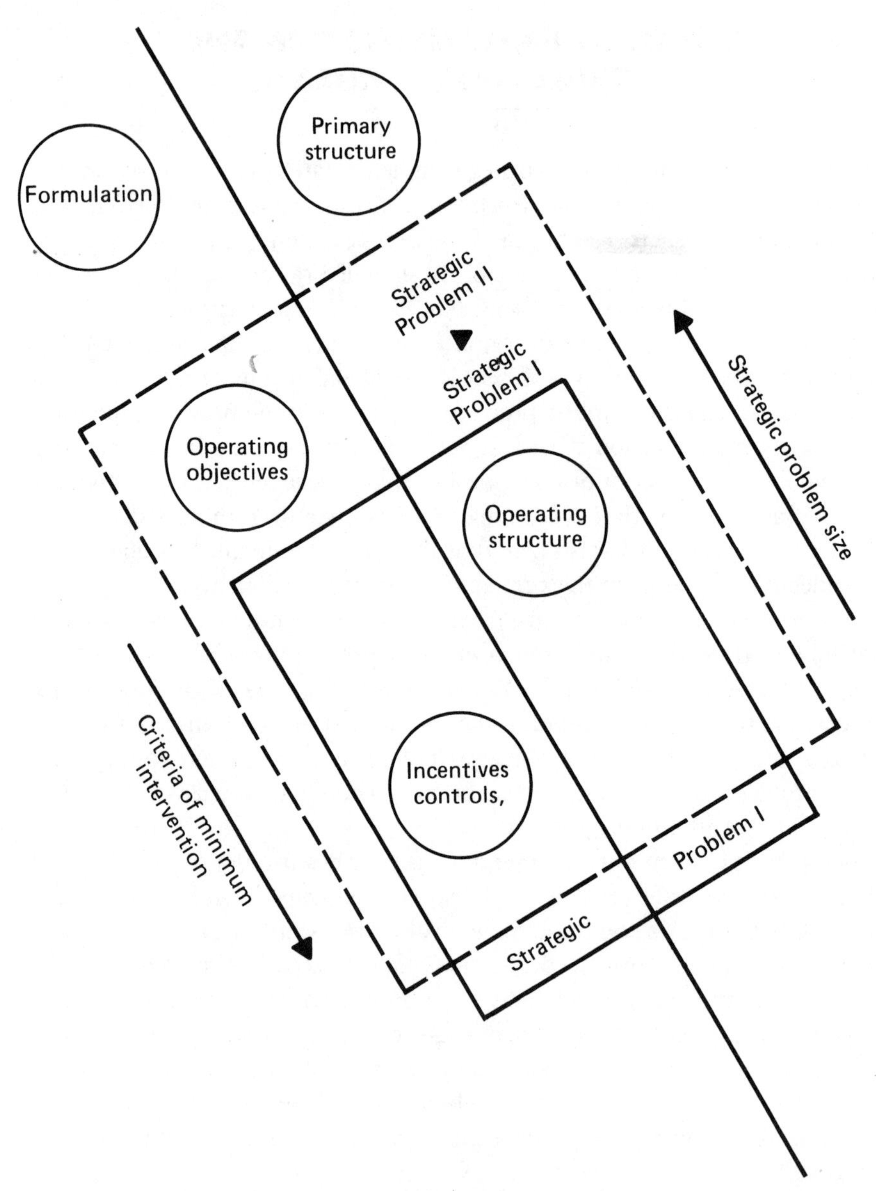

Figure 1-2. Effects of strategic problem size and criteria of minimum intervention on elements considered in implementing strategy.

in the order of the basic model, or whether they should all be considered jointly or concurrently. Generally, managers prefer to implement strategy sequentially because the type of interdependence among components of the implementation process can be managed by plan. Concurrent or complex interventions or changes imply that "everything depends on everything else," that all components of the process are reciprocally interdependent. This type of dependence must be managed by mutual adjustment, a more costly form of coordination than plan, leading managers to prefer sequential implementation.[28] However, other factors constrain this choice, the principle one of which we call the *implementation horizon.*

Implementation Horizon

Strategic problems have an additional important property beyond their size, and that is the time limit within which they must be solved. Ozbekhan calls this the planning horizon: the time within which implementation must be accomplished.[29]

The implementation horizon is determined by answering a number of questions, including "How long will the organization stay in business if it continues in its activities as it is today?" If the answer to this question is several years, sequential strategy implementations are feasible. It is possible in this case for managers to approach the problem or threat in parts, methodically moving on only after each preceding part is handled or treated appropriately. If the answer to the implementation horizon question is that time is of the essence—for example, three to six months—it is clear that generally complex concurrent interventions must be undertaken to implement strategy.

The effect of shorter implementation horizons is to increase the number of components of the basic model that must be considered *concurrently.* Generally, the shorter the implementation horizon, the more complex the change and, consequently, the more costly the adjustment in strategy. Under norms of rationality and the principle of minimum intervention, managers prefer to *sequence* implementation activities, beginning with the smallest component that will produce an enduring solution to the strategic problem.

The combination of these two primary characteristics of a strategic problem—size of problem and implementation horizon—determines the style chosen to implement strategy. Their combination implies that even small strategic problems can be difficult when coupled with short implementation horizons. The joint effect is a "velocity of change" that can produce costs approximating those of larger changes accomplished within longer implementation horizons.

A Typology of Strategy Implementations

The combination of these dimensions describes a rough taxonomy of types of strategy implementation efforts as shown in Figure 1-3. In implementing

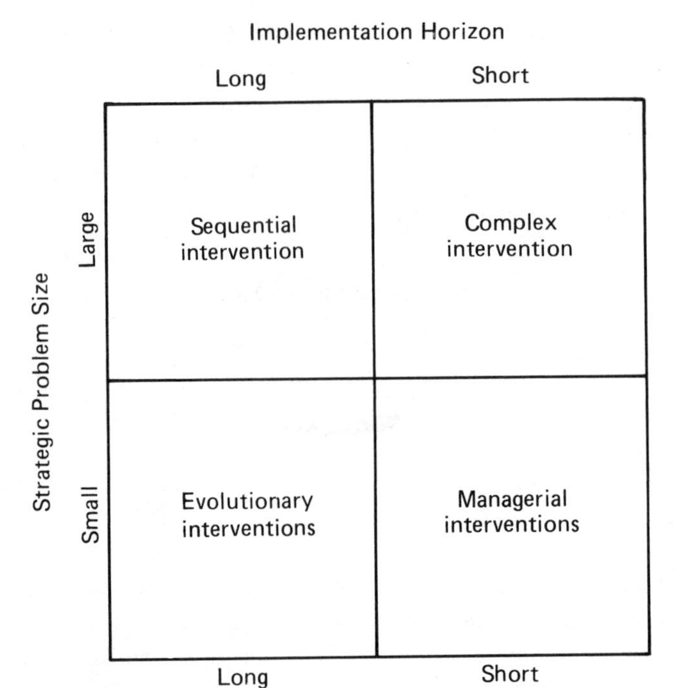

Figure 1-3. A typology of strategy implementations.

strategy, each of these generates specific problems arising from its use; these will be discussed in greater detail in Chapter 8. There is a logical progression of costs among the four strategies—from simple evolutionary strategic change, through managerial and sequential implementation, and ending with complex implementations. This sequence implies that the most significant costs of implementation arise from the sheer magnitude of the problems being undertaken and that for any such problem the time available for implementation will have a secondary but important effect. Each of the types is now discussed briefly.

Evolutionary implementations are utilized when the strategic problem is small and the implementation horizon is long. Usually such changes are not recognized as changes at all but rather simply as "differences" in the way in which things are done over time. Under norms of intended rationality, managers take local actions to improve organizational performance, but without reference to any implementation plan. Because the size of the problem is small, many implementations focus on latter stages of the implementation model and often are personnel related, as the emphasis is on incentives, controls, and motivations. Consequently, they are not sequential or complex interventions because only one component of the model is generally considered.

Connections between actions taken in evolutionary implementation are generally not recognized, and suboptimization occurs. Because such implementations are small, the costs of suboptimization are also small, and organizational slack is sufficient to absorb the minor inefficiencies. This type of implementation is effective as long as there are no major shifts in strategy and the organization has elaborated basic operating structures consistent with the strategic plan. Organizations implementing strategy in this mode are often "reactors" because of the few contingencies posed by their environment.[30]

Managerial implementations occur when the size of the strategic problem is small, but the time available to implement the strategy is short. This can occur due to minor shifts in the business environment that require adjustment, but for which evolutionary implementations are undesirable due to the short time frame and cost of suboptimization. By definition, the planning horizon is short, and concerted action is imperative. Under criteria of intended rationality, organizations will develop implementation plans focusing on only one of the latter components: for example, structure or personnel-related decisions. Because the problem is not serious, usually only one component of the model is considered, and the effects of decisions on other components are ignored. Slack is usually sufficient to absorb these costs because the implementation is small and secondary effects are usually minor. Business environments are still relatively stable, posing no significant threats but requiring relatively frequent small adjustments.

Sequential implementations occur when the size of a strategic problem is large, but the implementation horizon is long enough to allow several components of the implementation model to be implemented sequentially. Because the implementation involves several components of the model, successful implementation necessitates consideration of the dependencies among components as well as within them. Planning for such interdependencies recognizes that any significant strategic change will involve change in several areas. In such cases, concerted action is required to avoid suboptimization, for now slack is unavailable or too costly an alternative. Connections among components of the model are explicitly recognized and accommodated and are managed sequentially.

In this mode, an implementation begins with a specific component of the process and proceeds through all succeeding steps in turn, the key contingencies being posed by previous steps in the process. Because such interdependencies can be managed by plan, sequenced interventions are preferred to the next type, complex interventions, in which planning is very difficult.

Complex implementations occur when the size of strategic problems is large and the implementation horizon is too short to allow sequencing of implementation activities. In this case, managerial decisions about any one aspect of implementation both depend upon and influence decisions in all other areas. Because of this reciprocal dependence, coordination by plan is impossible, and generally more costly face-to-face mechanisms are necessary. Organizations may establish task forces for implementing strategy to accommodate the higher needs for information processing arising from mutually interdependent activities.

Complex interventions occur under a variety of circumstances. For example, complex implementation is required in the face of a severe environmental shock requiring immediate adaptation. Generally, complex interventions are becoming more common as business environments become more complex and turbulent. In the face of rapid change, large adjustments in strategy are needed more frequently, implying more costly and complex implementations that pose new challenges for managers. These are considered in detail in Chapter 8.

Summary

A great deal more may be said about implementing strategy, and that is precisely our intention. The purpose of the present chapter was merely to introduce and provide a brief overview of our approach to strategy implementation. The chapters that follow focus upon the key elements or aspects of Figure 1-1 and, more important, the linkages or interdependencies between and among them. Toward that end, Chapter 2 begins with the first key element of the model, strategy formulation.

Notes

1. James G. March and Herbert A. Simon, *Organizations* (New York: John Wiley & Sons, Inc., 1958).
2. Herbert A. Simon, *Administrative Behavior* (New York: The Free Press, 1976).
3. March and Simon, *Organizations.*
4. James G. March, "Decisions in Organizations and Theories of Choice," in Andrew H. Van de Ven and William F. Joyce, eds., *Perspectives on Organizational Design and Behavior* (New York: John Wiley & Sons, Inc., 1981).
5. Ibid., p. 212.
6. Charles Hofer and Daniel Schendel, *Strategy Formulation: Analytical Concepts* (St. Paul: West Publishing Company, 1978), p. 70.

7. Ibid., P. 70.
8. James D. Thompson, *Organizations in Action* (New York: McGraw-Hill Book Company, 1967), p. 70.
9. James Brian Quinn, *Strategies for Change: Logical Incrementalism* (Homewood, Ill.: Richard D. Irwin, Inc., 1980), p. 52.
10. Ibid., p. 58.
11. Paul R. Lawrence and Jay W. Lorsch, *Organization and Environment* (Boston: Division of Research, Graduate School of Business Administration, Harvard University, 1967).
12. Jay R. Galbraith, *Designing Complex Organization* (Reading, Mass.: Addison-Wesley Publishing Company, 1972).
13. Thompson, *Organizations in Action.*
14. Alfred Chandler, *Strategy and Structure* (Garden City, N.Y.: Anchor Books, 1962).
15. Roger Harrison, "Choosing the Depth of Organizational Intervention," *Journal of Applied Behavioral Science,* 6:181–202 (1970).
16. Galbraith, *Designing Complex Organization.*
17. Chandler, *Strategy and Structure.*
18. Harrison, "Choosing the Depth of Organizational Intervention."
19. March and Simon, *Organizations,* p. 5.
20. Ibid.
21. Thompson, *Organizations in Action,* especially Chapters 2 and 6.
22. Galbraith, *Designing Complex Organization.*
23. Stanley Davis and Paul Lawrence, *Matrix* (Reading, Mass.: Addison-Wesley Publishing Company, 1978).
24. Lawrence and Lorsch, *Organization and Environment.*
25. Galbraith, *Designing Complex Organization.*
26. Peter Lorange, *Corporate Planning* (Englewood Cliffs, N.J.: Prentice-Hall, Inc., 1980).
27. Edward L. Thorndike, *The Elements of Psychology* (New York: A. G. Seiler, 1905).
28. Thompson, *Organizations in Action.*
29. Hasan Ozbekhan, *Planning* (Unpublished Manuscript, The Wharton School, University of Pennsylvania).
30. Raymond Miles and Charles Snow, *Organizational Strategy* (New York: McGraw-Hill Book Company, 1978).

FORMULATING STRATEGY

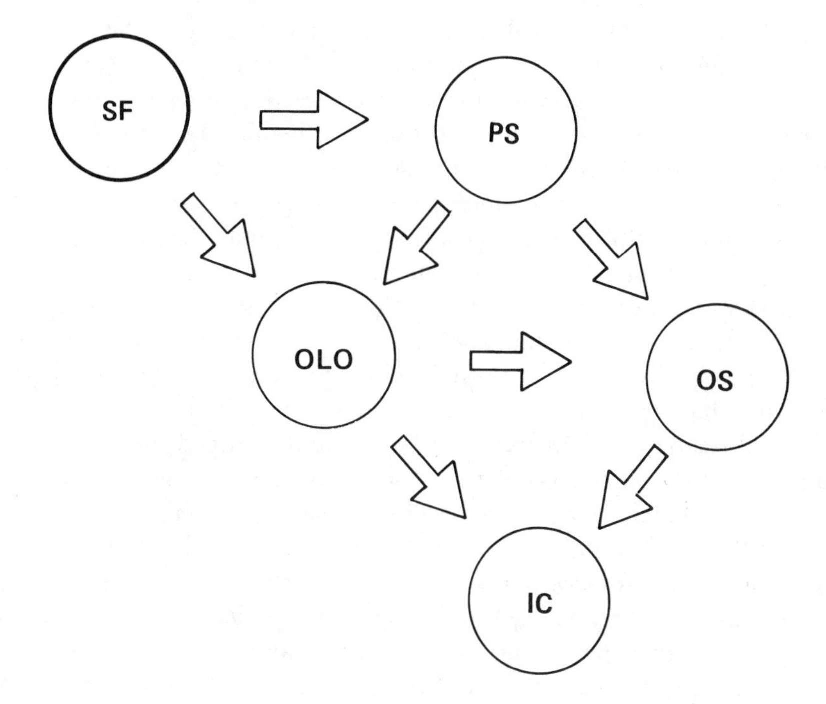

Strategy formulation affects and provides input to the implementation process. Strategic plans and objectives form the basis for subsequent implementation decisions.

Strategy formulation represents the logical starting point or origin for activities aimed at establishing and accomplishing organizational objectives. Strategy formulation is the first component of the implementation model developed in Chapter 1.

There are two obvious consequences of including strategy formulation as the first component of the implementation model developed in this book. The first is that the quality of the strategy formulation process itself will impact on organizational performance. Different strategies will result in differential effects on performance criteria, assuming that implementation activities are carried out equally well. Thus, strategy formulation is an important activity that affects organizational performance in its own right and is worthy of discussion on this basis alone. The second observation is that strategy formulation and implementation are highly interdependent and that the strategies and action plans developed during formulation form the basis for subsequent implementation activities. Achieving high degrees of agreement or consensus among top managers on what strategies are worthwhile, for example, clearly will affect ease of implementation and later commitment to the implementation process. A discussion of formulation is important, then, because an understanding of implementation is incomplete without reference to the contingencies and factors affecting strategic choice.

This chapter, therefore, has two purposes. First, we discuss strategy formulation. Because the techniques of strategy formulation have been presented elsewhere, the discussion focuses on developing an understanding of the process rather than on the procedures required for carrying it out. Preliminary sections distinguish definitions of strategy formulation and implementation and present rationale for the effects of formulation on organizational performance. Following this, formulation is discussed as a decision process that can be characterized in terms of the agreement among key decision makers concerning preferences for strategic outcomes and beliefs about the effects of strategic actions for achieving these outcomes. The specific components of the strategy formulation process are then presented along with a discussion of individual, organizational, and environmental factors affecting development and assessment of strategic options.

The second purpose of the chapter is to introduce the relationship between formulation and implementation activities. The latter sections of the chapter present a brief discussion of the role of formulation at the corporate and business levels of the firm, illustrate the functions of formulating strategy at multiple rather than single levels of the enterprise, and show the implications of corporate-level strategic decisions for the primary structure of the firm.

STRATEGY FORMULATION: DEFINITION AND IMPLICATIONS

There is no single consistent definition of "strategy" in the management literature. Even a cursory reading reveals many definitions that vary considerably along a number of important dimensions. This section presents a comparison of several of the more important definitions of strategy and justification of the specific concept of formulation adopted in this book. Strategy formulation and implementation are shown to be complementary, but distinguishable, components of the process of setting and obtaining strategic objectives, and formulation is discussed as producing several benefits that facilitate the strategic decision-making process and result in positive effects on organizational performance.

Defining Strategy Formulation

A number of definitions of strategy formulation have been used or proposed in the management literature. Chandler defined formulation as the determination of long-term objectives and the adoption of plans of action and allocation of scarce resources to achieve those objectives.[1] Drucker argued that formulation represents the response to two related questions: "What is our business?" and "What should it be?"[2] This clearly represents a very general and broad definition of business strategy. In contrast, other authors have adopted a more narrow view of strategy formulation, excluding the development of goals and objectives from the process. Hofer and Schendel, for example, define strategy as the "fundamental pattern of present and planned resource deployments and environmental interactions that indicates how the organization will achieve its objectives."[3] In seeming agreement with this differentiation between the process of strategy formulation and its outcomes, Richards provides a discussion of organizational goal structures as a separate strategic decision-making process.[4]

Other definitions of strategy formulation may be distinguished in terms of the degree of complexity they assign to the process. Some authors, most notably Andrews[5] and Ansoff,[6] emphasize that strategy involves a "pattern" of objectives or plans; it thus represents the common thread that pervades all of an organization's activities and product and market decisions. In seeming contrast to this complex view, there is the approach of Galbraith and Nathanson who view strategy as a "specific action, usually but not always accompanied by the development of resources, to achieve an objective decided upon in strategic planning."[7] The former view stressing a pattern or common thread argues for a complex concept of strategy. The latter view argues against such a concept, opting instead for a situation in which an organization can have many different, simple strategies (i.e., various specific actions to achieve different organizational objectives).

A third distinction among competing definitions of formulation may be made in terms of the planning horizon for strategic actions. Chandler, Drucker, and Andrews include long-term objectives in their definitions, whereas others, for example, Galbraith and Nathanson, at least imply the inclusion of shorter-term actions and plans.

The various definitions of strategy formulation disagree concerning whether formulation is broad or narrow, simple or complex, or long or short term. Part of this disagreement may stem from a basic problem in the analysis of decision-making behavior: that is, the inseparability of the means and ends of a decision process.[8] *Strategic decision making may be viewed as a series of means-ends decisions beginning with the determination of long-term, global objectives (ends) and the development of shorter-term, more local actions to obtain these objectives (means).*

As the process continues, the short-term, more local objectives are taken as ends and subsequently factored into progressively shorter and more local plans, which become the means for obtaining these new "ends." The inversion and alternate linkage of means and ends continue until long-term, global objectives are factored into a "size" that fits within the limited physical and cognitive capabilities of individuals who ultimately execute specific assigned tasks.

While most definitions of strategy stop far short of defining the process in terms of these ultimate short-term objectives, they do differ systematically in terms of their focus on means and ends in early stages of the strategic decision process. Drucker, Chandler, and Andrews, for example, emphasize long-term objectives (ends) in their definitions, whereas Hofer and Schendel as well as Ansoff emphasize the complex activities inherent in obtaining these objectives (means). These activities may then be taken as objectives or ends themselves and further means developed for their attainment, as when Galbraith and Nathanson describe strategy as a specific action undertaken to achieve an objective determined in strategic planning. Different definitions of strategy, therefore, depend to some extent on the particular issues on which authors have chosen to focus in their research and writing. The various definitions are not right or wrong but, rather, differentially useful, depending on the purposes at hand.

For the purposes of this book, we adopt the following definition of strategy formulation:

Strategy formulation is a decision process focusing on the development of long-term objectives and the alignment of organizational capabilities and environmental contingencies so as to obtain them.

This definition includes the deployment of financial resources as one form of organizational capability and focuses on early stages of the strategic decision-making process. It emphasizes long-term objectives and the means of obtaining them and, therefore, is most consistent with the definitions of strategy of Chandler and Andrews.

Strategy implementation will be defined as all the remaining components of the basic implementation model defined in Chapter 1. Thus, implementation begins with decisions concerning primary structure and continues through the components of the model dealing with incentives and controls. Some of what we are calling implementation would be defined by others as formulation (refer to Lorange, who includes short-term operating objectives within what he calls "strategic programming").[9] However, most definitions of strategy formulation are consistent with our usage, generally agreeing that organization design and related activities constitute the "beginning" of implementation and the "end" of formulation activities.

Strategy formulation and implementation are primarily analytical processes of decision making, consistent with the principle of intended rationality. With high rates of environmental change or many environmental uncertainties, comprehensive, long-range objectives become increasingly difficult to obtain. Under these conditions managers undertake less comprehensive planning activities and shorten their time horizons. Organizational design decisions facilitate implementation by reducing the complexity of the strategic task and assigning parts of it to more manageable, differentiated subunits of the organization. While formulation activities are generally most responsible for determining the ends of strategic action, and implementation activities are mainly responsible for the means, both decision processes represent *complementary portions of a recurring chain of means-ends relationships designed to factor large, complex, long-term objectives into smaller, less complex and manageable actions.* Where one chooses to draw the line in this process—separating ends from means and, thus, formulation from implementation—is partially arbitrary. It is important, however, constantly to keep in mind just *what* it is that is being implemented: in this regard, strategy formulation precedes and shows the way for implementation activities.

The Importance of Strategy Formulation

The concept of strategy has received much attention in the recent literature on management. The heightened interest can be attributed to the importance of the strategy formulation and implementation process, especially in industries characterized by uncertainty, competition, and limited access to scarce resources. Hofer and Schendel conclude that studies by a number of researchers indicate that formal attention devoted to strategy formulation indeed results in superior performance measured in terms of profits, sales, and return on assets.[10] This conclusion is supported by the research of Karger, which shows a clear relation between planning and organizational profitability.[11] These and other works indicate that, given external conditions that are becoming more complex and presenting a host of contingencies and problems to organizations, the process of formulating strategy provides important outcomes or benefits that affect organizational performance. These benefits include, but are not limited to, the following.

1. *Identification of major opportunities and threats.* An important outcome of the process of strategy formulation is a better recognition and grasp of the critical issues that will affect the organization in the future. These might include:
   a. Marketing issues, such as new product or market opportunities or threats to market share.
   b. Anticipated actions of competitors or changes in the structure or concentration of the industry.
   c. Technological innovations that, if accomplished, would provide a distinctive cost or quality advantage for the innovator.
   d. Efficiency considerations (e.g., the need to lower costs to remain competitive, given commodity-type, undifferentiated products).
   e. Human-resource issues, such as the ways in which to develop top-management talent for future expansion.
   f. Ways in which to meet present or anticipated government regulations or requirements.

The process of formulating strategy forces a long-term perspective that can help in the identification of problems and opportunities that could become increasingly salient to the organization.

2. *Determination of key result areas to guide the setting of objectives.* An important consequence of the identification of opportunities and threats in the strategy formulation process is the setting of specific, long-term objectives to guide organizational action. Top management can identify and attach priorities to key result areas, and objectives can be set and action plans developed to achieve them.

Key result areas represent the strategic analog of what is referred to in sociotechnical theory as "key variances." As discussed by Hackman, key variances "are the points of leverage that can make big differences in what is produced and what it costs."[12] Hackman suggests that it would be worthwhile to apply this idea to broad questions of organization design and management. The point here is that this idea *is* being applied as managers utilize strategic planning processes to determine key result areas. Faced with opportunities on many fronts, managers select a restricted set of areas within which to concentrate their resources and efforts, the assumption being that the major portion of variance in organizational performance can be accounted for by a relatively small subset of strategic actions. Other applications of the idea of key variances occur in the strategy formulation literature, as when Hofer and Schendel discuss "sensitivity" or "variability" analyses.[13]

Additional benefits of the planning and objective-setting process include provision of a direction for middle managers and positive psychological outcomes for individuals, points developed in greater detail in Chapter 4. Suffice it to say at present that strategy formulation aids in the setting of objectives and creation of action plans, which often results in additional favorable consequences for the individual as well as the organization.

3. *Improved resource allocation.* Another important benefit of the strategy formulation process and its identification of strategic issues and specific key result areas is that top management is able to develop priorities and a guide for resource allocation. With competitive and economic pressures looming as increasingly pervasive and constraining phenomena, this consequence of strategic planning will increase in importance in most industries.
4. *Provision of a direction for change.* An important aspect of the strategic planning process is the identification of areas for organizational change. Planned change is a critical aspect of the top manager's role. And change is inextricably involved with the setting of objectives and evaluation of performance against them. The process of formulating strategy highlights areas where change is essential or beneficial and guides the development of specific change objectives. Hofer and Schendel similarly note that formal planning helps to implement changes once they have been decided upon.[14] Because of the importance of change, a separate chapter is devoted to it in Chapter 8.

There are other benefits of the strategic planning process, but the four noted here seem to capture their essence. It seems clear that strategy formulation is a purposeful, intellectual decision process that can result in the accrual of important benefits for the organization.

Strategy Formulation as a Decision Process

The previous sections have defined and discussed the importance of strategy formulation as a decision process. If this is so, then strategy formulation must have some characteristics in common with other human decision processes. We have already discussed the importance of one such characteristic—bounded rationality—for strategy formulation and implementation. In the following discussion, we further explore the implications of viewing formulation as a decision process, arguing that (1) decision situations may be characterized in terms of agreement concerning objectives and the means of obtaining these objectives, (2) some decision situations are relatively more desirable than others, and (3) strategy formulation is partially concerned with managing the decision process toward these more desirable conditions.

Thompson argues that decision issues always involve two major dimensions, which he refers to as the *basic variables of decision*.[15] These dimensions are (1) beliefs about the effects of alternative decisions or actions and (2) preferences regarding possible outcomes. The former dimension can easily be recast as technological clarity and output certainty. (If A is done, how clear and certain is a result or outcome, B?) The latter dimension can be reconceptualized to include agreement or disagreement on objectives or desired outcomes. Combining the two dimensions results in Figure 2-1, which identifies four idealized decision situations.

Cause-Effect Relations and Outcomes	Agreement on Objectives or Desired Outcomes: Agreement	Agreement on Objectives or Desired Outcomes: Disagreement
Certain/clear	Computation (I)	Compromise (III)
Uncertain/unclear	Judgmental (II)	"Inspiration" (IV)

Figure 2-1. Strategic assessment as a decision affected by two major dimensions. [Derived from J. D. Thompson, *Organizations in Action* (New York: McGraw-Hill Book Company, 1967), pp 134–136.]

Where there is agreement on objectives or desired outcomes among managers involved in the assessment of strategic options, and when it is very clear how to achieve those objectives (quadrant I), a choice of strategy is clear-cut. Decision making, in fact, is *computational.* A programmed decision is likely, for what is needed simply is a rank ordering of strategic options on clear, predetermined criteria of effectiveness. Assume that managers agree on some measure of profitability (e.g., net present value of future cash flows). The test of strategic options and choice is relatively simple and straightforward, for it is only necessary to perform some basic computations to determine the attractiveness of strategic proposals on the profitability criterion.

If managers agree on their preferences or desired outcomes, but the ways in which to achieve them are unclear, the assessment of strategic options is more difficult (quadrant II). Decisions are *judgmental.* Reliance on judgments increases the difficulty of decision making and the possibility that decisions may detract from measures of organizational-level performance. Given such problems over time, we would postulate a heightened interest in the need to clarify or crystallize the technologies involved. The agreement on desired ends simply creates or fuels a drive to seek better, more predictable ways or means of achieving preferred outcomes.

To illustrate this case, consider the use of strategic planning in a psychiatric hospital. Organizational members involved in the process agree on the primary objectives of cure and rehabilitation. Under these circumstances, the assessments or judgments of strategic options are likely to reflect this agreement, barring some clear-cut sign to the contrary. Decision making would only be problematic with respect to the means of obtaining the desired outcomes. Judgment would be employed to choose from among options potentially impacting on the agreed-upon objectives, and decision making would focus on such variables as discharge rate, treatment modality, and so on. Current discharge rates and treatment methods, for example, would be evaluated with respect to previous, historically successful levels and methods. As long as the hospital is seen as successful in meeting its primary objectives, such judgmental decision making is only slightly more difficult than computational decision making.

A mass murder by a discharged patient alters the case. In addition to obvious repercussions, such an action emphasizes the lack of certainty inherent in the treatment technology. It implies that previous judgments concerning the means of obtaining organizational objectives are subject to question. It may also increase the likelihood of future disagreements on values, perceptions, or desired outcomes (e.g., rehabilitation versus incarceration). Thus, assessment of strategic options is more difficult where cause-effect relations are unclear. Agreement on objectives or preferences helps the assessment and choice process, but decisions clearly are more fallible than those under the computation condition noted in the previous example.

If managers charged with the responsibility of strategy formulation disagree on the appropriate outcomes to attain, but the technological clarity of cause and effect is still high, decision making and choice of strategy ultimately reflect a *compromise* between or among individuals or coalitions (quadrant III). Power differences here may become quite salient and instrumental as the dominant individuals or coalitions control the assessment and affect the choice of strategy. With equality of power or influence, the compromise will of necessity reflect the disparate views and values of the disagreeing parties. In this case, the assessment of options and choice of strategy can be a longer and more arduous process compared with the situation in which there is widespread agreement on values and desired outcomes. Compromise may also describe decision making under conditions where management must consider the objectives of formal groups outside the organization (e.g., the perceptions of a large national union whose influence is felt in the definition and assessment of strategic options).

The most difficult case of decisions regarding strategy is the situation marked by both disagreement on desired outcomes and uncertain cause-effect relations (quadrant IV). Clearly, this represents a trying and unstable condition. Short of divine guidance or *inspiration,* some agreement on objectives, values, or desired outcomes must be negotiated. Only then is assessment of strategic options possible.

Decisions regarding the choice of strategy, then, are similar to other managerial decisions, except that the stakes may be a bit higher. Clearly, too, some decision situations are more preferable than others. Inspiration, compromise, and judgmental decisions are problematic in varying degrees, and managers would in general prefer computational decision making. Formal strategic planning processes are aimed in part at translating difficult and problematic decision situations into simpler, more certain, and more manageable ones. In the following sections, we argue that this is accomplished by first establishing agreement concerning strategic objectives and then systematically considering the merit of various strategic alternatives or options for obtaining these outcomes. In carrying out this process, decision makers respond to a number of organizational and environmental contingencies so as to maximize the probability of obtaining the desired objectives. This decision process also may be subject to a number of disturbances that affect the quality with which it is carried out. The next sections present our view of the strategy formulation process in detail.

THE STRATEGY FORMULATION PROCESS

Strategy formulation is a decision process concerned with developing long-term objectives and aligning organizational capabilities and environmental contingencies so as to obtain them. This process has several components that are presented in Figure 2-2. These components can be broadly segregated into two groups: the first deals with the *identification* of a set of strategic options; the second deals with *assessment and choice* from among those options.

We argue that it is useful and realistic to view strategy formulation as a search process influenced by considerations of limited rationality; the performance experience of the firm; the location, quality, and level of slack resources present; and the aspiration levels of key decision makers. The influence of search activities is most important during the identification of strategic options, so we discuss it along with the factors that are influential in developing such options. The desired outcome of the search process is consensus or agreement concerning a set of potential strategic options. This is achieved by considering what options are indeed feasible and then narrowing the range of feasible options through political compromise. The consequence is that the decision situation from that point on is better characterized as judgmental or computational rather than as a compromise or inspirational condition, facilitating further decision making.

The latter portions of the formulation process, then, typically employ judgment and computation to select from a set of acceptable options a smaller subset that will actually be pursued. This assessment will still be problematic because agreement resulting from the search process usually is not perfect, and a variety of rational, nonrational, and organizational factors will impact the final decision process. The following sections discuss each of these aspects of the formulation process in greater detail.

FACTORS CONSIDERED IN DEVELOPING STRATEGIC OPTIONS

In developing strategic options, a number of factors or "sources of contingency" must be accommodated, including the firm's current strategy and structure; environmental conditions; and its internal resources, capabilities, and distinctive competence, as shown in Figure 2-2. Strategic options result when the search process identifies locations of fit or complementarity between or among these areas.

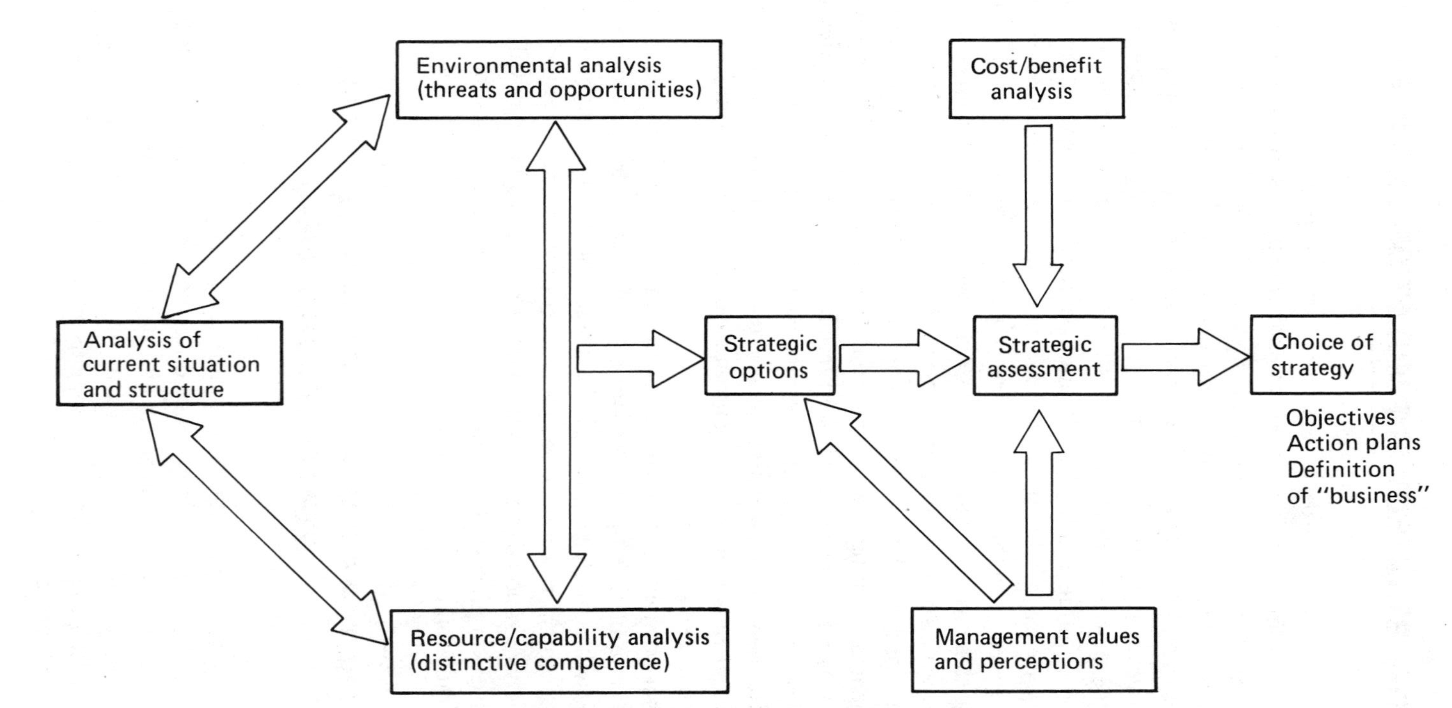

Figure 2-2. Strategy formulation process.

TABLE 2-1. Partial Correlations: Top-Management Agreement on Strengths and Weaknesses and Organizational Performance.

Agreement on Strength of	*Organizational Performance*
General management	32*
Financial management	26**
Sales and marketing	30**
Research and development	32*
Engineering	18†
Production	24**

*$p < .01$.
**$p < .10$.
†$p < .05$.
Source: From L. G. Hrebiniak and C. Snow, "Top-Management Agreement and Organizational Performance," *Human Relations,* Vol. 35, No. 12, (1982), pp. 1139–1158.

outcomes or even serendipitous consequences, leading to the reinforcement of strengths and the correction of weaknesses.

A recent empirical study provides some evidence supporting this view. Hrebiniak and Snow examined the relationship between top managers' agreement on their firm's strengths and weaknesses and the profit performance of the enterprise.[20] The research was based on a large sample (247 top-level managers in 88 organizations) and eliminated the effects of other variables (types of planning, prior performance, industry) when examining the relation between level of managerial agreement and current organizational performance. They found that there was a *positive* relation between top management's agreement on the firm's strength and weaknesses, in relation to its environmental context and the measure of organizational performance used—return on assets (see Table 2-1 for examples of the partial correlations obtained).

The data suggest that an ongoing assessment of organizational capabilities and external needs can have positive results. If the process of assessment and analysis of relevant internal and external variables results in agreement, top management can more easily build on strengths and develop plans to compensate for weaknesses when positioning the organization in its task environment. The study also suggests that the *process* of interaction or participation among top-level managers and the resultant commitments to action plans and objectives hold positive implications for the subsequent successful implementation of strategy.

THE SEARCH PROCESS

The truly interesting and important issues underlying traditional concerns with the matching of internal competence with external needs or opportunities really involve the nature of the *search process* in organizations. While we have argued that an analysis of endogenous and exogenous variables is an essential part of strategy formulation, it is essential that we not limit our inquiry to that basic fact. The search process is more complex than the need to focus on fit between organization and environment would indicate. Clearly, there are more central and interesting issues that can be raised regarding the nature of search activities in organizations.

The relevance of search processes to the development of strategic options is clearly seen as March discusses the consequences of limited rationality: "Rather than all alternatives being known, alternatives have to be discovered through search—search is seen as being stimulated by a failure to achieve a goal and continuing until it reveals an alternative that is good enough to satisfy existing goals." During this process "new alternatives are sought in the 'neighborhood' of old ones, and new information is obtained."[21]

Thus, search processes for strategic options in organizations are not random but, rather, are stimulated by a discrepancy between current performance and the aspiration levels of key decision makers. Once search processes are begun, they are influenced by a number of factors, which we consider next.

Possibility, Acceptability, and the Feasible Set of Strategic Options

As has just been indicated, a desired outcome of the process of selecting strategic options is the development of agreement concerning what objectives are sought by the firm. Agreement is accomplished by identifying a set of technically and politically acceptable strategic options. Because there is consensus that these options are in fact desirable, further choice from among them is judgmental or computational, facilitating decision making.

Clearly, the first critical issue is to determine what is and is not feasible for the firm to achieve. Thompson writes that "Members of a dominant coalition are, of course, free to prefer anything; but for purposes of control over the organization, . . . only those preferences which conceivably are outcomes of possible action by the organization are therefore relevant."[22] This suggests that there are criteria for agreement on a strategic option, two of the more important ones being *technical possibility* and *political acceptability*.

Technical possibility refers to the constraints imposed by the firm's understanding of cause-effect relationships as they relate to a specific option. Some options are more "do-able" than others, and, subject to the criteria of intended rationality, decision makers will prefer options that meet at least some standards of attainability. Identification of options that meet these standards determines what we will call the possible set of options.

Political acceptability further reduces the number of options that may be pursued. All the options within the possible set are not acceptable to all parties, and, building upon the previous argument, compromise takes place among politically influential groups both within and without the organization to generate a smaller subset of strategic options acceptable to all. Compromise results in a smaller subset of strategic options selected from among the possible set. Although many options may be possible, fewer are politically acceptable, and those that are both determine what we will call the *feasible set* of options.

Two factors, technical possibility and political acceptability, determine what we define as the feasible set of strategic options. The search process, which identifies options that are technically possible and that meet the first tests of political acceptability, can now be examined in greater detail.

Factors Affecting the Search Process

A number of specific factors influence the nature of the search process and the feasible set of strategic options. The first three—organizational learning, distinctive competence, and the qualitative type of search engaged in—affect the development of strategic options by localizing search activities so as to maximize the likelihood of quickly discovering *possible* options. The last two—power differences and absorption of environmental uncertainty—influence the acceptability of strategic options through processes of compromise.

Organizational Learning. Over time, key decision makers learn that a particular activity or strength can be applied to a variety of external needs. This momentum or "inertia" is strongest when the organization feels comfortable with certain activities or ways of doing business and when those patterns of behavior have typically been associated with positive results. This phenomenon can be interpreted as a process of "organizational learning," much like individual models of behavioral change and adaptation. Organizations learn from the consequences of their previous strategic behaviors. Strategic actions that have produced successful results are repeated, and those that have not are abandoned. The results of these actions are internalized by the firm as a sort of organizational "memory" that is drawn upon as decision makers search for strategic options when facing a problematic situation. This memory resides in key decision makers, rules and procedures, and the organization's strategic and operating systems.

Miles argues that " a strategic choice may be viewed as a voluntary behavior of the organization. . . . The propensity for managers to employ a specific strategic choice is conditioned—strengthened or diminished—by the consequences it has elicited from the environment in previous situations."[23] The search process is therefore influenced by organizational learning as key decision makers search for strategic options in the locality of previous successes. The competencies of the firm, distinctive in relation to others with which it competes, also influence the identification of feasible strategic options by "localizing" and directing the search process.

Distinctive Competence and the Location of Slack Resources. We have argued that organizations will search for strategic options that are possible or attainable. It is logical, then, to posit that the location of these possibilities is influenced by the nature of the firm's slack resources. *Slack resources denote an advantageous capability or excess capacity that, under norms of rationality, the organization seeks to apply to establish a strategic position and avoid underutilization of capacity and inefficient performance.* We propose that organizations with a distinctive competence tend to build upon it and that the strategies identified will vary with the type and amount of slack resources available.

In our view, distinctive competence denotes a type of slack resource or excess capability. Given this excess capacity, organizations will seek to use it productively. Thus, search for strategic options will be driven by distinctive competence and a desire to maintain the competitive advantage it denotes. Assume, for example, a distinctive competence in the area of production or technology. Strategic planning will likely identify options or new applications, first, in products or services *related technologically*. This follows simply because it is the easiest and most efficient option and results in the greatest possibility of success. Thompson notes that the simplest form of diversification springs from excess technological capacity and results in new products to which that capacity is closely allied and easily adapted.[24]

It is also possible that a firm may enjoy excess capacity or distinctive competence in marketing or distribution. In this case, the development of strategic options would center on identifying products or services that are *market related*. In the ideal situation, of course, new products and/or services are also related technologically, but it often happens that they enjoy little similarity technologically. This strategy generally necessitates the acquisition of additional technical capacity and is often more drastic than diversification through technologically related products.

Diversification that involves developing strategic options that are related technologically and marketwise is sometimes referred to as *concentric* diversification. The term is used to suggest that the firm is expanding its domain from a "center" of distinctive competence. Rumelt suggests that firms pursuing strategies of concentric diversification frequently outperform those selecting strategic options that are unrelated in a technical or market sense.[25] While other unrelated options could be adopted on the basis of portfolio analyses, for example, these options pose greater risks to the firm. Some of these risks include management's inability to run a business that is unrelated to its own and, in the case of an acquisition, to correct possible weaknesses of the acquired firm that its own experienced management was unable to resolve.

The higher performance of a firm pursuing market- or technically related strategic options suggests that, by searching for such options in the locality of the firm's distinctive competence, some of the aforementioned problems can be avoided and the firm's critical resources can be exploited more efficiently. Given a distinctive competence, then, the search for strategic options will reflect management's desire to build on it and the excess capacity it implies. Products or services related technologically and in a market sense will logically be sought first, with diversification into unrelated areas the next likely step.

Past Performance and Type of Search Activity. Depending upon the previous performance of the organization, qualitatively distinct types of search activity are employed for the identification of the feasible set of strategic options. March refers to these processes as *solution-driven* and *slack-search* activities.[26] In the former, search focuses on developing solutions for problems; in the latter, search is not as tightly linked to organizational objectives but, rather, represents experimentation or even "dabbling" with new or untried activities, processes, or products. March argues that when the firm has been performing well, its solution-driven search activities will diminish but that slack-search processes will increase and adopt a more risky stance. Conversely, if the firm has been performing poorly, its central or solution-driven search will become more important, correspondingly more constrained, and, consequently, more risk taking as the organization seeks results in specific problem areas.

Figure 2-3 summarizes these observations. As the performance of the firm improves, slack-search activities take precedence over solution-driven search, decisions are less centralized, and risk taking is seen as options are uncovered

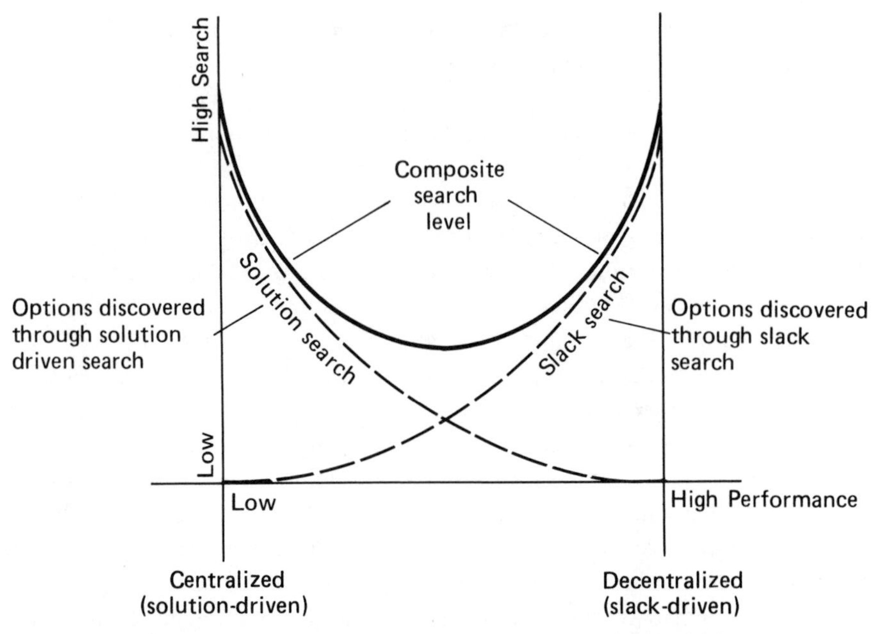

Figure 2-3. Organizational performance and search activities.

during slack search. The converse also obtains: when performance is poor, solution-driven search is preferred, slack search disappears, decisions are more centralized, and there is greater risk taking among the problem-oriented options developed.

Another way in which to consider March's arguments and fit them into our perspective of search for feasible options is to clarify further the qualitatively different types of search being discussed. Under conditions of poor performance, search is solution driven as the organization is concerned with improving its position. It may be that the organization is running extremely lean or is in trouble due to an external "shock" that looms as a growing threat. Problem-oriented search activity increases, and requisite levels of important performance criteria decrease in an effort to identify feasible solutions. Thus, a greater number of external opportunities become salient and are defined as satisfactory options for organizational action.

Under conditions of high performance or low threat, search occurs as a part of the slack-generated activities of the organization, according to March. This type of slack search, as noted, at times may even represent a form of legitimized dabbling. With more than ample resources, pet projects more readily are funded. Individuals are indirectly encouraged to experiment with new markets, applications, or innovative approaches to existing conditions.

Given the relaxed, nonthreatening conditions, slack search has a chance of discovering something of considerable value. And even if innovations are not forthcoming, this type of search produces a *reservoir* of ideas. While opportunities identified during the process of slack search may not be acted on immediately, they form a pool of options that can be stored in the organizational inventory or managerial memory and activated later when and if they are needed. Thus this reservoir provides potential additions to the feasible set of strategic options for future organizational use.

In sum, Figure 2-3 shows that there is a composite level of search activity within the firm and that this level can be approximated by an inverted U shape. The total level of search is high when the firm has been performing well or poorly (although the type of search differs) and moderate when performance has been average. It follows, then, that the number of strategic options generated will be high during times of plenty and adversity and correspondingly lower when the firm's performance has been moderate. Many of these identified options will be viewed as possible or feasible because, under both high- and low-performance conditions, the firm is risk prone with respect to the options generated by the search process that is predominant. However, because search and decision making are more centralized and linked to organizational goals when the firm has been performing poorly, it also follows logically that more of the options discovered under this condition will be viewed as possible solutions to the problems at hand.

Organizational performance, therefore, influences the level and type of search activities in which the firm engages as well as the extent to which decision processes are risk prone or risk averse and centralized or decentralized. The net effect is to increase the number of feasible strategic options when the firm has been performing either well or poorly, thereby heightening the importance of further political processes of compromise to determine the acceptable set of options to be pursued. The next two factors describe these processes.

Power Differences Within the Organization. Power is social influence—the ability to influence others to do something, including concur with a decision or plan with which they might not normally agree. In utilitarian organizations, power usually is the *obverse of dependency;* that is, if B is dependent on A for something essential, and if A is successful in controlling (at the extreme, monopolizing) what it is that B needs, A has power over B.[27]

If an individual or unit within an organization solves the critical problems facing an organization, or is able to control important scarce resources, the dependency of others results in power differences. The individual or unit can exercise power or social influence. And one such exercise among top managers is the formulation of strategy, including definition of external needs or opportunities to which the powerholder's knowledge and expertise can be applied. By becoming central and pervasive, managers with power can do a great deal to determine or define specific external factors that deserve the attention of the organization.

Having power and using the social influence it denotes to control resources and decision making, including strategic planning, clearly represents an example of internal political forces shaping the process of identifying acceptable strategic options for the organization. *Given a number of options that represent possible outcomes and courses of action, the exercise of power identifies those that are most feasible or desirable.* Power differences are also important in explaining the process of assessment and choice from among acceptable strategic options, a point to which we return shortly.

Absorbing Environmental Uncertainty Through "Politics." Faced with uncertainty, the organization has a problem, for it cannot operate well without determinateness and certainty. It must try to absorb or eliminate problems and uncertainty and achieve some rationality, even if it is bounded and incomplete. Thus, we observe a strategy of vertical integration backward to reduce the uncertainties associated with erratic or unpredictable supplies (assuming, again, the existence of slack resources). Given the risks or implied threats of seasonality, organizations expand lines of activity and diversify products and services to compensate for seasonal fluctuations. But the organization may also engage in "political" behavior to reduce uncertainty. To acquire power and reduce a problematic dependence on another organization or class of organizations within a market or domain (e.g., financial institutions), the organization contracts, co-opts, or enters a coalition with those external entities.[28]

While entering contracts, absorbing new elements into the organization (e.g., representatives of banks onto the board of directors), and entering joint ventures with other organizations reduce uncertainty for the organization, they also produce new constraints. Contracting, co-opting, and coalescing give other individuals and organizations some say in the operation of the firm *and thus possibly a voice in the political process of compromise that selects an acceptable set of strategic options for final assessment and choice.* In effect, the organization must reduce uncertainty and increase determinateness so that it can operate. But if the absorption of uncertainty includes contracting, coalescing, and co-opting, additional voices are introduced into the process that identify aceptable strategic options.

Summary: Identifying Strategic Options. The preceding discussion suggests that search in organizations and the resultant formulation of a feasible set of strategic options depend on a number of key factors:

1. Organizational learning
2. Distinctive competence and the location of slack resources
3. Past performance and type of search activity
4. Power differences within the organization
5. Absorption of uncertainty through politics

We have examined some of the more important factors influencing the search process as well as their effects on strategy formulation. In essence, we have argued that these five factors can affect or cause a differential salience among external stimuli or internal variables in the identification of strategic options.

The next logical step is to consider the assessment process by which these options are evaluated and that leads inexorably to the choice of an operative strategy for the organization. This is the purpose of the next section.

STRATEGIC ASSESSMENT AND CHOICE

Strategy formulation has been presented as a decision process focusing on determination of long-term objectives and the alignment of organizational capabilities and environmental opportunities so as the achieve them. The discussion has also implied that this matching process may reveal a number of different strategic options: to achieve its objectives, an organization may be able to choose among various acceptable plans or ways in which to proceed. How, then, are priorities assigned to the feasible options beyond their political acceptability, and what determines the final choice of strategy?

The assessment process by which strategic options are evaluated may vary by organization or industry, depending on previous experience, changing economic concentration or market structure, and the amount of anticipated change.[29] Still, it will be useful to classify the factors affecting the assessment and choice process into two categories: rational and nonrational factors (Figure 2-2). We have found that use of these two categories has a strong basis in reality. While managers typically present the paradigms and variables that affect strategic choice with a cold, stated logic, the "logic-in-use" occasionally includes additional factors, subjective or nonrational, that occasionally have a large impact on the assessment and choice process.[30]

The Rational Factors. A rational approach assumes that the organization's purpose or *raison d'être* is primarily the pursuit and achievement of economic or utilitarian objectives. It presumes that even seemingly noneconomic factors support the basic ends of the organization.

To some, the mention of economic objectives surely denotes a perspective focusing on private sector, profit-making institutions. While clearly these organizations are included, the present discussion of the rational approach is broader. It also includes, for instance, strategic planning in a general hospital where the emphasis is on the provision of quality care at reasonable cost. Similarly, emphasis on cost containment or avoidance of duplication of expensive diagnostic equipment or procedures within a defined health care region also would be included under a rational or utilitarian approach.

The crux of this approach is an emphasis on (1) organizational ends and (2) utilitarian outcomes. Consistent with the principle of intended rationality, top management focuses upon important utilitarian factors that will strengthen the position of the organization in its task environment. Top-level decision makers then evaluate strategic options against these factors, well-known examples of which include the following:

1. *Economic costs versus benefits.* Use of break-even analysis, payback periods, and net present value or discounted cash flow methods is consistent with the notion of measuring costs and benefits of competing strategies.
2. *Market share.* Emphasis is on variation in market penetration as a result of various strategies. The assumption usually is that increase in market share will result in increased profitability in the longer term as well as a broader base for future expansion and penetration.
3. *Profitability, liquidity, or leverage indexes.* These, to some degree, may be implied by or subsumed under (1) above. Because of the attention paid to certain specialized indexes or measures when evaluating strategic options, however, it is our view they should be mentioned separately. These include, but are not limited to, such indexes as earnings per share, current ratio, net working capital, inventory turnover, and the debt-to-equity ratio.
4. *Opportunity costs.* Strategic options may be evaluated against an opportunity cost criterion, most notably, when a single strategy looms preeminent or obvious. The purpose really is to force consid-

eration of other options or activities and the potential benefits forfeited by their exclusion.
5. *Turnover and other human resource issues.* Such criteria as reductions in turnover or improvement in management training are used in assessing strategic options primarily because of the cost savings or other utilitarian benefits involved (e.g., source of future general managers to take over new divisions).

Managers routinely and overtly stress economic or utilitarian measures when considering different strategies. They attempt to make appropriate and profitable decisions for the organization. Ultimately, managers face the test of performance evaluation and review; supervisors, directors, or external stakeholders typically seek an accounting of the uses to which scarce resources have been applied. Occasionally, the utilitarian test is delineated prior to strategic assessment and choice. Recent strategic decisions at U.S. Steel, for example, clearly delineated the minimum growth criteria that must be met before investments can be made in its various operations, including steel, chemicals, and manufacturing.

Other organizations routinely exhibit similar pre- and postperformance controls. To presume that managers flaunt reason and ignore the inevitable accountability built into organizational planning and control systems is naïve. That is *not* to say, however, that arational or nonrational considerations do not affect the assessment of strategic options.

Nonrational Factors: Individual Needs, Values, and Perceptions. The mention of arational elements in the assessment and choice and strategies should not connote arbitrary, capricious, or foolish behavior on the part of managers. We are not introducing "irrational" behavior, but arational factors—factors that are not solely economic or utilitarian, as in the rational approach, but rather ones grounded in or affected by the *needs, values, and perceptions* of the managers making the strategic choices.

One rather clear example of the role of personal values in the strategic planning process was seen in 1977 when the president of Holiday Inns resigned after the company approved its first venture in casino gambling. The strategy formulation process had generated a pervasive belief among Holiday Inn executives that such a venture was clearly consistent with the company's distinctive competence and, hence, represented a prudent and profitable business decision. The president, however, had long disapproved of gambling on moral and religious grounds. These values or beliefs prompted him to oppose strenuously the development of plans or objectives premised on a move into the casino business. When his influence failed, he felt that he had no other alternative but to resign his position; his values and beliefs were not consistent with those of the remainder of the top-management team. While personal values were rejected in this case, the influence attempt based on those beliefs supports the contention that nonutilitarian or noneconomic factors enter the strategy formulation process.

Evidence of the effects of individuals' values on objectives and strategy abounds in the history and folklore of organizations. Howard Head's long insistence that metal skis were far superior to their plastic counterparts and the long-lived strategy based on that premise provide one example. And the impact of Edwin Land on Polaroid is well known. As both *Fortune* and *Time* magazines have noted, Polaroid has been shaped in Land's image; its approach to business is that of the rational scientist and the humanitarian philosopher.[31] Who can analyze the business decisions of Harold Geneen (IT&T), Lee Iacocca (Ford, Chrysler), Henry Ford, Reginald Jones (General Electric), or George Romney (American Motors) without sensing that their values had or still have a profound impact on the strategy formulation process?

Although central values and beliefs are occasionally *the* determining factor in the assessment and choice of strategic options, rational factors notwithstanding, there are three more usual and prevalent cases of the effects of individual needs or values on strategic decision making. The first occurs when *strategic choice is among options with apparently satisfactory utilitarian outcomes, so that the decision ultimately made really reflects preferences that are personal or value driven.*

The very clear example of this impact is shown by some recent work suggesting why organizations develop the particular strategies they do. Miles and Snow studied organizational adaptation in over eighty organizations and their data were striking.[32] They found that top management consciously and purposely develops and articulates an organizational type and image when choosing a strategy and market niche. In the presence of information regarding environmental opportunities, top-level decision makers focus on subsets of it, depending on what they feel the organization should do or be like. The four organizational types of images that Miles and Snow identified are [33]

Defender: *This type of organization attempts to locate and maintain a secure niche in a relatively stable product or service area. The organization tends to offer a more limited range of products or services than its domain by offering higher quality, superior service, lower prices, and so forth. Often this type of organization is not at the forefront of developments in the industry—it tends to ignore industry changes that have no direct influence on current areas of operation and concentrates instead on doing the best job possible in a limited area.*

Prospector: *This type of organization typically operates within a broad product-market domain that undergoes periodic redefinition. The organization values being "first in" in new product and market areas even if not all these efforts prove to be highly profitable. The organization responds rapidly to early signals concerning areas of opportunity, and these responses often lead to a new round of competitive actions. However, this type of organization may not maintain market strength in all the areas it enters.*

Analyzer: *This type of organization attempts to maintain a stable, limited line of products or services, while at the same time moving out quickly to follow a carefully selected set of the more promising new developments in the industry. The organization is seldom "first in" with new products or services. However, by carefully monitoring the actions of major competitors in areas compatible with its stable product-market base, the organization can frequently be "second in" with a more cost-efficient product or service.*

Reactor: *The type of organization does not appear to have a consistent product-market orientation. The organization is usually not as aggressive in maintaining established products and markets as some of its competitors, nor is it willing to take as many risks as other competitors. Rather, the organization responds in those areas where it is forced to buy environmental pressures.*

An important point for the present discussion is that all four types can be found in the same industry and all can perform well on a list of popular utilitarian criteria. Given a defined market or domain, organizations can approach it differently, depending on what top management decides is most appropriate. The identification and/or the assessment of feasible strategic options developed in the rational search process, then, are affected by managerial perceptions or values. In similar terms, given strategic options that are *equally* viable from an economic or utilitarian standpoint, managerial beliefs, attitudes, or values provide the "tie-breaker."

The second case occurs when *individuals pursue ends that for them are eminently rational and worthwhile, but the summation of individual motivations and achievements does not result in appropriate outcomes for the organization.* Individual rationality, that is, does not result in organizational-level rationality. In extreme cases, logical pursuit of ends at the individual level militates against organizational performance. This leads observers to believe, mistakenly, that individuals and organizations do not attempt to behave rationally, even in a bounded sense. Indeed, the inference occasionally derived from the observed results is that anarchy, lack of structure, and disorder comprise or characterize the decision-making process in organizations, not rationality and its attendant means-ends analysis.

This case actually provides support for intended rationality in organizations. The problem it raises is primarily one of level of analysis and control. The task or challenge it defines is the need to ensure that motivations and logical behavior at the individual level are consistent with utilitarian outcomes at the organizational level. Because of the importance of motivation and the control function, additional attention is devoted to it in part in Chapter 4 but especially in Chapter 7, on incentives and controls.

The preceding example suggests that individual rationality in pursuing needs and values might not necessarily culminate in organizational-level rationality. Another interesting but different case can be observed when studying political processes in organizations. That is, *individuals acting in their own self-interests—following their own beliefs, values, and political predispositions—may positively affect organizational rationality, despite the exercise and predominance of nonrational factors in the decision process.*

As indicated previously, differences in power are inevitable in organizations. Externally generated contingencies and problematic dependencies usually affect organizational structure and process and the allocation of resources; those responsible for the handling or solution of major problems or dependencies confronting the organization receive the resources, status, and rewards commensurate with that important task. This unequal endowment or distribution of scarce resources provides the basis for an uneven distribution of power—social influence—in the organization, power being the obverse of dependency, as indicated earlier. Those who have resources, and who are successful in monopolizing them over time, can influence the behavior of those who depend on and need those resources. Other factors also influence power, of course, but in utilitarian organizations, the distribution of and control over scarce resources (money, people, information, etc.) are predominant.

Obviously, power can be used to determine the assessment and choice of strategic options. Individuals who are central, pervasive, and highly visible because of their ability to solve major problems or handle critical dependencies confronting the organization clearly will affect decision making more than will managers with far less of a base of social influence. Obviously, individuals with power can yield their influence in a variety of ways, including the use of covert, political activities. The work of Pfeffer, Hrebiniak, Dahl, and others vividly portrays the effects of power on decisions in political-economic systems.[34]

It should be clear, however, that power or social influence often is employed to support a decision or strategy that is viable and competitive with other options on some set of utilitarian criteria. Managers surely do play politics and lobby for a preferred option or alternative. But to do so consistently to support a strategy that is clearly deficient in its utilitarian outcomes vis-à-vis other strategies is certainly not very wise. Even allowing for individuals' hedonism, need for power, and purely personal objectives, "organization," by definition, denotes control and evaluation. Satisfying personal needs without contributing to the utilitarian outcomes deemed important by others inside or outside the organization can culminate in a loss of resources, influence, and status over time.

Thus the exercise of power, engaging in politics, and satisfaction of individual needs can result in positive outcomes for the organization that, in turn, reinforce the existing distribution of influence. The existence of power differences and politics does not always result in negative or debilitating consequences for the system within which these influence processes occur.

One additional point should be emphasized to complete the discussion of power and politics. Our arguments assume that social influence is wielded in utilitarian organizations where outcomes are measurable and many, if not all, cause-effect relations are at least fairly crystallized. Certainly, political behavior is more prevalent in organizations where outcomes are not measurable and, consequently, technologies or means-ends relations are unspecifiable. One could even argue that a fair proportion of the research on power in the literature has taken place in these types of organizations (e.g., hospitals, universities, and political organizations), a fact that may go far in explaining the importance of and infatuation with power and politics that pervade these systems.

To recapitulate, the assessment and choice of strategy usually represent a process that emphasizes utilitarian outcomes. Top-level managers perform a purposeful role in strategy formulation that is directed toward achieving an alignment between external market needs and organizational capabilities. Personal attitudes and values play an important role in the process primarily when it is difficult to choose between or among options that have similar economic or utilitarian outcomes, when organizational factors create an inconsistency between individual and organizational needs, or when political processes are active.

LEVELS OF STRATEGY

Up to this point we have employed the singular term "strategy" almost exclusively, which implies a single organizational action plan. In reality, this may or may not be true. An organization can have a single strategy or many strategies. The multidivisional firm has a *corporate-level* strategy as well as *divi-*

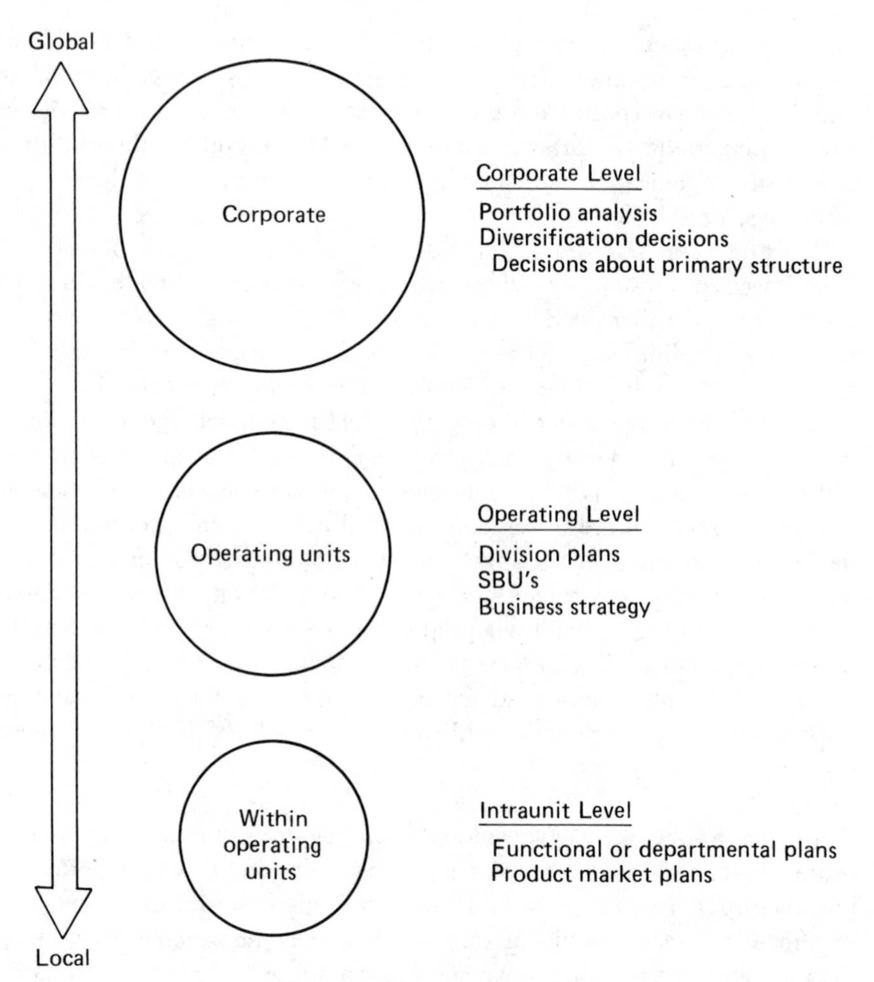

Figure 2-4. Levels of strategy.

sion- or *business-level* strategies. Within divisions or businesses, there may be additional distinct *functional area* strategies and similar formulations that vary by level or task.[35]

Figure 2-4 shows the different levels of strategy formulation and how they vary on a global-local continuum. Corporate strategy is the most "global"; planning at this level typically involves "portfolio" decisions regarding what businesses the firm is in or should be in. Portfolio analysis at the corporate level directs attention to questions regarding the attractiveness of entire businesses in terms of important operating or strategic criteria, such as markets, industry growth, or expected contribution to corporate earnings over some period of time.

Operating units of the organization include the divisions, businesses, or strategic business units (SBUs) that are created by the corporate level. The operating level is more "local" than the corporate level, and the former can be subsumed under the latter. The strategies of operating divisions or businesses can be viewed as the plans of the "parts" that comprise and define the whole organization. Figure 2-4 also indicates that strategic planning may be carried out by functions or departments within the major operating units, indicating even smaller or more "local" concerns within the major operating divisions or businesses.

Discussion of the interactions or relations between or among organizational levels can be found in Lorange as well as in Hofer and Schendel, among others.[36] Some of what we develop in the paragraphs that follow, while expanding and explaining the implementation model, will add to that discussion, as, for example, when considering strategic decisions and their effects on primary structure. For present purposes, it is only necessary to stress that *the essence of strategy formulation is grasped by Figure 2-2 but that elements or key variables in that process vary by organizational level or part.*

To pursue this point, consider a hypothetical multidivisional firm. Examination of the planning process reveals at least two different levels of strategic concern (see Table 2-2). Decisions at both levels—corporate and divisional or business—include external and internal factors in the strategy formulation process, consistent with Figure 2-2. The nature and type of those factors, however, may or may not vary as a function of level. Planning decisions at the corporate level include analyses *across* divisions or businesses; in contrast, decisions in the latter units are confined primarily to *within*-business concerns and more specific product and/or market considerations. The corporate level decides on the retention or elimination of entire businesses, whereas individual divisions decide on the expansion or consolidation of only its own products or services. Values, perceptions, and differences in social influence come into play at both levels, as the more powerful and central managers affect the planning process. If the corporate level should ever decide to "clamp down" on a specific division, however, the resultant centralization would increase the relative power or influence of the corporate staff over division managers.

Thus, it is clear that there are differences in levels within organizations and often multiple strategies. It is also true that the nature and type of specific influences on the planning process may or may not vary as a function of level, as the preceding discussion and Table 2-2 indicate. Again, the reader is

TABLE 2-2. Strategy Formulation at Two Levels in a Multidivisional Firm.

Organizational Level	Examples of Variables Entering Strategic Decision Process,*
Corporate Level	*External Factors* Changes in government antitrust legislation Worldwide fluctuation in currency exchange and interest rates Rates of growth or decline in GNP Changes in economic concentration or competition in key industries Educational-level changes affecting work force composition and career expectations Employment levels and demands of large national unions
	Internal Factors Relative competitive strength and profitability of the different divisions or business units Differences in distinctive competence among units Market growth rates across businesses Relative degree of demand volatility and price elasticity across businesses Varying levels of political power or influence among individuals heading divisions or businesses Values and perceptions of C.E.O. and key decision makers or gatekeepers
	Strategic assessment and choice Portfolio analysis evaluating industry attractiveness and competitive position of divisions vis-à-vis other firms in industry Analysis of past and projected performance in terms of relative business growth, profitability, net present value of future cash flows, and related utilitarian measures of effectiveness
Division or Business Level	*External factors* Stage of market evolution, product demand, or product life cycle Competitive trends or changes in specific product-market niches Government regulatory changes affecting a specific business or product-market niche (e.g., EPA regulations or OSHA standards) Trends in cost-price structure and price elasticities Corporate portfolio analyses and projected strategies of central planning staff or top management team

Organizational Level	Examples of Variables Entering Strategic Decision Process,*
	Trends in financial factors in industry (e.g., capital structure, working capital needs)
	Uncertainty due to sales and price volatility specific to a division's task environment
	Changes in market concentration within industry
	Internal factors
	Excess capacity or distinctive competence of business or division over competition
	Extent of or opportunity for vertical integration
	Adequacy of the number and type of distribution channels
	Technological or production adequacy
	Relative power or social influence of heads of functional areas
	Incentive and control systems
	Values and perceptions of division head and key functional people
	Strategic Assessment and Choice
	Analysis of trends in profitability, market share, and growth vis-à-vis competitors
	Calculation of net present value of future cash savings and outlays due to contemplated vertical integration
	Evaluation of financial, managerial, and physical resources needed to pursue different growth, defender, or turnaround strategies
	Political compromise process to "break ties" when more than one "preferred" or viable strategy is identified

*From Figure 2-2.

advised to consider the in-depth analysis of strategy formulation at both the corporate and business levels by Lorange, Hofer and Schendel, and others who have spent a good deal of time differentiating and discussing the nature of decisions that predominate by organizational level. Finally, more is said in Chapter 4 about strategy at the business level when considering operating-level objectives and their relationship to organizational or corporate strategic decisions.

Despite the different loci or levels of strategy formulation, two points should be kept in mind. First, those charged with the job of strategy formulation usually focus most of their attention at a single level. The head of a division will exert most intellectual effort on the division's strategy. The C.E.O. in the organization will be concerned primarily with corporate strategy and how the divisions and businesses fit under one unifying umbrella. This is not to say that there is little or no interdependence between levels; clearly, strategy at one level incorporates and is consistent with strategy at the next lower level, as has been indicated. It is to say that there exists a predominantly unitary focus on strategy formulation because of level. Managers rarely are blessed with the cognitive abilties and time to comprehend fully the complex strategies and related data that exist at different locations in the organization. Thus, use of the singular term "strategy" is not necessarily inappropriate or misleading.

The second point is an extension of the first, namely, that the model of strategy formulation (Figure 2-2) is useful, regardless of level. Constraints, resources, or type of environmental variables differ by level, but the formulation approach is basically the same. In addition to market factors and divisional strengths and weaknesses, a president of a division would likely include corporate level variables or factors in his or her analysis of the "external" environment. Analyses at the corporate level, including consideration of the type, nature, and salience of external factors, may be quite different, although the process or approach to identifying and assessing them would resemble that at the divisional or SBU level. While the nature, number, and type of variables included at various organizational levels in strategic planning clearly can differ, all the variables can be subsumed under the headings of the formulation model.

It should be emphasized, finally, that formulating strategy on multiple levels is consistent with what we described in Chapter 1 as the principle of intended rationality. Faced with large, difficult, and unmanageable tasks, the strategy formulation process factors these tasks into smaller, less difficult, and more manageable components. Corporate-level strategy creates the portfolio of businesses that represent these more local and smaller units. In similar terms, the outcomes of strategy formulation at the corporate level impact on the primary structure of the firm by suggesting appropriate or desirable levels of horizontal and vertical self-containment, for example, extent of divisionalization and vertical integration.

It is clear, therefore, that strategy formulation at the corporate level impacts on choices of primary structure (Chapter 3) as well as on business-level strategies and operating-level objectives (Chapter 4). It is fitting, then, that the next two chapters treat these topics in greater depth.

Summary

The present chapter was designed to present an overview of the strategy formulation process. A number of conclusions or implications for managerial action and strategy implementation are suggested.

Formulating strategy is a decision process that selects and fosters utilitarian outcomes, helps to position the organization in its task environment, and enables management to build on competitive advantage. To the extent possible, formulating strategy reflects a concurrent analysis of external and internal variables. The process also attempts to foster agreement among managers on the key result areas on which to focus, for we have suggested that agreement is related to organizational performance. Agreement on strategic ends and plans is also very likely to be related in a positive way to ease of implementation because of the participation and commitment implied by it and by the improved decision situation it fosters.

The identification of a feasible set of options under strategy formulation is affected by organizational learning, distinctive competence, and the type of search process conducted. Responses to environmental contingencies and the existence of power differences and political processes influence the acceptability of the strategic options identified. The present chapter intended to show how organizations build on or are affected by these variables and how the search for strategic alternatives or options is conducted and consummated.

Search processes are central to decisions regarding strategy and long-term objectives. Under conditions of duress, search activity is problem oriented and is intended to thwart the threats to organizational position. Under conditions of high performance and slack resources, search is more relaxed and often not tied tightly to organizational objectives. In our opinion, the latter type of search is critical to long-term adaptability and success. Search under conditions of slack resources generates a pool of potential options that can be mobilized under less munificent conditions, thereby offering an additional buffer against environmental volatility or unforeseen exigencies. Slack-generated search may also result in serendipitous consequences, as the relaxed climate that prevails compared with search under duress may allow for more "tinkering" and occasionally may result in innovation, with positive, if unanticipated outcomes, for the organization.

Assessment of strategic options occurs using both rational and nonrational criteria. The former include the assessment of options against such utilitarian measures as return on investment, net present value, and expected changes in market penetration. Nonrational factors include managerial values and preferences that typically represent "tie-breakers" after some minimum level of performance on utilitarian measures has been established. It is important to note, however, that different strategies can prosper in a given industry, depending upon managerial desires or values. That is, managers can exercise discretion over strategic approaches to task environment, selection of market niche, or "type" of organization. The critical task for the implementation process, given such strategic choice, is to align type of strategy or market approach with the appropriate organizational design, distinctive competence, and incentives of controls, topics considered in greater detail in later chapters.

A final implication of the present chapter is one that is critical to the implementation process and one that provides the topic of the next chapter: namely, that choice of strategy can affect the primary structure of the organization. Strategy formulation clearly reflects existing constraints or conditions, including how the organization is designed and how it functions. This fact notwithstanding, this chapter has also suggested that corporate-level decisions include those that create structure and affect the primary operating units of the organizations (e.g., businesses or divisions). It is time now to consider this important link in the implementation process and consider the relation between strategy and structure, as we do in Chapter 3.

Strategy formulation occurs at different levels of the organization. Corporate strategic planning may focus on portfolio analysis to determine the businesses worth pursuing; business-level strategies are of a more "local" nature, focusing on a more limited and smaller set of environmental contingencies or market conditions; and functional plans may exist to support activities at the business level of analysis. Despite the different levels of strategy formulation, the model developed in this chapter has utility in explaining that process, for the general approach to identifying feasible options, assessing them, and making decisions holds across levels of analysis.

Notes

1. Alfred Chandler, *Strategy and Structure: Chapters in the History of American Industrial Enterprise* (Cambridge, Mass.: M.I.T.Press, 1962).
2. Peter Drucker, *The Practice of Management* (New York: Harper & Row, Publishers, 1954).
3. Charles Hofer and Dan Schendel, *Strategy Formulation: Analytical Concepts* (St. Paul: West Publishing Company, 1978), p. 25.
4. Max Richards, *Organizational Goal Structures* (St. Paul: West Publishing Company, 1978).
5. Kenneth Andrews, *The Concept of Corporate Strategy* (Homewood, Ill.: Dow Jones-Irwin, 1971).

6. Igor Ansoff, *Corporate Strategy: An Analytical Approach to Business Policy for Growth and Expansion* (New York: McGraw-Hill Book Company, 1965).
7. Jay Galbraith and Daniel Nathanson, *Strategy Implementation: The Role of Structure and Process* (St. Paul: West Publishing Company, 1978), p. 3.
8. Herbert Simon, *Administrative Behavior* (New York: The Free Press, 1976).
9. Peter Lorange, *Corporate Planning* (Englewood Cliffs, N.J.: Prentice-Hall, Inc., 1980).
10. Hofer and Schendel, *Strategy Formulation.*
11. D. W. Karger, "Integrated Formal Long-Range Planning and How to Do It," *Long Range Planning,* 6:31–34 (1973).
12. J. Richard Hackman, "Sociotechnical Systems Theory: A Commentary," in A. Van de Ven and William Joyce, eds., *Perspectives on Organizational Design and Behavior* (New York: John Wiley & Sons, 1981), pp. 82–83.
13. Hofer and Schendel, *Strategy Formulation.*
14. See Hofer and Schendel, *Strategy Formulation*; and Galbraith and Nathanson, *Strategy Implementation.*
15. J. D. Thompson, *Organizations in Action* (New York: McGraw-Hill Book Company, 1967).
16. L. G. Hrebiniak, *Complex Organizations* (St. Paul: West Publishing Company, 1978); Thompson, *Organizations in Action;* David Jacobs, "Dependency and Vulnerability: An Exchange Approach to the Control of Organizations," *Administrative Science Quarterly,* 19:45–59 (1974); and Jeffrey Pfeffer and Gerald Salancik, *The External Control of Organizations: A Resource Dependence Perspective* (New York: Harper & Row, Publishers, 1978).
17. Philip Selznick, *Leadership in Administration* (New York: Harper & Row, Publishers, 1957).
18. W. H. Newman, "Selecting Company Strategy," *Journal of Business Policy,* 2(2):60–71 (1972); M. L. Kastens, "Outside-In Planning," *Managerial Planning,* 22(5): (1974); P. Kotler, *Marketing Management: Analysis, Planning, and Control,* 3rd ed. (Englewood Cliffs, N.J.: Prentice-Hall, Inc., 1976); A. Thompson and A. Strickland, *Strategy Formulation and Implementation* (Dallas, Tx.: Business Publications, Inc., 1980).
19. David Sills, *The Volunteers* (New York: The Free Press, 1957).
20. L. G. Hrebiniak and Charles Snow, "Top Management Agreement and Organizational Performance," *Human Relations,* 35(12):1139–1158 (1982).
21. James March, "Decisions in Organizations and Theories of Choice," in Andrew Van de Ven and William F. Joyce, eds., *Perspectives on Organization Design and Behavior* (New York: John Wiley & Sons, Inc., 1981), p. 212.
22. Thompson, *Organizations in Action,* p. 137.
23. Robert Miles, *Macro Organization Behavior* (Santa Monica, Ca.: Goodyear Publishing Co., 1980), p. 288.
24. Thompson, *Organizations in Action.*
25. Richard Rumelt, *Strategy, Structure, and Economic Performance* (Cambridge, Mass.: Harvard University Press, 1974).
26. March, "Decisions in Organizations and Theories of Choice; also, see Paul Lawrence, "Organization and Environment Perspective," in Andrew Van de Ven and William F. Joyce, eds., *Perspectives on Organization Design and Behavior,* pp. 311–337.

27. Hrebiniak, *Complex Organizations;* Thompson, *Organizations in Action;* Jacobs, "Dependency and Vulnerability": and Pfeffer and Salancik, *The External Control of Organizations.*
28. Thompson, *Organizations in Action.*
29. Hofer and Schendel, *Strategy Formulation;* Thompson, *Organizations in Action;* see also L. G. Hrebiniak and Charles Snow, "Industry Differences in Environmental Uncertainty and Structural Characteristics Related to Uncertainty," *Academy of Management Journal,* 23:750–759 (1980).
30. Abraham Kaplan, *The Conduct of Inquiry* (New York: Chandler Publishing Co., 1964).
31. *Fortune,* November 1970; *Time,* June 1972.
32. Raymond Miles and Charles Snow, *Organizational Strategy, Structure, and Process* (New York: McGraw-Hill Book Company, 1978).
33. Charles Snow and L. G. Hrebiniak, "Strategy, Distinctive Competence, and Organizational Performance," *Administrative Science Quarterly,* 25:317–336 (1980).
34. Jeffrey Pfeffer, *Power in Organizations* (Marshfield, Mass.: Pitman Publishing, 1981); Hrebiniak, *Complex Organizations;* and Robert A. Dahl, *Modern Political Analysis* (Englewood Cliffs, N.J.: Prentice-Hall, Inc., 1963).
35. Lorange, *Corporate Planning;* and Hofer and Schendel, *Strategy Formulation.*
36. Ibid.

PRIMARY STRUCTURE

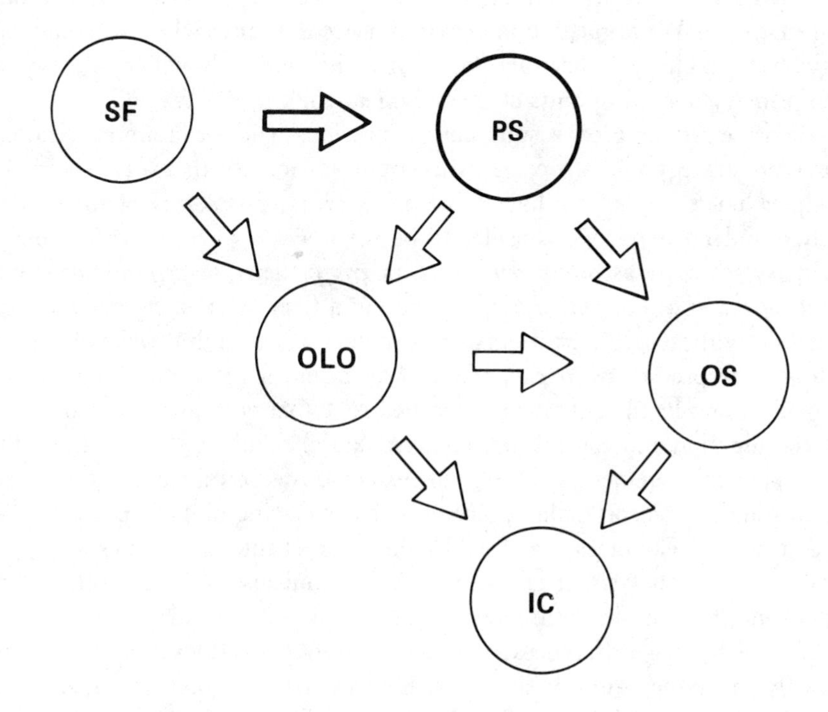

Strategy formulation at the corporate level can affect the structure of the organization. Given the demands and economic and administrative costs associated with different strategies, there are better ways than others in which to organize to implement strategic plans.

The previous chapter discussed strategy formulation, emphasizing the choice of strategic objectives and plans and the influence of slack resources, distinctive competence, production and market relatedness, past organizational performance, and the impact of individual values on these decisions. Formulation was discussed as occurring at several levels within the firm, including corporate, business, and functional levels.

The present chapter focuses on one important result of strategy formulation at the corporate or organizational level. The contention of this chapter is twofold: (1) that choice of strategy can affect decisions regarding overall structure and (2) that managerial decisions to alter structure in the face of strategic change result primarily from an assessment of relevant economic and administrative costs. We argue that under certain circumstances where a given strategy has been effected, there are better ways than others in which to designate the primary operating units of the organization.

Before embarking on a summary of previous works examining relations between strategy and structure, it is important to note that analysis in this chapter looks at what we have labeled the *primary structure* of the organization and not what we consider to be the *operating structure.* We define primary structure as the *major elements, components,* or *differentiated subunits of the entire organization.* Describing a firm as (1) a functional organization with geographically dispersed plants, (2) a multidivisional organization with product or market-oriented divisions, or (3) a worldwide matrix organization identifies its primary structure. Other structural decisions such as coordination and control mechanisms, lateral relations strategies, product or project management systems, and extent of decentralization versus centralization in decision making *within* major operating units focus on operating structure (Chapters 5 and 6). While some of the same issues appear at both levels of analysis, it is useful to define and discuss both primary and operating structure in the interest of clarity.

To clarify the differences between the types, consider two firms with exactly the same primary structure, for example, the multidivisional form (Figure 3-1). Both look identical on paper,with *n* number of separate divisions clearly identified on the organization chart. Entrance into the organization and close examination of operations and decision processes might reveal, however, that the amount of authority inherent in the division manager's role varies a great deal between organizations. The divisions of one organization may be organized along functional lines, whereas those in the other exhibit both functional and matrix forms (see Figure 3-1). Finally, it is seen that the methods of coordinating across functions or projects within divisions are quite different. In one division, for example, task forces and work teams solve cross-functional problems, whereas management in another

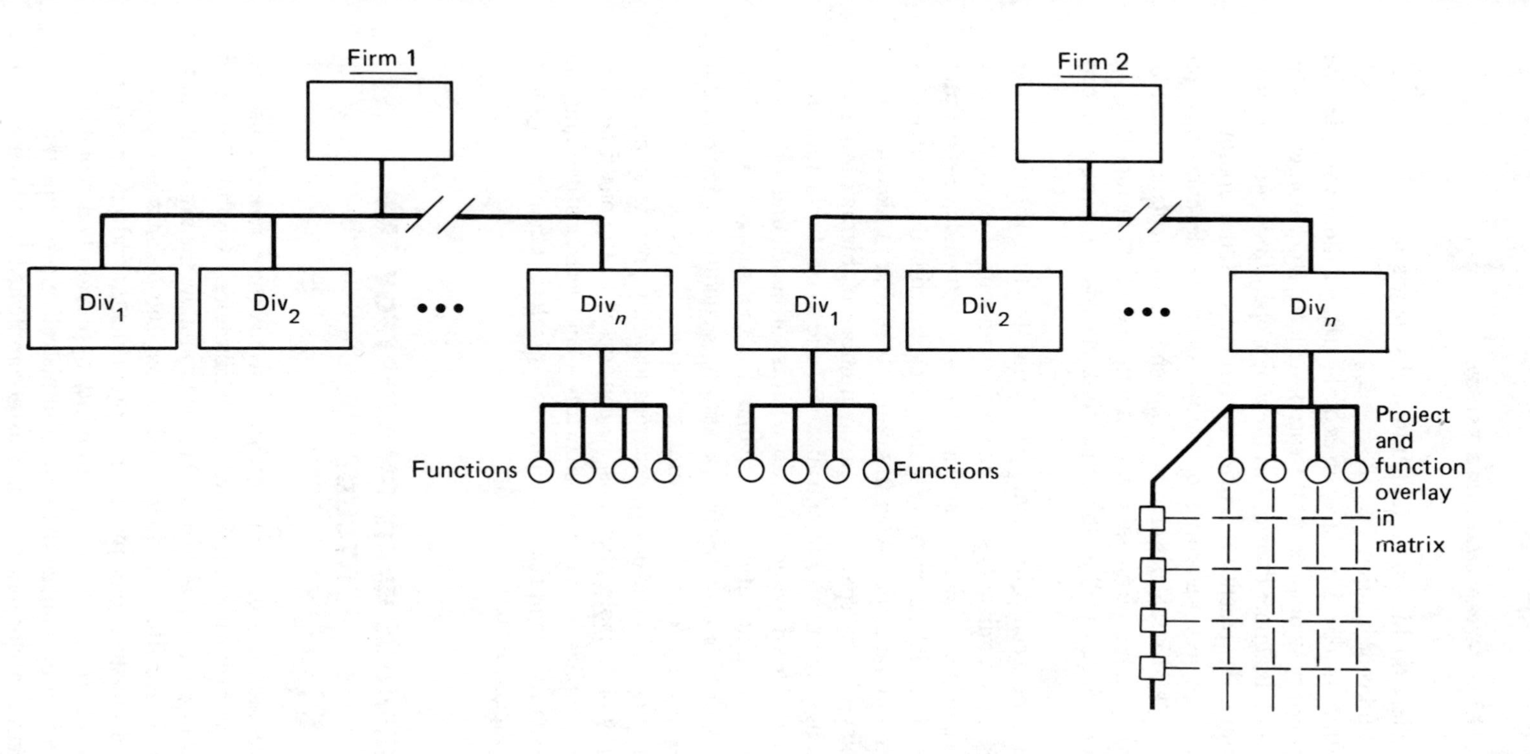

More centralized: division managers in firm 1 have less autonomy than managers in firm 2
Coordination by rules and plans

Division managers in firm 2 work in more decentralized setting with greater autonomy in decision making
Coordination by plan and mutual adjustment

Figure 3-1. Two hypothetical multidivisional firms with different operating structures.

division relies solely on hierarchy and informal contacts to achieve lateral communication and coordination.

The point is that the operating structures of the organizations vary, despite their identical primary structures. At the corporate level, a decision was made to differentiate and designate divisions as the major operating units; the divisional configuration represents the primary structure of the organization. Within divisions, choices regarding operating structure depend more on "local" conditions and strategies. Managerial choices of structure, that is, vary as a function of the business, environment, and other factors that the different divisions face as well as the constraints placed on them by the corporate level.

The distinction between primary and operating structure is often blurred in the literature on organizations, causing a fair amount of conceptual and empirical confusion. Discussions of structure routinely include consideration of a vast array of variables or factors, including functional and divisional structures, matrix organization, coordination, job routine, task interdependence, job manageability, spans of control, number of hierarchical levels, extent of rule usage, autonomy, decentralization, and so on. In the final analysis, one is left bewildered, wondering just what is subsumed under the heading of "structure" or, alternatively, just what it is that supposedly "follows strategy." Distinguishing primary from operating structure suggests that all design variables are not equally relevant at various stages of the strategy implementation process. Some design decisions logically precede others, simplifying the array of variables that must be considered at any one time. The present chapter emphasizes primary structure—the decisions defining the major components that comprise the entire organization; Chapters 5 and 6 deal with operating structures in detail.

PREVIOUS WORK ON STRATEGY AND STRUCTURE

Study of the relationship between strategy and structure received its first major impetus with the now-classic work of Chandler.[1] Chandler showed that historically organizational structure tended to follow the growth strategy of the firm. With growth, according to Chandler, the organization experienced various administrative or managerial problems that adversely affected economic performance. To increase profitability to previously acceptable levels, it was necessary to manage the new administrative problems that were negatively affecting performance. This was accomplished by altering organizational structure. A change in growth strategy, then, ultimately resulted in a change in structure.

Besides providing a thesis that has become central and pervasive in the strategy literature—namely, that strategy affects structure—Chandler discusses the various types and stages of growth strategy and the predominant structural modifications that occur. These are summarized briefly in Table 3-1. What is suggested by Chandler is a sequence of growth and development over time, characterized by (1) an accumulation of resources by the organization, (2) an expansion into new market areas to take advantage of the resources, and (3) the development of new structures to handle the increased-product and market diversity and the administrative problems it creates. Thus, structure not only follows strategy, but the pattern of relation over time is fairly predictable as resources are accumulated and growth strategies create the need for new structural forms.

Chandler's work has generated additional conceptual work and empirical analysis. Wrigley, for example, identified four different strategies and related them to organizational structure.[2] The strategies were (1) *single-product business;* (2) *dominant business,* accounting for 70 to 95 percent of sales; (3) *related businesses,* with less than 70 percent of sales in one business, but with some overlaps or similarities across businesses (e.g., common production or technology, same sales and distribution channels); and (4) *unrelated businesses* (different markets, technologies, or production processes for the various products). His main finding was that strategy affected structure, with increased diversification positively related to acceptance of multidivisional forms and low diversification associated with functional types of structure.

TABLE 3-1. Chandler's Stages of Growth with Resultant Structural Changes.

Stage or Type of Growth Strategy	*Structural Response*
1. Simple volume Expansion	1. Central administrative office
2. Geographic expansion	2. Functional organization (to achieve coordination and control geographically dispersed units)
3. Vertical integration	3. Functional organization (with more sophisticated planning techniques and operating structures)
4. Product diversification	4. Multidivisional organization (separate divisions or businesses), with a central corporate control center (to achieve coordination across divisions)

All the single business types studied by Wrigley, for instance, were functionally organized; in contrast, 100 percent of the unrelated businesses employed the divisional form of organization to manage the diverse products, markets, or technologies involved.

Rumelt elaborated upon the types of diversification strategy, and his findings were consistent with those of Wrigley and Chandler.[3] He employed nine different strategic types that represented increased diversity and dissimilarity in terms of products and markets. His major findings included the facts that (1) American businesses had become increasingly diversified and complex over the period 1949 to 1969 and (2) single and dominant business strategies employ functional organizations, whereas increased diversification is associated with the use of multidivisional structures. The suggestion is that diversity, complexity, and dissimilarity of products, markets, and technologies require a different type of structure than do simpler strategies based on little or no diversification.

Similar conclusions were suggested by Franco and Stopford and by Wells.[4] Their work indicates that international diversification of products and markets resulted consistently in the adoption of multidivisional forms of organization.

Other studies using national and international samples of organizations provide additional empirical data that suggest relations or links between strategy and structure similar to those already discussed.[5] Generally, the data indicate that domestic and foreign product diversifications are best managed and controlled by multidivisional organizations. Similarly, firms following like strategies adopt similar structures, whereas the pursuit of different strategies is related to the adoption and use of dissimilar structures to achieve management control and optimal economic performance. Galbraith and Nathanson provide a good review of many of these and other studies and, as suggested, the similarity of findings provides support for a strategy-structure relationship.[6] These findings, *in toto,* also suggest support for the principle of intended rationality, as their overriding suggestion is that *structure develops or changes logically in the face of economic or administrative problems wrought by increased diversification and the concomitant technical and market complexity.*

It is this last point that we think requires further elaboration and clarification. Much of the work in the strategy area describes the observed relations between strategy and structure. Causality and the factors underlying such a relationship are implied, but it often is unclear as to *why* changes in structure occur. Consistent with our presentation in Chapters 1 and 2, we feel that it is necessary to pay attention to the planning and design *decisions* that underlie the formulation and implementation of strategies. We argue that choice or alternation of a strategy can have clear effects on measurable organizational outcomes and that control over these outcomes or consequences can vary with the choice of organizational structure.

We should emphasize at the outset that changes in primary structure are rare compared with changes in operating structure, in part because of implicit reliance on the principle of minimum intervention. Decisions about strategy that greatly affect the administrative or economic costs of doing business are not an everyday occurrence. However, the frequency of these decisions is expected to increase as business environments become increasingly complex and dynamic. Because of their impact on organizational performance, it is necessary to examine closely the relation between corporate strategy and primary structure, including the planning decisions that result in structural modifications.

STRATEGY AND STRUCTURE: ANALYSIS OF DECISIONS AND CHOICES

Chapter 2 argued that strategy formulation is affected by such factors as an organization's distinctive competence, extent of production and market relatedness of new products, amount of slack resources enjoyed by the organization, managerial values, and the severity of external threats and competitive pressures confronting the firm. In the present chapter, we contend that choice of organizational design or primary structure represents decisions that reflect a managerial desire to *achieve greater rationality and control* by reducing complex objectives and strategic plans to more manageable pieces, in order to both, (1) *ensure efficiency and optimal performance* in terms of economic and related criteria, and (2) *reduce the complexity* of administrative and managerial tasks.

To reach a better understanding of the relation between strategy and structure, it is necessary to identify and discuss some key planning and design decisions that are central to the strategic process. To help with this identification, consider, first, the case of an organization selling a single commodity-type product under perfectly competitive conditions. The familiar horizontal demand curve and other industry characteristics dictate the price of the product. Lacking control over price, but able to sell virtually all the product it manufactures, top management focuses primarily on costs and output as relevant factors in decision making. Efficiency and the control of variable costs over large ranges of production become extremely salient.

Given these conditions, the functional organization is a logical choice of

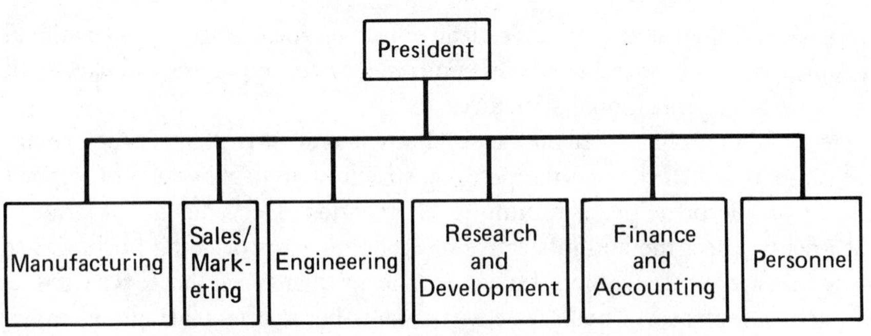

Figure 3-2. Example of a typical functional organization.

primary structure (see Figure 3-2). The firm is designed around common processes or functions, with coordination of the flow of work through common facilities. This enables the component divisions of the organization to specialize according to the processes that they perform. Specialization and emphasis on large numbers to achieve economies of scale have positive effects on economic performance. The organization is also likely to develop a distinctive competence in the area of manufacturing, including production, cost, and quality control.[7]

In the single-business, single-product case, the distinction between primary and operating structure is blurred. In terms of the present implementation model, the corporate and operating levels are virtually identical, and the term "functional organization" describes the entire organization. As the strategy and resulting structure become more complex, the distinction becomes clearer. The research of Wrigley, Scott, Rumelt, and others cited earlier reveals that the single-product firm represents a decreasing proportion of current organizations. *To pursue the relation between strategy and structure further then, it is necessary to add products to our hypothetical firm.* The planning and design decisions that underlie the choice of products and the consequences of that choice will then be clearer.

Assume that the firm in our illustration develops a distinctive competence in production or manufacturing. Distinctive competence reflects an *excess capacity* of the organization. It represents something that an organization does especially well vis-à-vis others in the industry, suggesting a competitive edge and a store of energy or knowledge on which the firm can build in its planning decisions. This excess capacity or pool of special capabilities that defines distinctive competence represents an important source of opportunity for the organization. Recalling Chapter 2, we noted that organizations with a distinctive competence will tend to build on it and that search processes will proceed logically, with the degree of (1) production or technological relatedness and (2) extent of market relatedness determining the choice of new products.

In essence, the organization will increase the number of products or services it offers or, as Thompson argues, expand its domain by seeking related products first.[8] In terms of our example, the single-product firm with excess capacity or distinctive competence in the area of manufacturing or production will seek products to deploy that capacity and build on that competence. For purposes of illustration, let us focus on three situations that the firm could face after engaging in such search activities: (1) high relatedness in terms of both production and markets, (2) high relatedness in terms of production but low relatedness in terms of markets, and (3) low relatedness in terms of production but high relatedness in terms of markets. We examine each of these situations and explain what we believe to be the likely effects on the primary structure of the organization.

Case I: High Relatedness in Both Production and Markets. The firm here is manufacturing similar products and is using existing marketing mechanisms and channels of distribution. But the introduction of multiple products to the single-product firm actually raises a *design* issue, which can be expressed as the choice between *purpose* or *process specialization* (Figure 3-3).[9] The former denotes self-containment whereby, in our example, each of the products or product groups would have and control its own productive and related functions (sales, R&D, etc.); the latter denotes common processes through which all products are scheduled or on which all products or services rely. The task interdependence between or among primary units under purpose specialization is pooled, whereas it may be pooled, sequential, or reciprocal under process specialization. Management decisions regarding specialization of necessity must reflect the costs and benefits of the alternative forms.

When the firm chooses to introduce additional, new, but highly related products, the choice of primary structure is relatively simple and straightforward. The organization *retains* a functional organization with its emphasis on process specialization (Figure 3-2). The obvious benefits that accrue with specialization are *economies of scale* from the use of common functions for all the products involved. Utilization of machinery and equipment can reach a sufficiently high percentage of capacity to achieve and take advantage of low unit costs or, alternatively, high economic efficiency. Individuals within functions become highly specialized and expert at their tasks, leading to greater efficiency and positive movement along some experience curve.

The functional organization, with its emphasis on process specialization, however, is not necessarily free of all problems. The benefits are those of

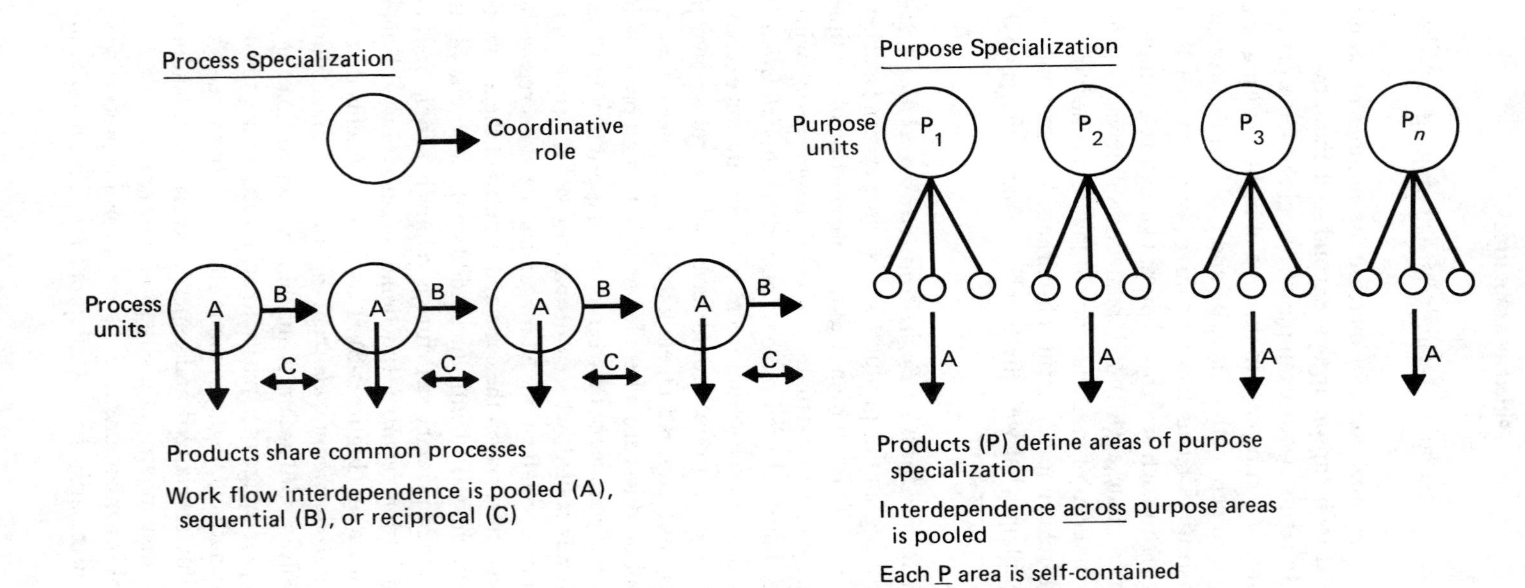

Figure 3-3. Process and purpose specialization.

specialization and economies of scale, but potential problems include those that arise from the increased *need for coordination* of the various products across all the functions. Obviously, coordination or scheduling problems become worse as the number of products increases; given Y products, administrative complexity and the costs of coordination in terms of time and money increase as Y becomes larger. There is indeed a point when the economic benefits of process specialization in the functional organization are outweighed by the costs of coordination and administration. Despite their market and production similarity, eventually the sheer volume of products requires further adjustment in primary structure. We shall consider the case of large numbers of products and high coordination costs below, arguing that the design response in this special case is similar to the situation of products unrelated in a market sense.

Case II: High Production Relatedness but Low Market Relatedness. In this case, search activities uncover product opportunities that still use the firm's excess productive capacity and build on its distinctive competence, but the products now are aimed at markets that are different from those previously served. Included here, for example, would be the discovery of retail, consumer-based possibilities for products that heretofore had only industrial applications. While technological or production processes remain the same, the degree of market relatedness is low, raising concerns or questions about such factors as channels of distribution and marketing techniques. As Chapter 2 indicated, decisions regarding the appropriateness of such new ventures often depend on the nature of the opportunity and amount of monetary slack resources available. Assuming that the resources are available and that the diversification into new ventures is attempted, our example organization confronts a major structural or design decision.

The low degree of market relatedness across products creates a need for separate and selective attention to different problems and customer needs. Sales and marketing efforts for new products vary from those previously used. Customers are quite different, and the pricing tactics, demand elasticities, and ways of differentiating products for retail consumer consumption are drastically different from those for industrial products. New distribution channels and warehousing facilities may have to be created or old channels and facilities expanded. These and related issues increase the need for better managerial control of work and resources within the diverse markets.

The structural response of the organization is most likely to be some form of purpose specialization, such as the multidivisional form where discrete units or divisions are formed on the basis of product, customer, or geography (e.g., Figure 3-4). The low degree of market relatedness creates a need for

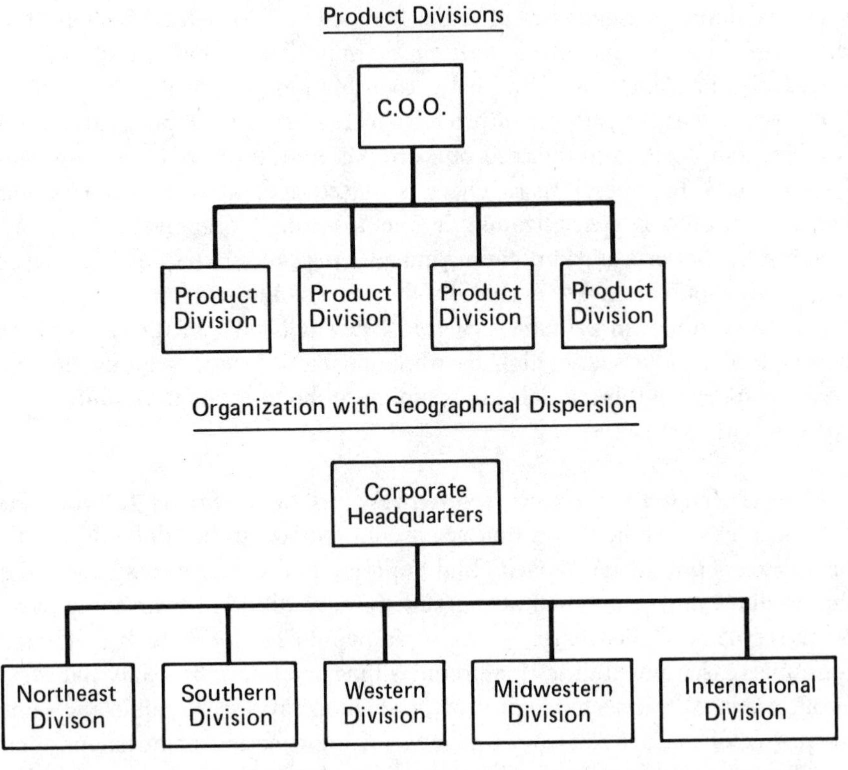

Figure 3-4. Product division organization and organization with geographical dispersion.

specialized, differential attention on the part of management. Purpose specialization under the multidivisional form produces greater *self-containment,* and interdependencies or reliance on common functions across divisions are reduced or eliminated. This results in greater attendant managerial control as division heads individually focus on smaller, more select, and thus less complex portions of the entire organization's marketing effort.

Returning to the previous case of high production and market relatedness, but large numbers of products, the structural response is similar. Given increasingly high costs of coordination due to scheduling difficulties, the economies of the functional organization are soon reduced drastically or negated. To eliminate this problem, top management can combine purpose specialization with process specialization in a divisional structure and reap the benefits of each. When costs resulting from integration requirements approach the economic benefits derived from process specialization, the organization should be structured again according to product, geographic, or customer type, but with the divisions organized along functional lines. The most obvious cost of such a structure is duplication of resources and effort, as each division is somewhat self-contained to maximize the attention paid to the chosen market segments. The critical assumption here, of course, is that the costs of duplication are *less than* the costs of coordination and diseconomies of scale associated with the functional organization that serves unrelated markets or handles a large number of products.

Case III: Low Relatedness in Terms of Production but High Market Relatedness. In contrast to the previous example, the organization discovers new products or services that require technologies or production processes grossly different from those currently in use. For example, a firm serving a well-defined retail market with established channels of distribution may discover that it can appeal to the same set of consumers with new products it has never manufactured before. The production or technological requirements are sufficiently divergent from existing skills to be potentially problematic, but the expected returns due to high market relatedness are attractive.

The necessary structural response will focus on the need for purpose specialization and the self-containment it denotes. A likely response would again be the divisionalized structure with the new products and new production technologies in a separate business unit. Managers in the new division can more easily cope with the problems specific to the unfamiliar technologies because of the separation and low interdependence of production across divisions. Self-containment allows for the attention that is needed to cope with unexpected technological challenges and become specialized and proficient with the new production techniques. Due to the high market relatedness of the new products, the division will use and build on existing sales and marketing skills as much as possible. In this case, there are few costs of duplication due to self-containment.

Strategy and Structure: The Effects of Product and Market Relatedness

The creation of a divisional structure to reap the benefits of self-containment given widely divergent markets or production processes provides a good example of how strategy affects structure. In the hypothetical cases just given, strategic planning decisions to enter new markets or create new technologies that were quite different from existing ones placed great pressure on the efficiencies and coordination mechanisms of the functional form. A strategy of expansion or diversification increased costs of coordination and negated the economies of scale that had accompanied the distribution and marketing of only highly related products. The new strategies created a need for a differentiation of production facilities and markets as well as managerial attention to more select and distinguishable market niches or production requirements rather than what had been "the market" or "manufacturing" for the entire organization. In essence, the changes in strategy created a need to focus on distinct, homogeneous segments of technologies or markets that overall had become heterogeneous at the corporate level of analysis.

The examples also highlight the differences between primary and operating-level structure. At the corporate level, decisions regarding the need for and appropriateness of divisions created that primary structural form. Each division or business was then in a position to analyze its own peculiar environment—competition, product or service mix, production, level of external uncertainty, rates of technological change—to determine the optimal operating structure, given the more local business conditions. The entire organization was structured along divisional lines, but any given division could adopt a different structure from that of another division because of important variables at the operating or business level.

To summarize, a number of points should be emphasized. Under norms of rationality, decisions regarding primary structure are intended to ensure efficiency and optimal performance for the entire organization in terms of economic and administrative criteria. Design decisions reflect strategic planning decisions; long-term objectives and complex strategies must be reduced in size and scope, and choice of primary structure serves this purpose.

Thus far we have emphasized two variables that describe expansion of products or services: the extent of technological and market relatedness. We contend that product and market strategies that vary on the two factors evoke different structural responses for the organization. Lower levels of relatedness denote higher levels of diversification, which create a need for purpose specialization and the attendant self-containment and control inherent in the multidivisional form. High relatedness on the two dimensions, coupled with small numbers of products, dictate a need for the efficiency and large-scale economies of process specialization as found in the functional organization.

It appears that there are better ways than others in which to organize to implement strategy. To pursue this important point further, let us consider two additional cases that relate important strategic planning and primary design decisions.

Vertical Integration Strategy: Managerial Decisions and Effects on Structure

The work of Chandler and others has directed the attention of organization theorists to vertical integration as a type of growth strategy. We would like to consider that strategy from our perspective, viewing it and consequent structural responses in the context of the implementation of strategy. In so doing, we shall emphasize relevant market-related variables and cost criteria in the choice of organizational strategy and structure.

Traditionally, economists have viewed vertical integration as a form of organizational growth. *Horizontal* growth implies economies of scale, lowered average cost curves, and more of the same products. *Vertical* growth indicates expansion or extension of the firm by integrating preceding or successive productive processes, with or without more productive capacity for existing products. The automobile firm mines its own iron ore and makes its own engines to ensure supplies. It also controls its own system of dealerships to ensure retail outlets for its products. The continuous-process oil refinery seeks land leases and develops its own drilling capacity to ensure a constant supply of crude oil. It may also expand into retail operations by owning or licensing gasoline stations, thereby guaranteeing itself customers. It is important to note that the organization under vertical integration is not diversifying into different products or businesses; it remains in the same business, but it assimilates preceding or successive production processes to support its core technology.

The primary *raison d'être* of vertical integration to the economist is that it positively affects the costs of production. Bain expressed the rationale underlying it as well and succinctly as anyone.

> *Some such integration may give rise to economies in production, such that the integrated firm can perform a series of successive productive functions more efficiently than they could be performed by a number of individual firms each of which performed only one function. Economies of vertical integration are especially apparent in cases where technologically complementary productive processes can be brought together in a single plant. For example, the integration of making pig iron, converting iron into steel, and shaping of steel into semifinished products—all in a single plant—permits considerable savings in the total fuel requirement for heating the iron and steel. If all functions are performed in a single plant, neither the pig iron nor the steel ingots have to get cold and then be reheated before passing to the next productive process. Some economies of vertical integration are also claimed in instances wherein the firm performs successive functions which are not technologically complementary and are not subject to unification in a single plant: production of the components of a machine, assembly of the components into a finished machine, and distribution of the machine. In such cases, economies are usually attributed to improved coordination of the rates of output at the successive stages (through placing them under one management), consequent reduction of intermediate inventories, and elimination of the expense of purchase-sale transactions in moving goods from one stage to the next. In addition, pecuniary economies may result if the firm can, by integrating backward or forward, eliminate the payment to suppliers or*

customers of profits in excess of a basic interest return on the added investment required to integrate.[10]

Williamson makes more explicit what is implied by the work of Bain and other economists: namely, that markets and firms represent *alternatives* for the conduct of economic transactions and that organizational structure can make a difference in terms of costs.[11] Under certain conditions, the market mechanisms may not perform efficiently. Give a small number of firms—at the extreme, a bilateral monopoly—bargaining and reliance on the market are not efficient. Instead, a vertically integrated firm that controls its own source of inputs and does not pay a monetary premium for them is more efficient in terms of economic and transaction costs.

From our perspective, additional clarification is useful. We shall try to focus on the planning decisions that bring vertical integration about. The question is, "What types of strategic objectives or market conditions lead to that investment strategy and related structural changes representing vertical expansion of the firm either forward or backward?" We shall rely on the principles of intended rationality and minimum intervention. Consistent with Chandler, Thompson, and Williamson, we shall assume that management is interested in achieving economies by reducing production and transaction costs.[12] We shall also assume that there may be different ways in which to solve problems or achieve economies. Faced with a number of viable options, managers will choose the minimum path or intervention needed to accomplish desired ends. As we shall stress, vertical integration and the consequent changes in structure represent a feasible option only if certain conditions are satisfied.

The view of the organization as an open system (Chapter 2) emphasizes that it routinely interacts or deals with a number of important external groups. These boundary activities usually serve to identify or highlight the major problems, critical dependencies, or greatest vulnerabilities facing the organization. It may be, for example, that an organization (1) faces severe competition in marketing its product lines, (2) is forced to purchase raw materials from a small number of large firms in an oligopolistic industry, or (3) must worry constantly about technological changes that may render its major products virtually obsolete in a short period of time. Whatever the problems, dependencies, or vulnerabilities, it can be said that they represent sources of uncertainty that must be eliminated or reduced if the organization is to function and achieve a satisfactory level of performance. Figure 3-5 shows that the existence of these sources of uncertainty results in search and planning processes that seek solutions or options to increase determinateness and certainty for the organization so that it may operate and make decisions.

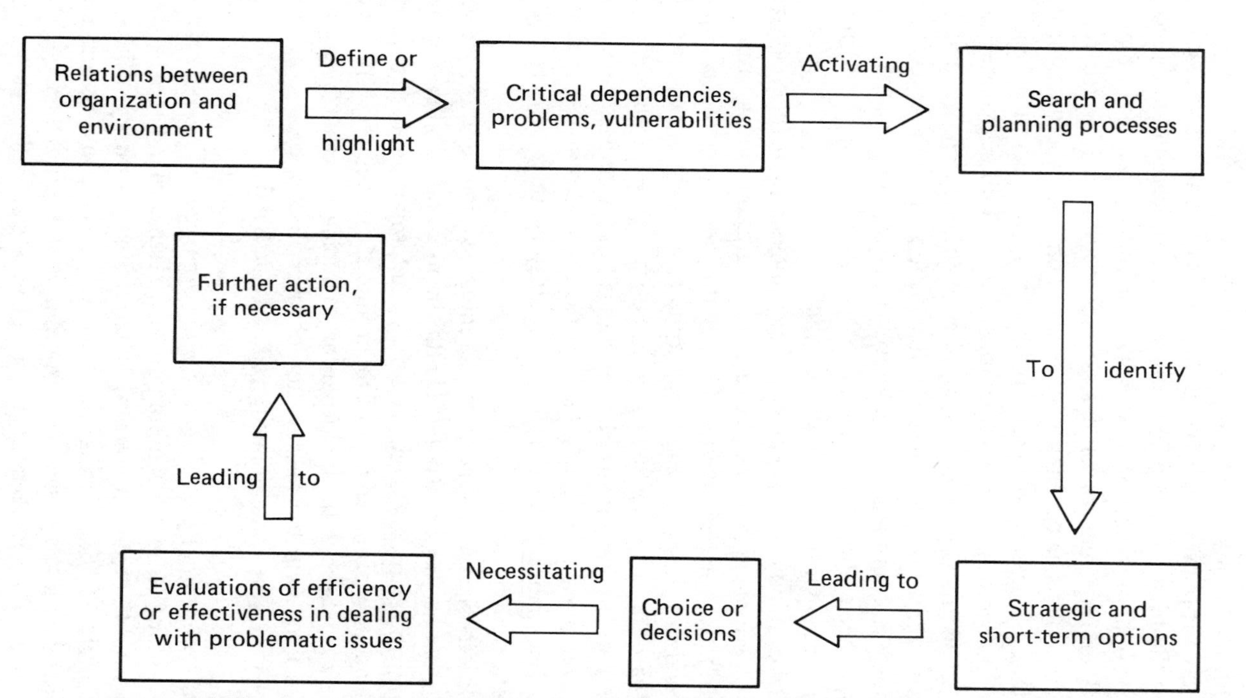

Figure 3-5. Sources of externally generated uncertainty and levels of organizational response.

Consider one such source of uncertainty—a concern about the adequacy of supplies of inputs for a mass production technology. A corollary concern is the cost of these supplies. Clearly the organization will want to reduce uncertainty, but at the least cost possible to allow rational decision and efficiency. Consequently, options identified by search or planning processes in Figure 3-5 at first will not represent corporate strategies at all but will reflect middle-management decisions or changes in standard operating procedures or other aspects of basic operating structure (Chapter 5) or operating objectives (Chapter 4). Decisions might focus upon such areas as buffer inventory levels, stockpiling versus the cost of excess supplies, volume purchases, and long-term contracts to ensure critical inputs at fixed prices. If, however, evaluation of these tactical or operating decisions reveals that the problem of vulnerability has not been eliminated, additional possibilities will be identified, including, ultimately, corporate strategic options.

One strategic option to achieve independence and eliminate the problematic dependency on suppliers, of course, is vertical integration. But this represents a major decision for the organization. Despite the increasing costs of supplies and the dependency the organization wishes to eliminate, the expansion vertically backward in the production process implies large expenditures and an important impact on the organization. It stands to reason that the *costs and benefits of integration will be weighed against the costs and benefits of not integrating*. The planning decision regarding strategy, then, reflects the costs underlying the options available.

The conditions or factors that affect planning decisions to integrate vertically include, but are not limited to,[13] (1) the amount and stability of demand for the organization's products or services, (2) the proportion of *new* productive capacity actually absorbed or used by products, (3) the prospects or probability of new products with production or technological relatedness, or (4) the costs associated with the coordination of scheduling of products or semi-finished goods over the contemplated productive activities.

1. *Amount and stability of demand for the organization's products* are important inputs to the planning process. High demand or sales volatility would not support vertical integration as a strategy. With the high levels of fixed costs that usually accompany integration attempts, low levels of sales and especially stable, but depressed, levels of demand over extended periods of time can lead to extremely dire economic circumstances. The relatively recent poor performance of companies in the automobile industry and other industries marked by heavily vertically integrated firms and excessively low demand bears witness to this point.

2. Another issue is *the proportion of new productive capacity actually absorbed by existing products.* The smaller the proportion, the lower the possibility of achieving economies of scale in the preceding or successive production activities being contemplated. In similar terms, consideration of horizontal or scale economics of the new plants and equipment is an important factor in the planning decision.
3. The low anticipated economies of scale associated with (2) can be mitigated by *the prospects of new products with high technological or production relatedness.* The planning decision now anticipates that strategic objectives include the addition of new products and services over time that will use up or deploy the excess capacity created by the strategy of vertical integration. In essence, the strategic plan builds in excess capacity purposely, anticipating the application of that capacity to achieve a future expansion of products and market or domain.
4. Finally, *transaction costs associated with the need for increased coordination or scheduling of semifinished goods through the various stages of the production process must be considered.* Clearly, administrative transaction costs must be weighed against expected economies of production in the planning decision.

A decision regarding the feasibility of vertical integration, thus, reflects the anticipated costs and benefits of that strategy. And choice of integration as a growth strategy *clearly affects the primary structure of the organization.* Expansion and integration of productive capacities, backward or forward, add new units to the organization. Vertical integration introduces new technologies and methods of operation and control that increase diversity within the organization. As shown in the cases cited above, diversity can lead to increased structural differentiation, as managers at the corporate level create-self-contained units to cope with smaller, more manageable portions of the needs and problems that accompany diversification.

Similarly, it can be argued that vertical integration results in lower production or technological relatedness within the organization. Expansion backward in the production process introduces new technologies with which managers have little or no experience. To cope with the new, nonroutine problems that arise, a likely structural response would be divisionalization or creation of self-contained units. Managerial attention, then, can be devoted more easily and exclusively to the new technologies.

The following schematic summarizes the discussion of the strategy of vertical integration and its effects on primary structure:

Strategy →	Problems or Concerns →	Effect on Primary Structure
Vertical integration	Increased diversity	New business units
(to reduce uncertainty,	New technologies	Divisional structure
costs, or dependencies)	Lower production relatedness	
	↓	
	Increased administrative costs	

Decisions regarding the integration strategy are based on analysis of its costs and benefits to the organization. A positive decision to integrate vertically, however, creates additional problems or concerns that ultimately can result in increased managerial or administrative costs. The result, in part, is a change in primary structure, as divisions or business units are created to handle the increased diversity and lower levels of production relatedness within the organization.

Strategy, then, affects structure; the former gives rise to issues, needs, or problems that new forms of structural differentiation are created to handle or solve. Decisions regarding costs and the reduction of uncertainty result in a growth strategy such as vertical integration, which adds new structural units and affects levels of administrative complexity within the organization. Exxon, with its own onshore and offshore drilling rigs and its own retail stations, clearly is larger and more structurally differentiated than is an independent firm with only refining capacity. A company such as Campbell Soups, which produces tin packer cans for its own consumption, has a different primary structure and set of administrative needs that does the firm without such production capacity. Strategies that come about for various reasons, then, can affect structure and change drastically the way in which the organization operates.

Matrix Organizations

Most discussions of the matrix form of organization focus on what we have labeled operating structure. Indeed, Chapter 6 dedicates considerable time to the discussion of lateral relations and integration mechanisms, including the contribution of the matrix organization to the solution of coordination needs.

The matrix form, however, can also represent primary structure. The key variable for us is *size or extent of application of the matrix.* The worldwide application of the matrix form in such companies as Chase Manhattan, Citibank, and Dow Chemical clearly presents a different structural picture than does the use of a matrix organization in only one division of a multidivisional firm. In Figure 3-6, for example, the manager of corporate banking for Italy

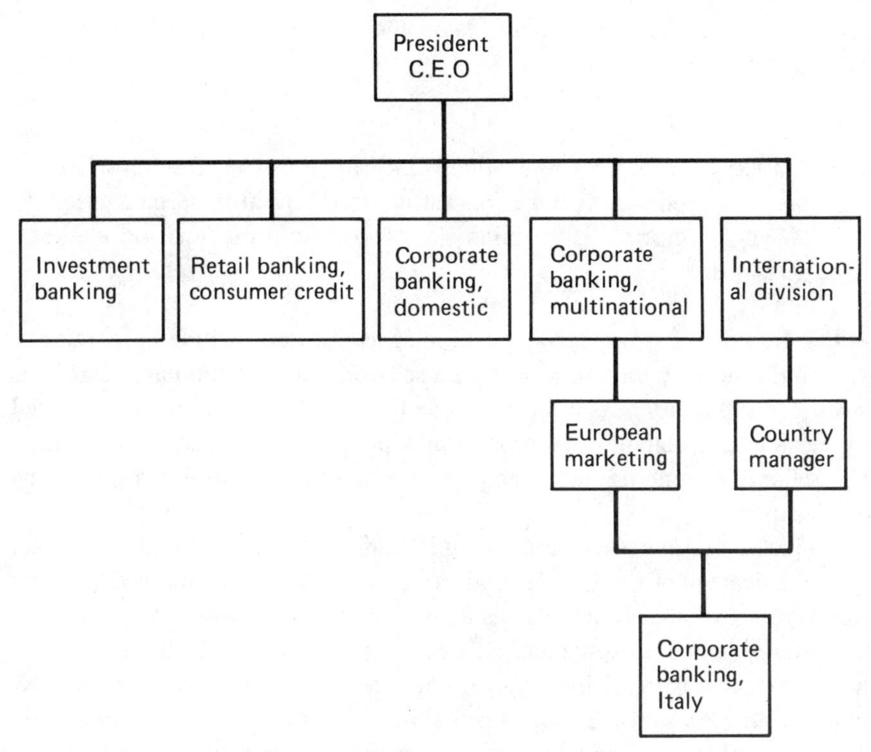

Figure 3-6. Primary matrix structure.

reports to both a country manager and the director of European marketing. The matrix intersects at a point determined by markets and geography. Only one marketing function is involved with the international division in the matrix shown in Figure 3-6, but clearly other functions or product and/or service areas can be involved. Similarly, the figure shows an international matrix, but the same intersection of markets and geography can occur in organizations without an international division.

The majority of the discussion of matrix organizations, as indicated, appears in Chapter 6. There, attention is paid to the definition and use of the matrix form as an operating structure that superimposes one type of organization (e.g., project or product orientation) on another (e.g., functional organization) to achieve lateral integration. For present purposes, it is only necessary to discuss briefly the characteristics of strategies or planning decisions that result in the deployment of the matrix form as the primary structure of the organization. The following conditions lead to the adoption of the matrix as a primary structural form. These conditions or strategic factors have been discussed by others, most notably Davis and Lawrence and Galbraith, and may be summarized as follows[14]:

1. Need for a dual focus.
2. Scarcity of resources and opportunity for cross-fertilization across projects, products, or major operating units within the organization.
3. Need to improve the ability to process information and make decisions.

The benefits of process and purpose specialization include economies of scale and efficiency for the former and self-containment and ease of administration for the latter, as indicated. The three limiting conditions just noted argued for a combination of process and purpose specialization and imply that reliance on one or the other creates real and opportunity costs for the organization.

A *need for a dual focus,* for example, indicates that the product/market mix and strategy of the firm in a given industry or set of countries demand that *both* technical or functional issues *and* the specific needs of the consumer or customer be met simultaneously. Focusing only on project needs—performance characteristics, delivery time—may result in poor cost performance, which ultimately detracts from profitability and even customer satisfaction and future sales. Attention only to costs or efficiency criteria may lead to violation of performance standards deemed important by the customer and may detract from the tailor-made attention to detail the customer seeks. The structural problem, then, is to *balance* the power and inputs of the functions, projects, products, or major operating units so that both contribute to task performance.

Similarly, consider the case of *scarce resources* and the *opportunity for cross-fertilization* across the major operating units. Competent engineers in a certain speciality may be scarce industry wide, but application of their knowledge across business units is vital to organizational learning and task performance. Reliance on either process or purpose specialization is costly when there are such interdependences, communication requirements, and opportunities for technical applications across product areas or operating units. Consider an organization such as the National Aeronautics and Space Administration (NASA). Many projects are the rule, but the organization is not separated into divisions. Manufacturing an advanced radar or communications system for one project creates new technologies that can be adapted for use in other projects. Similarly, in organizations such as RCA and General Dynamics, the same needs may be apparent. Developing high-technology systems for satellites or aircraft may result in an opportunity to apply those same systems, with variations, to other satellites or aircraft. An organizational design such as the matrix that allows functional areas to serve different projects or businesses for varying time periods is well suited to organizations with many similar projects and a scarcity of critical resources.

The last condition may be subsumed under and implied by the previous two, but a separate mention is worthwhile. That is, the organization is confronted by a need to *improve its ability to handle or process information.* Environmental uncertainty, task complexity, and task interdependencies create a heightened need for information processing capabilities within an organization. If this need occurs across major structural units, the matrix form of organization becomes a viable design option at the primary structural level.

Summary: Strategy and Structure

This section has analyzed the factors that affect managerial choices of primary structure. Toward that end, we discussed a number of variables or "strategic conditions" that have an impact on managerial decisions, given the principle of intended rationality. These variables or conditions include degree of production and market relatedness, stability or volatility of product demand, costs of coordination or administration, need for economies of scale, and the benefits of process or purpose specialization. The point was to suggest how these conditions affect the choice of strategy and how that choice, in turn, affects the primary structure of the organization.

Table 3-2 summarizes many of the salient points of the discussion of the relation between strategy and structure. It shows how certain product or market conditions lead to choice regarding strategy and, consequently, decisions-regarding primary structure. The table also suggests that, under certain conditions, there *are* better ways than others in which to organize.

DOES STRUCTURE ALSO DETERMINE STRATEGY?

One final point must be considered. A question is frequently raised regarding the direction of effect or causality in the relation between strategy and structure. We believe that raising this question amounts to the creation of a false dichotomy of causation and a resulting irrelevant dilemma. There is no satisfactory answer to this question because it is the question itself which is wrong. Stategy affects structure *and* structure affects strategy, as should be apparent from the discussion within this chapter, as well as that contained in

TABLE 3-2. Strategic Conditions, Strategy, and Primary Structure.

	Strategic Conditions, Product and Market Factors, and Other Key Variables	*Strategies*	*Primary Structure*
I	Commodity-type products	Volume expansion (horizontal growth)	Functional organization (process specialization)
	Small numbers of products and services	Geographical expansion	Central administrative unit
	High degree of production and market relatedness		
	Need to focus on efficiency criteria, cost reduction, or economies of scale		
II	As in I above, plus	As in I above, plus	As above in I, plus
	High stability or low demand volatility for products	Vertical integration	More sophisticated operating structures (Chapter 5 and 6)
	Prospect of adding new products with high production or technological relatedness		
	High proportion of potential new productive capacity being absorbed by existing or new products		

III	Large numbers of products or services Low production relatedness Low market relatedness Excess productive capacity (distinctive competence) Slack resources Need to reduce coordination costs	Product diversification	Multidivisional organization (purpose specialization by product, customer, or geography) Strategic business units (discrete units, highly self-contained) Holding companies and conglomerates
IV	Need for dual focus—products and functions Scarcity of resources, with opportunity for cross-fertilization or synergy across products or projects High uncertainty, complexity, and interdependence, increasing need to process information and make decisions more efficiently	As in I, II, or III above	Matrix organization

Chapter One. This is true both within and between levels of analysis in the basic implementation model for the following reasons.

As this chapter has indicated, choices of strategy influence the development of primary structures. Primary structures are selected to complement, facilitate, and enact strategic decisions. In this sense *strategy determines structure.* But these primary structural units in turn affect the development of operating level strategies, as we shall argue in more detail in Chapter 4. Decisions regarding primary structure can have an impact on future planning decisions. Primary structure defines constraints and clarifies conditions (extent of decentralization, size of business unit, competitive conditions) that affect the importance or perceived salience of certain inputs to subsequent planning activities. In this sense *primary structure affects strategy* by constraining future decisions at the operating strategic level.

There *is* a dominant direction of influence in strategy-structure relationships, but it is primarily a logical rather than causal, or even temporal one. Strategy implementation refers to a process through which large, complex, and potentially unmanageable strategic problems are factored into progressively smaller, less complex, and hence more manageable proportions. The process as we have described it involves a logical, alternating, and complementary series of planning and organizing decisions arranged to accomplish this purpose in accordance with the "principles" elaborated in Chapter 1. It is logical then to assume a dominant direction of influence in which decisions at the level of the "whole" lead to the creation of the "parts" and their more local, less complex perspectives.

However, even this argument should not be pushed too far. Action in latter components of the strategy implementation model can affect logically previous components of the model, as this example suggests. Consider briefly one correlate or consequence of structure in organizations—the uneven distribution of power or influence that typically exists. As Dahl, Jacobs, Pfeffer, Hrebiniak, and others suggest, some operating decisions are clearly more central to organizational performance than others.[15] It follows that those managers who handle the major issues or solve the largest or most problematic dependencies facing the organization or subunit typically are the largest benefactors in an uneven distribution of resources within it. If we define "resources" broadly to include influence in decision making, clearly the most central and pervasive managers can play an important policy role and can affect the planning process. An influential functional head within a division of a multi-divisional firm can affect the strategic planning of that local unit more than less influential functional heads. Therefore, structure and decision processes in the division reflect differences in influence or power among individuals at the same hierarchical level, resulting potentially in differences in contributions to planning at the divisional level.

These observations make it clear that *strategy both affects and is affected by structure*, but that there is a dominant direction of influence in strategy-structure relationships from logically previous components of the implementation model to subsequent components. This direction is due to the system nature of both organizations and the implementation model itself. In analyzing systems, Katz and Kahn argue:

> *The first step should always be to go to the next higher level of system organization to study the dependence of the system in question upon the supersystem of which it is a part, for the supersystem sets the limits of the variance of behavior of the dependent system.*

Posing the direction of causality between strategy and structure as simple, exclusive, competing hypotheses violates the complexity of the relationships between these variables across the several levels of strategic analysis important to the organization.

Summary

We have argued that the link between strategy and primary structure is an important consideration in the implementation process. Given strategic conditions and product and market factors, it is imperative for the organization to develop strategies that reduce costs, realize economies, or have some other beneficial effect on performance. The critical next step is to ensure that the primary structure of the organization is such that it aids in the attainment of those benefits and does not hinder the economic performance that the strategy is intended to achieve.

It follows, too, that the primary structural units of the organization develop strategic and operating objectives that tie into more global plans. Chapter 2 has discussed levels of strategic decisions; the next chapter (Chapter 4) contributes further to the model of implementing strategy by discussing the function, characteristics, and development of operating objectives within primary structural units.

Notes

1. Alfred D. Chandler, *Strategy and Structure* (Cambridge, Mass.: MIT Press, 1962).

2. Leonard Wrigley, *Divisional Autonomy and Diversification*. Unpublished Doctoral Dissertation, Harvard Business School, 1970.
3. Richard Rumelt, *Strategy, Structure, and Economic Performance* (Boston: Harvard Business School, 1974).
4. Lawrence Franko, "The Move Toward a Multi-divisional Structure in European Organizations." *Administrative Science Quarterly,* 19:493–506 (1974); John Stopford and Louis Wells, *Managing the Multi-national Enterprise* (London: Longmons, 1973).
5. For a good summary see Jay R. Galbraith and Daniel A. Nathanson, *Strategy Implementation: The Role of Structure and Process* (St. Paul, Minn.: West Publishing Co., 1978).
6. Galbraith and Nathanson, op. cit.
7. Charles C. Snow and Lawrence G. Hrebiniak, "Strategy, Distinctive Competence, and Organizational Performance." *Administrative Science Quarterly,* 25:317–336 (1980); Philip Selznick, *Leadership in Administration* (New York: Harper and Row, 1957).
8. James D. Thompson, *Organizations in Action* (New York: McGraw-Hill Book Company, 1967).
9. James G. March and Herbert A. Simon, *Organizations* (New York: John Wiley & Sons, 1958).
10. Joe S. Bain, *Industrial Organization* (New York: John Wiley & Sons, 1959). pp. 156–157, w. permission.
11. Oliver Williamson, *Markets and Hierarchies* (New York: The Free Press, 1975.)
12. A. Chandler, J. D. Thompson, and O. Williamson, op. cit.
13. See Joe Bain and A. Chandler, op. cit., for other discussions of vertical integration.
14. Jay Galbraith, *Designing Complex Organizations* (Reading, Mass.: Addison-Wesley, 1977).
15. Robert A. Dahl, *Modern Political Analysis* (Englewood Cliffs: Prentice-Hall, 1963); David Jacobs, "Dependency and Vulnerability: An Exchange Approach to the Control of Organizations." *Administrative Science Quarterly,* 19:45–59 (1974); Lawrence Hrebiniak, *Complex Organizations* (St. Paul, Minn.: West, 1978); Jeffrey Pfeffer, *Power in Organizations* (Marshfield, Mass.: Pitman Publishing, 1981).
16. D. Katz and R. L. Kahn, *The Social Psychology of Organizations* (New York: John Wiley & Sons, 1966), p. 22.

4

OPERATING-LEVEL OBJECTIVES

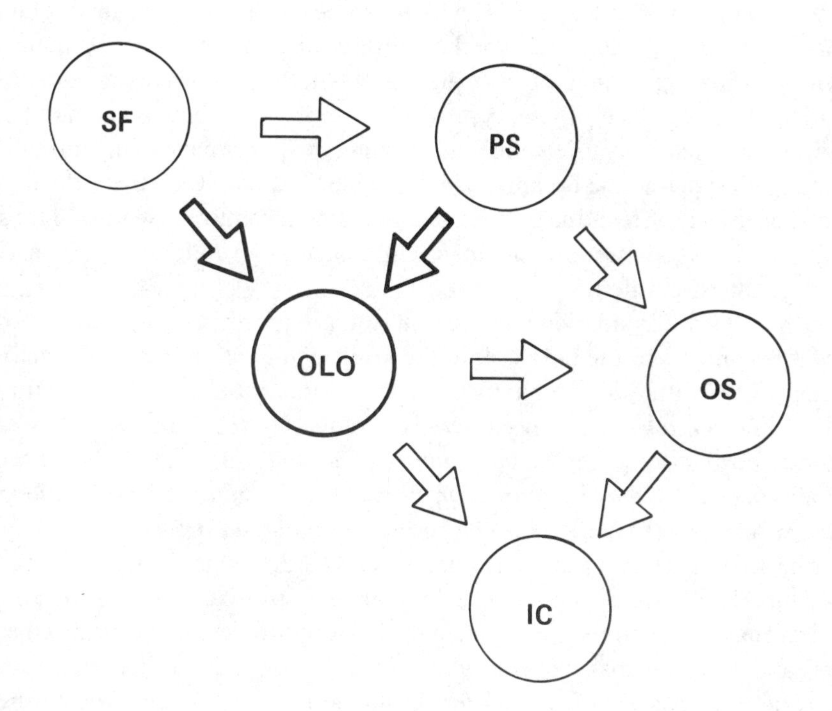

Prior commitments to strategy and choices of primary structure affect the development of strategic and short-term objectives at the operating level (businesses, divisions, SBUs) of the organization. Relating plans at the operating and corporate levels and ensuring the consistency and integration of short-term and strategic objectives are important steps in the strategy implementation process.

The previous chapter considered primary design variables and the relation between strategy and structure. The argument was that global strategic objectives of the organization must be reduced to smaller, more manageable pieces. One step in this process is the structuring of the organization, which refers to the differentiation process by which, under norms of rationality, the organization is able to take complex strategies and objectives and assign them logically to smaller structural units. Once the organization has been segmented appropriately and the relation between "parts" and the organizational "whole" is determined in the corporate strategy formulation process, the role of differentiated subunits is better understood and the total system is ready to function at its various levels. At the corporate level, decisions are made about organizational direction and whether different businesses or self-contained units are consistent with corporate plans and objectives. The creation or elimination of businesses or divisions provides an example of how corporate strategic decisions directly affect the number and type of primary structural units that together define the organizational "whole." At one level, there exist the units, parts, subsystems, or businesses that define the entire system, and those units are added, allowed to remain, or eliminated as a result of strategic decisions at the corporate level.

Given this differentiation and the concomitant determination of the appropriate organization, the next task in the implementation process is the delineation of operating-level objectives for the primary subunits or structural parts. The central issue or need here is twofold: (1) *the formulation of strategic objectives and plans for the primary structural units* and (2) *the setting of objectives that link the short-term functioning of subunits with the long-term requirements identified in the strategy formulation process.*

The first issue or need—formulation of strategic objectives for primary structural units—has been addressed in part in our discussion of formulation and primary structure. It is impossible, obviously, to develop strategic objectives and plans for major operating units until these units have been created by corporate-level decisions and are in operation. In this sense, operating-level objectives depend on previous decisions regarding primary structure, as our model indicates.

In most organizations, however, the majority of primary structural units are in place. Notwithstanding corporate decisions regarding the creation or elimination of select businesses or divisions, other primary structural units are long-lived, relatively permanent businesses or divisions under the corporate aegis. While primary structure follows strategy, most organizational units are enduring or long-lasting products or creations of strategic decisions that occurred years in the past. Strategy formulation may always result in an evaluation of primary structure, but not always in the creation, elimination, or modification of the number or type of primary structural units.

Although operating-level strategy follows from and depends on corporate-level decisions, strategy formulation at both levels may occur virtually simultaneously. This is especially true when certain operating-level units represent large, dominant parts of the corporate whole. In this case, there is a fairly close relation between the corporate and operating unit strategic planning process. This "overlap" in planning, coupled with the fact that the basic elements of our strategy formulation model are applicable across organizational levels, with some modification (Chapter 2), supports the fact that the setting of strategic objectives at the operating level has partly been addressed when discussing strategy formulation.

To complete the picture of the strategic planning process, the present chapter begins with a discussion of strategic operating-level objectives. Emphasis is on the distinction raised in Chapter 2 between global corporate strategy and strategy formulation for businesses, divisions, SBUs, or other operating-level units. Another purpose is to stress that, in our implementation model, the formulation of operating objectives is affected by and follows logically from corporate-level strategic plans and prior decisions regarding the creation, elimination, or retention of primary structural units.

After a brief consideration of strategic objectives and decisions, it follows logically then that the remaining thrust and relative emphasis of this chapter should be on short-term, operating-level objectives and plans. These operating objectives and plans are critical to the strategy implementation process, for they affect the integration of short term and long term in the planning process. Consistent with our discussion in Chapter 2 of means-ends relations and the required translation of long-term global ends and plans into shorter-term, more local concerns, the thrust of this section of the chapter is to define the necessary and important characteristics of operating-level objectives that serve this integrative function. A related concern is the discussion of operating objectives that do not tie directly to long-term, strategic objectives but are needed to identify and confront problems or opportunities of a purely *local* concern. Even here, of course, interdependence between operating-level objectives and corporate strategy is pooled,[1] at a minimum, so that short-term objectives that seemingly are specific to only operating subunits and their particular circumstances really can be considered part of the process of implementing strategy for the entire organization.

The purpose of this chapter, then, is to discuss operating-level objectives and their role in the implementation of strategy. Emphasis is on the integration of the short and long term and the coordination of means and ends, as plans and objectives are handled by successively lower levels in the organization, often within increasingly shorter time frames. Additional benefits of planning and the integration process are discussed. The way in which objectives are negotiated and determined is presented, and the criteria that characterize sound operating objectives are developed. The motivational consequences of setting objectives and the attendant dysfunctions of poor objectives are also introduced as central elements in the implementation process.

STRATEGIC OPERATING-LEVEL OBJECTIVES

Following and consistent with the development of corporate strategy and the creation, elimination, or retention of primary structural units in the organization, attention can turn to strategic operating-level objectives. *As Chapter 2 indicated, the purpose of strategy formulation, regardless of level, is to enable the organizational unit (corporation, division, SBU, business) to develop long-term objectives and align its capabilities optimally with environmental contingencies so as to obtain them.* Regardless of level, search processes are activated to identify relevant strategic options and evaluate their relative importance and contribution to unit effectiveness and adaptation. In essence, there are similarities in the strategy formulation process across organizational levels, including the categories or headings under which important variables and decision processes were discussed in Figure 2-2.

Chapter 2 also indicated, however, that there are differences in strategy formulation by organizational level in terms of the specific variables or factors that affect strategic choice and the types of outcomes that are related to strategic performance. Table 2-2 provided some examples of important environmental and internal variables that might characterize and influence strategy formulation at the corporate and divisional or business levels of organization. The table and related discussion also suggested ways in which the formulation process is similar or different across levels. The reader is referred back to that portion of the discussion of the strategy formulation process in Chapter 2 to examine again examples of the factors affecting planning decisions at different levels of the organization.

Characteristics of Strategic Planning at the Operating Level

For present purposes, it would be helpful to discuss briefly the characteristics of strategic objectives and plans for the major operating units of the organization. Strategy formulation at the level of businesses, divisions, or SBUs has received a good deal of attention in the recent literature,[2] and our intention is not to repeat unnecessarily what others have described adequately. Rather, we present a brief summary of some of the major characteristics or elements of strategic objectives that seem to appear consistently within this body of existing literature. Comparing the characteristics of strategic objectives at the operating level with those at the corporate level can highlight the differences that exist and provide insights into what authors in the strategy formulation area have emphasized.

Table 4-1 presents the characteristics of strategic planning at the two organizational levels, placing them on a corporate–operating-level continuum. The purpose of the framework is simply to show a relative picture of factors emphasized at the two levels. For example, the literature suggests consistently that strategic planning at the corporate level is necessarily more *global* than is that at the operating level. While the former emphasizes *interindustry* analyses and multiple *businesses,* the latter typically stresses *intraindustry* analysis or a single *business.* Corporate decisions regarding *resource allocations across businesses* can be compared with *internal* allocations and controls at the operating level. A *portfolio of businesses* is determined by evaluating the relative *attractiveness of industries* at the corporate level; in contrast, businesses, divisions, or SBUs are concerned more with *product and market evolution* and development of a *portfolio of products and/or markets.*

Another interesting difference focuses on the amount of self-containment and type of interdependence at the two levels. We would argue that the perception of top managers at the corporate level often is one of an organization

TABLE 4-1. Strategic Operating-Level Objectives and Corporate Objectives: A Brief Comparison.

Corporate Level	*Operating Level (Business, Divisions, SBUs)*
←	→
Global (broader)	Local (more specific)
Interindustry analysis; businesses	Intraindustry analysis, business
Resource allocations across businesses	Internal allocation and controls, financial liquidity analysis
Industry attractiveness	Product and market evolution
Portfolio of businesses	Portfolio of products and/or markets
Self-containment, pooled interdependence	Higher degrees of interdependence across functional areas and even products and/or markets
Many general managers	Few, even one, general manager (division head) with more specialists

with *pooled interdependence* and a high degree of *self-containment* across businesses or major units. Operating entities, that is, are seen as independent, rarely if ever facing a need to work together closely on a task or problem. For the entire organization to perform well, however, individual businesses, divisions, or SBUs must perform well, with the individual performances added together or pooled to determine organizational performance. In contrast to the pooled interdependence or unit independence at the corporate level, there are usually higher *degrees of interdependence across functions or product and market areas* within businesses or divisions. Each operating unit is a type of cooperative system marked by high needs for coordination and internal integration, but each unit is self-contained and independent, rarely having to engage in collaborative efforts with other businesses or divisions.

Finally, the picture derived from the formulation literature is one of *many general managers* or generalists at the corporate level to handle interindustry analyses and portfolio evaluation and development. The contrasting picture at the operating level is one of *few general managers and a greater number of specialists.* While this and the other characteristics in Table 4-1 hardly constitute inviolate facts or rules, we feel that they generally describe differences in strategic planning at the corporate and operating levels of the organization.

Another way in which to differentiate between corporate- and operating-level strategies is to consider what Hofer and Schendel define as the four components of organizational strategy,[3] which are

1. *Scope or domain,* which is the extent of the organization's present and planned interactions with its environment.
2. *Resource deployments* to enable the organization to achieve its goals and objectives. This component is sometimes referred to by them as the organization's *distinctive competences.*
3. *Competitive advantages,* or the unique position an organization develops vis-à-vis its competitors.
4. *Synergy,* which refers to the joint effects that are sought from the organization's resource deployments and/or scope decisions.

In essence, their argument is that corporate- and operating-level strategies vary in their emphasis on the four components. Corporate strategy, we stressed, is concerned primarily with portfolio analysis and the determination of the appropriate industries and businesses to be in. In Hofer and Schendel's terms, corporate strategy is heavily concerned with decisions about organizational scope or domain and the proper resource deployment between or among businesses or major operating units. Competitive advantage and synergy may or may not be important at the corporate level, depending on what we have called the extent of production and market relatedness across businesses or strategic operating units.

Strategy at the operating level, we have argued, is more local and specific, focusing on products and markets and such concrete issues as pricing decisions, product or market evolution, competitive analysis, and certain "generic" strategic issues.[4] The latter include share-increasing or market penetration strategies, growth strategies, or turnaround strategies aimed at a reversal of business fortunes in a given market. In Hofer and Schendel's terms, competitive advantages or distinctive competence are critical components of strategy at the operating level. Scope clearly is far less important than it is at the level of corporate strategy. In contrast, synergy at the operating level is much more important because of greater interdependence within businesses and the need to integrate common functions and processes to achieve product and market objectives. Resource deployments are more common and central to corporate decisions regarding appropriate industries or businesses than they are to operating-level decisions about intraunit allocations and budgets.

Table 4-2 borrows from Hofer and Schendel and shows what they feel to be some major differences between corporate- and operating-level or business strategies. Again, our point is to emphasize that operating-level objectives are related to corporate strategic decisions and prior choices of primary structure but that the specific variables or salient components of the strategy formulation process can vary by level in the organization. Focusing on these variables or components has enabled us to complete the picture of the strategic planning process by considering strategic objectives at the operating level. We, thus, have focused on the first dimension or aspect of operating-level objectives as it appears in our implementation model, namely, the formulation of strategic objectives and plans for the units comprising the primary structure of the organization. We next can turn to a consideration of the second dimension or issue related to operating-level objectives, that is, the integration of the short and long term in the strategy implementation process.

Summary: Strategic Operating-Level Objectives

Strategic operating-level objectives follow logically from and are related to corporate planning efforts and decisions regarding the primary structure of the organization. When operating units such as businesses or divisions have been in existence for a period of time, corporate- and operating-level strategic planning may occur virtually simultaneously, but with each level considering different types of variables or inputs to the process. When corporate decisions

TABLE 4-2. Some Basic Characteristics of Corporate and Business Strategies.

	Corporate Strategy		Business Strategy
Goals and Objectives	*Survival* *Purpose and Mission Overall* *Growth and Profit Objectives*		*Constrained* *Product/Market Segment* *Growth and Profit Objectives*
Relative importance of strategy components	Conglomerates	Related product Multiindustry firm	
Scope	✓ ✓ ✓	✓ ✓ ✓	✓ ✓
Distinctive competence	✓	✓ ✓	✓ ✓
Competitive advantage	✓	✓ ✓	✓ ✓
Synergy		✓	✓ ✓
Characteristics of strategy components			
Scope	Scope of business portfolio and Conglomerate Diversification		Product market segment matches and concentric diversification

Distinctive competences	Primary financial, organizational, and technological		Varies with the stage of product/market evolution involved
Competitive advantage	Versus industry		Versus specific competitors
Synergy	Among businesses		Among functions
Major functional policy decisions	Financial policies Organizational policies	Diversification policies Make-buy policies Technological policies Financial policies Organizational policies	Manufacturing system design Product line policies Market development policies Distribution policies R&D policies
Nature of resource allocation problem	Portfolio problem		Life-cycle problem

✓ ✓ ✓ Very important
✓ ✓ Important
✓ Occasionally important
Not important

Source: From Charles Hofer and Dan Schendel, *Strategy Formulation: Analytical Concepts* (St. Paul, Minn.: West Publishing Company, 1978), p. 28.

result in an alteration of primary structure (e.g., creation of a new division) the development of operating-level strategic objectives clearly follows from and is affected by that corporate strategy.

Corporate planning decisions affect business, divisional, or SBU planning decisions, especially by providing constraints, guidelines, or resource parameters around decisions at the operating level. In this sense, planning decisions at the business level are affected by those at the corporate level, as our model of implementation holds. Strategic operating objectives, however, are also constrained by choices of primary structure. Portfolio analysis at the corporate level creates businesses or divisions to work in defined product and market areas. This definition of businesses represents a differentiation process by which the organization takes complex, global strategies and objectives, reduces them to manageable proportions, and assigns them logically to the units or "parts" whose performance together determines the performance of the "whole." This differentiation process represents a segmentation by which primary structure is created; primary structural units, with their attendant task environments and market niches, further constrain and affect the development of operating-level objectives. Thus, primary structure as well as corporate planning decisions serve to affect and delimit strategic objectives at the operating level, as the present implementation model holds.

SHORT-TERM OPERATING-LEVEL OBJECTIVES

One could argue convincingly that a most critical step in the successful implementation of strategy is the setting of short-term operating objectives that relate logically to long-term aims and that, when accomplished, add up to successful strategic performance at the operating unit level. Of course, performance at the level of businesses, divisions, or SBUs is pooled to represent organizational performance, as indicated. Consequently, one could argue that the integration of short- and long-term needs at the operating unit level clearly impacts on the successful implementation of corporate strategic plans and objectives.

This section of the chapter pursues this point further and shows the central importance of developing sound short-term operating-level objectives for the strategy implementation process. We shall argue that

1. There are important utilitarian and psychological benefits to be derived from attempts at integration of short and long run in the planning process.

2. The integration of short- and long-term objectives is essential for successful strategy implementation as well as the development of important organizational processes, such as participation in decision making and communication.
3. There are criteria that define good objectives or, alternately, criteria that, if not met or paid attention to, can lead to dysfunctional consequences that will detract from performance at the operating unit level and ultimately at the corporate level.

Two additional points should be made regarding the importance of the following discussion of operating-level objectives for the successful implementation of strategy. First, the presentation purposely and consciously attempts to include materials that traditionally have *not* been included in the literature on strategy. Our aim here is to meld points or issues from various literatures and integrate them in such a way as to exhibit their impact on the implementation process. Second, while emphasis presently is on short-term objectives at the operating or business level, it is imperative to note that the benefits of the planning process and the criteria or characteristics of sound objectives developed in this chapter apply similarly to long-term strategic objectives.

Benefits of the Objective-Setting Process and Integration of Short Term and Long Term

Chapter 2 in its discussion of strategy formulation mentioned briefly some of the benefits that are derived from the planning process. Included in that presentation were the identification of opportunities for the organization, the ability to place priorities on strategic options, and the definition of criteria to serve as a guide for the allocation of scarce resources. It was emphasized that these and other benefits of planning positively affect important outcomes, including the profitability of the firm.

One purpose of the present chapter is to add to this list of benefits. The outcomes of planning may indeed be self-evident, but that is not the assumption here. On the contrary, we would argue that most of the positive effects of setting short-term operating-level objectives are rarely identified and discussed. In the strategy literature, the benefits of the involvement and integration of individuals in the planning process are usually overlooked or, at best, assumed. It is necessary, then, to expand upon the central issue raised in Chapter 2—the rationale for, and the benefits of, the setting of objectives. Our position is that there are both utilitarian and psychological benefits of that process. To no small extent, these are interdependent, but each is presented separately to facilitate discussion.

Utilitarian Benefits. It is possible that businesses can prosper and grow without planning and the attendant integration of long- and short-term objectives. However, the complexity of organizational environments and technological developments in most industries suggest that poor planning and a lack of integration of short- and long-term needs present a poor prognosis for success. In fact, research suggests that the ability to remain effective and prosper over time depends to a large extent on strategy formulation and implementation, including the integration of long- and short-run concerns.

One relatively recent study, for example, examined the pretax profits of firms with formal planning and objective-setting mechanisms relative to the profit performance of firms with only informal approaches to the planning process.[5] Examining data for a ten-year period, the study indicated that profits and rate of increase in earnings over time were significantly higher for firms that had formal planning. The study suggests that performance is positively affected when managers focus on both long-range and short-term concerns. The implications of the data include the fact that organizational effectiveness, when profitability is the relevant criterion, is positively related to the process of planning and the purposeful attempt to translate long-term into short-term needs.

In addition to profit performance, studies have identified other utilitarian benefits of planning and the setting of short-term operating objectives. One study looked at various service-related jobs and found that goal setting improved performance.[6] Examining the effects of objective setting within a manufacturing firm, another study reported that having operating objectives resulted in better performance than just being provided with informal or implicit standards on the job.[7] Yet another study indicated that productivity was higher and absenteeism lower when goal setting was used to structure and guide desired performance.[8] Other evidence and data exist that show the utilitarian outcomes associated with sound planning and objective-setting processes.[9]

It seems clear that there are tangible utilitarian outcomes associated with planning and the process of setting objectives. A purposeful attempt to reduce long-term strategic aims to short-term relevant objectives to guide behavior and task needs, not surprisingly, results in increased performance on a varied set of utilitarian outcomes.

Psychological and Other Benefits. In addition to purely utilitarian outcomes, it is possible to identify and label another class of benefits as "psychological." Clearly, these benefits are related to the types of instrumental outcomes previously noted. We do not mean to imply that utilitarian and psychological benefits are separate, independent categories; in fact, there is no small amount of interdependence, as the latter often have an important impact on the former. The distinction is made and separate discussion devoted to the psychological benefits to draw attention to an often unconsidered topic—the importance of setting short-term objectives for the individuals working within the organization and its operating units.

Objectives and the process by which they are determined, for example, are intended to *create discontent* within organizations. While this at first may appear to be bordering on heresy, the point is that objectives are guidelines for performance. As such, they are intended to motivate individuals to surpass them. As Moynihan has emphasized, "the creation of discontent is in part the object of goal setting. Discontent is commonly a condition of creativity in an individual or a society: it is at all events an immensely useful spur to progress."[10] Thus, objectives and the rewards contingent upon them are intended to motivate superior performance and show where opportunities exist. Similarly, the process of planning and the setting of both strategic and short-term objectives are meant to foster a redefinition of purposes and spur new heights for individual as well as organizational action.

Related to the previous point is the fact that objectives are intended to provide "a kind of myth to which hopes and commitment can be attached. Thereby, goals provide a symbolism for creating the future."[11] Objectives and the planning process, that is, can help to *develop a commitment* to the organization or operating unit as the vehicle for the attainment of ends, individual and organizational. As March and Simon suggest, in the literature on organizations the objective has generally been associated with motivation and identification.[12] Individuals involved in the process of planning who feel that they have some control over and input to the resultant objectives are likely to feel committed to them and to the organization that fostered the involvement.

Turning to the literature in the area of participative management,[13] the planning process, with its negotiations over outcomes and resource allocations, is an important vehicle for individual involvement in decision making. The greater the participation in the process, the greater the identification is likely to be with the results. Similarly, the greater the involvement of individuals in objective setting, the more likely is the successful implementation of strategic decisions or short-term tactics that emanate from the process. It should be mentioned too that the idea of the objective representing a myth to which "hopes can be attached" further implies an affective dimension that might represent yet another factor to positively affect the commitment of individuals.

Another important function of objective setting is the *reduction of uncertainty* for the individual as well as the organization. The reduction or absorption of uncertainty surely denotes utilitarian benefits for the organization. It provides a factual basis for organizational action. The provision of a single sales forecast in the face of environmental uncertainty or volatility at the business level results in a consistent premise to serve as a guideline for ordering materials, determining the length and type of production runs, and hiring personnel, at least in the short run.

But the reduction of uncertainty also provides psychological rewards as it provides for agreement on what can be done. Consider the point of March and Simon—that satisfaction is positively related to predictability of instrumental relationships on a job or in a role.[14] Objectives, by acting as facts to guide behavior, increase the predictability of cause-effect relationships (e.g., between work and rewards or effort and feedback; see Chapter 2). Thus, they eliminate some of the stress associated with ambiguity or uncertainty. Also, reaching agreement on what can be done in itself is often satisfying. As Michael states,

> *Goal-setting is attempted as a psychological means for reducing uncertainty, and when participants succeed in stating and agreeing on goals, it symbolizes a reduction in uncertainty. It is, in this case, an agreement, usually tacit, on a prediction: "This is what can be made to work out." Thus, implicit in the wish or expectation that goals can be set is the hope that a consensus will be forthcoming on what constitutes reality and what legitimates selecting aspects of that reality that merit attainment or avoidance. In this state of mind, if agreement on goals could really be reached it would imply a greater likelihood of order, and this anticipated reduction in uncertainty is comforting to contemplate.*[15]

Another important correlate or consequence of the reduction of uncertainty is what is commonly referred to as "providing direction." A recent study identified a number of causes of common organizational problems, including lowered productivity and poor task performance.[16] One of the conclusions is especially germaine to a discussion of operating objectives: namely, that task performance suffers when a clear-cut direction and plan of action are lacking. An important function of goal setting, then, is to reduce uncertainty and provide such a direction, for both short and long term.

It may be argued, finally, that objectives and the process of setting them are inextricably involved with individual and organizational learning. The assessment of performance against goals represents a learning exercise. It forces a response to the questions of where the individual or organization is versus where he or she or it should have been, and why this is the case. Similarly, objective setting is not done only to commit to getting from A to B; as Michael emphasizes, the process also helps people to discover where they are and where they might go, given a better understanding of both A and B.[17] In our opinion, this examination and evaluation of actual versus desired performance, and the learning or insights that occur from such consideration, are important benefits of both the strategic and the short-term objective-setting process.

There surely are other points worthy of mention, but the preceding discussion is sufficient to emphasize our contention that the process of setting short-term operating objectives is an important and worthwhile endeavor. It is now time to consider that process in greater detail and focus more specifically on the integration of strategic and operating objectives.

Strategic and Operating Objectives: The "Linking-Pin" Notion Revisited

The previous chapter noted the importance of primary structure for the implementation of strategy. The next two chapters on operating structure emphasize further the processes of differentiation and integration at the operating level of the organization. Detailed attention is also paid to structural configurations that facilitate coordination and the flow and processing of information throughout the organization. The present discussion of the relation between strategic and operating objectives introduces this concept of integration or coordination. Specifically, it employs Likert's notion of the "linking pin" as it shows how strategic objectives are translated into short-term operational foci of behavior.[18]

A brief example can help to illustrate the process of translating long-term needs into short-run operating-level objectives and show the integration denoted by the linking-pin concept. The case was one of a company that faced a dependency on suppliers and that, consequently, decided to eliminate supply problems via a strategy of backward vertical integration (see Table 4-3 for a summary of facts). The integration plan was premised on both acquisition of existing production capacity and construction of new facilities.

Clearly, an important issue was the funding of such a venture, given the substantial amount of cash needed to implement the strategy. One option to raise the needed capital was entrance into the debt market to borrow what was needed. However, the company's long-term debt-to-equity ratio was already at a level that most commercial banks considered high, given prevailing money market and general economic conditions. Another option considered was a common stock offering. This raised many additional issues, but for present purposes, it is not imperative to relate all of them. The important point is that *short-term* steps or actions had to be taken to ensure successful implementation of the strategy within the five-year period.

Table 4-3 shows two short-term profitability objectives that supported the strategic plan. The basic reasoning is clear: to allow for the planned acquisitions and to enable new construction to commence within three years and

TABLE 4-3. Implementing Strategy: Integrating Long-Term Needs with Short-Term Operating Objectives.

The problem	Dependence on a few suppliers (oligopoly) for essential raw material inputs Recent price increases for the raw materials that could not be passed on easily to industrial customers Labor unrest in the supplier's industry, threatening the continuous source of materials
Strategy formulation	The long-term objective To eliminate the problematic dependency on the suppliers and become completely independent and self-sustaining with regard to the essential raw material inputs in five years The strategy Vertical integration backwards, both through acquisition of existing firms and construction of new facilities Resources required Substantial
Implementing strategy	Short-term objectives To increase earnings per share by 10% next year To reduce the long-term debt-to-equity ratio by 8% next year and a total of 20% in the next two years

be completed within five, top management felt it necessary to begin improving the profitability picture immediately. A succession of short-term improvements would allow for either debt financing or a stock offering in the longer term. Thus, a strategy of vertical integration was formulated to solve a specific set of problems, and this created a situation in which the long-term needs of the organization had to be translated into short-term performance considerations.

But this one aspect of the strategy implementation process—integrating short-term operating objectives to long-term plans—did not end with the determination of the profitability measures noted in Table 4-3. The business plan for the year indicated how the objectives would be achieved. Specifically, the plan to increase profits was premised primarily on an increase in sales, a reduction in cost of goods produced, and a price change for a product that was considered to be relatively inelastic in the price range considered.

It is probably obvious what occurred at the next lower level of the organization, as vice presidents were formally involved in the negotiation of objectives and functional plans. (Part of the company's functional organization is shown in Figure 4-1.) The vice president of sales assumed primary respon-

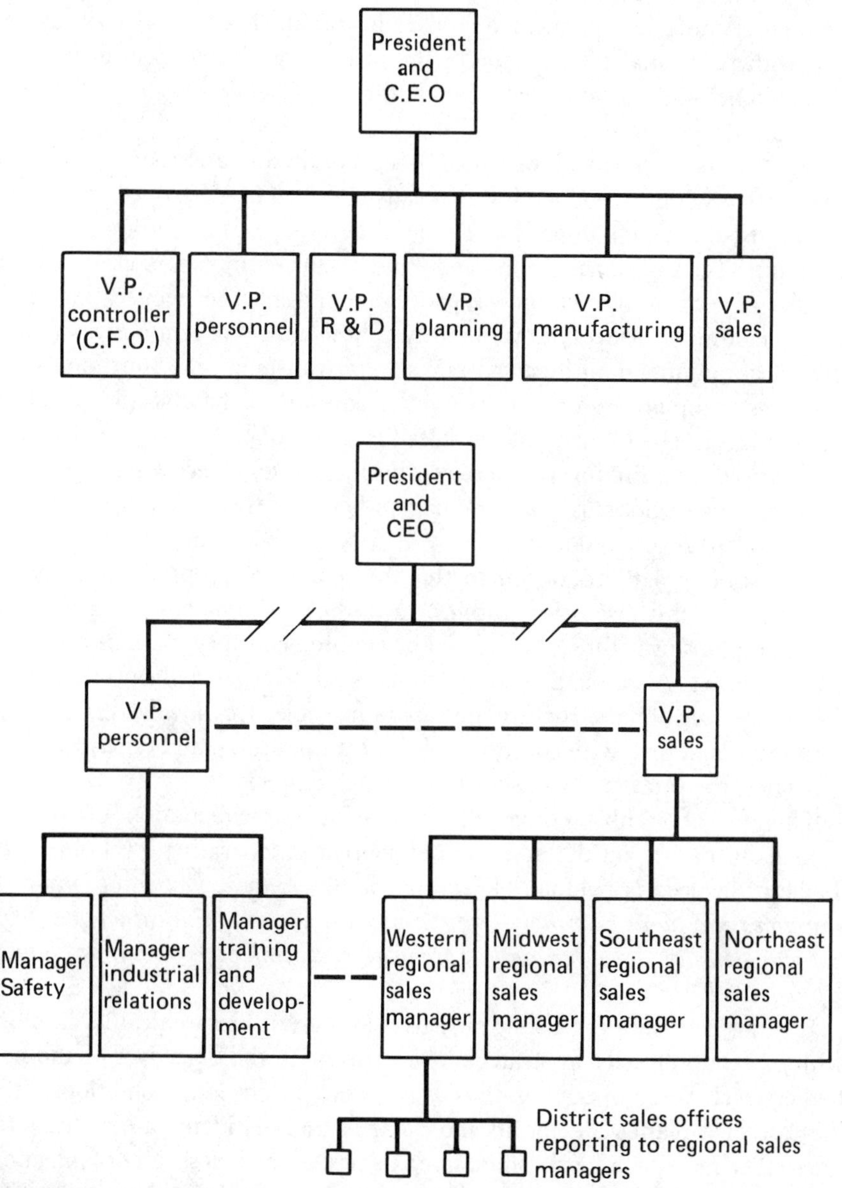

Figure 4-1. A functional organization and integration of strategic and operating objectives.

sibility for the sales objective, the vice president of manufacturing for the objective to reduce cost of goods produced, and so on. What is important to note is the fact that action plan items at the business level became operating objectives at the functional level. Tasks or activities that supported business-level profitability objectives were translated into objectives within the various functions. Similarly, operating objectives at the functional level were associated with functional plans; some of the tasks or activities identified on the plan then became operating objectives at the next level down, within the functional areas, and so on.

What we observe is a hierarchical process of linking and coordination that is consistent with the notion of the "means-ends" chain developed in Chapter 2. That is, the means to ends at one level become ends at yet another level, generating yet additional means and ends. In the case being considered, the strategy of vertical integration was translated into short-term operating objectives, including measures of profitability. These indices of organizational performance and attendant business plans were translated into functional-level objectives and plans, which, in turn, affected some of the objectives at lower hierarchical levels. In terms of the sales function in Figure 4-1, the vice president served as a linking pin between business-level objectives and those at the operating regions, regional managers between the functional head and district sales offices, and so on.

It must be recognized, of course, that the actual linking process may not be sequential, as this discussion implies. Instead of a simple cascading of objectives and plans over time, there could be simultaneous negotiations occurring between levels. Also, the present example is relatively straightforward, given the simple functional structure and operating objectives involved. In a large multidivisional firm with corporate-, business-, product-, and functional-level strategies, the process obviously can be more complex.

This fact notwithstanding, the successful implementation of strategy depends in part upon the definition of short-term operating-level objectives. The critical need is twofold: (1) *the segmentation or reduction of long-term objectives and plans into short-term targets* and (2) *communication and negotiation vertically, as adjoining hierarchical levels link objectives and plans in a purposeful way.*

It is not necessary for all the objectives at a given hierarchical level to link with or relate directly to strategic objectives or to the objectives of the next higher level. Some operating objectives reflect purely *local* conditions, as in the case of a plant reducing its inordinately high accident rate or a district sales office meeting a local competitor's tactics. Nonetheless, all organizations are characterized, at a minimum, by pooled interdependence. It is imperative, then, to engage in the vertical linking process and negotiate short-term operating objectives to ensure the achievement of strategic ends and the optimal use of resources.

One other type of integration or linking should be mentioned briefly, even though it will receive a great deal of attention in Chapter 6—that is, the case of *lateral relations* when formulating and implementing operating objectives. Turning again to the example in Figure 4-1, the dashed lines are intended to illustrate a simple case of the lateral relations that arose from functional interdependence. To achieve his sales objectives, the western regional manager negotiated targets with the vice president of sales and identified a number of action items or tactics that would positively affect sales in his region. One of these was an added emphasis on technical training for sales personnel in two of the district offices. This seemed particularly appropriate because of (1) recent surges in demand for products in a growing geographical area, (2) increases in the amount of competition on technical specifications and the performance characteristics of products, and (3) the relative youth and concomitant lack of experience of the sales people in the districts.

Despite the clear relevance of the technical training, that task was not the responsibility of sales but that of training specialists within the personnel function. To ensure the appropriate training, the regional manager contacted the training and development group, and the program was planned accordingly. The regional manager, then, provided an important link between two functions; he served in an integrating role laterally, recognizing the interdependence of the two separate areas. If delivery of the program were problematic (e.g., due to manpower shortages or scheduling constraints), the regional manager could have requested his supervisor to intercede with the vice president of personnel to help pave the way for program delivery.

The example introduces the point that operating structure, specifically, lateral relations and integration across functions, must support the development and implementation of operating objectives. If cross-functional interdependence grows over time and becomes increasingly important for planning and the setting of objectives in a subset of functions, we argue that the organization should formalize the process of lateral relations with appropriate modifications in operating structure (see Chapter 6).

It is worthwhile to note once again the importance of vertical and lateral links to the implementation of strategy. To achieve long-term aims, it is necessary to develop operating objectives that purposely translate strategy into manageable short-term pieces for implementation. This suggests further that the process of communication that underlies vertical and lateral relations is also critical to the successful setting of operating objectives.

In summary, managers involved in strategic planning can take a number of basic steps to ensure successful implementation:

1. *Identify key result areas and supporting objectives.* The integration of short-term operating objectives with strategic objectives is less difficult when strategies and long-term objectives are clearly targeted and communicated as important concerns. Similarly, the negotiation and determination of operating objectives at one hierarchical level of an organization should serve as key guidelines and constraints for the next level. It is useful to recall here the benefits of objective setting, especially those dealing with the commitment of individuals, provision of direction, and reduction of uncertainty that result from the identification of key result areas.
2. *Formalize the process of setting short-term operating-level objectives.* The integration of short-term and strategic objectives is best achieved when the process is formalized, with time and attention explicitly devoted to the setting of objectives and concomitant plans of action. While planning and negotiation of objectives across or between levels of organization typically reflect a formal managerial process (see Chapter 2), the same is not always true *within* units or levels. Heads of businesses or divisions, for example, formally negotiate objectives, plans, and budgets with the corporate level. In contrast, intradivisional planning processes and the integration of short-term operating objectives and action plans down through the hierarchy *within* the business unit may enjoy less formality and attention.

We find this divided attention and usage curious indeed, for it suggests an ambivalence regarding the merits of planning and the setting of objectives. Of course, it may simply be that intralevel or intraunit needs for integration are best served by other means less costly or time consuming than objective setting (e.g., use of performance programs, standard operating procedures, or other aspects of basic operating structure; see Chapter 5). Nonetheless, where it is necessary to link the organization vertically and laterally via the use of short-term operating objectives and action plans, we contend that the process should be formalized, with time and attention devoted to it, to optimize its credibility and effectiveness.

3. *Develop "good" operating objectives.* This statement seems obvious, but we often find that problems in implementing strategy stem from poor objectives. They are deficient in a number of ways and, in fact, occasionally create unintended or dysfunctional consequences for individuals and the organization. Because of the pervasiveness and centrality of objectives in the successful implementation of strategy,

it is necessary to devote some attention to the characteristics of "good" objectives.

Developing Sound Objectives

The majority of managers deal routinely with strategic or operating objectives, so it may seem redundant and less than useful to devote time and space to their consideration. Notwithstanding this familiarity, we argue that the implementation of strategy will be easier and more effective if managers emphasize the importance of objectives. Despite the apparent widespread use of objectives in organizations, we feel that the additional attention is warranted for at least three reasons.

The *first* of these was suggested in the discussion of vertical and lateral relations. That managers routinely, if informally, set objectives may be true; *that the objectives are integrated and coordinated to achieve or contribute to some clear superordinate purpose, however, is not always true.* Successful implementation of strategy depends on this integration and the development of short-term operating objectives that relate to strategic plans.

Second, experience indicates that managers in the same organization will develop objectives differently. Left on their own, individuals in different functions, departments, or units will often focus on and emphasize different criteria when writing objectives. Results of this include poor comparability of objectives across units, different levels of commitment to the value of objectives, and dysfunctional consequences of one unit's objective for the operations of another. The value of performance appraisal and review can vary as a function of the soundness of objectives, as can the efficacy and worth of the control system (Chapter 7). Thus, an approach to the definition of objectives that relies on a set of identical or similar criteria in their development has merit.

The *third* point flows logically from the previous one, but it is worth emphasizing. That is, poor objectives create dysfunctional consequences and additional problems. The manager in a complex organization is confronted with a large enough number of problems emanating from a variety of external and internal sources. To compound the difficulty and complexity of the situation by setting objectives that create additional woes is foolish.

It is imperative, then, to set short-term objectives that aid in the implementation of strategy or, alternatively, that do not create dysfunctions or problems that detract from successful implementation. In our opinion, sound objectives are marked by and satisfy a number of important characteristics or criteria.

Negotiated. The discussion of vertical and lateral relations mentioned that objectives are negotiated, but this point should be stressed again. Strategic objectives are formulated based on the data collected, analyses performed, and decisions regarding means and ends noted in Chapter 2. Short-term operating objectives then tie into long-term targets and plans. A sound process of integrating the long and short term and one organizational level's objectives and plans of action with another's relies on negotiation and discussion of the important data, premises, and assumptions involved. Included under negotiation is the "sign-off": the parties negotiating objectives sign or initial the final agreement, denoting a contract of sorts on what is to be done, how it will be accomplished, and the resources needed to achieve agreed-upon outcomes. The sign-off usually has the added consequence of clarifying objectives and eliminating ambiguities or unclear plans, primarily because individuals typically will not contract to ends and means that are ambiguous or imprecise.

The benefits of participation in planning and the setting of objectives have already been noted. To reinforce those arguments, it is only necessary to consider the eventual and inevitable consequences of unilateral imposition of objectives or performance criteria over time. The results of such unilateral determination and control include an increasing emphasis on conformity and a decrease in creativity or risk taking; dysfunctional utilitarian consequences when the individuals imposing the performance criteria are incorrect in their assessments; and negative effects on the motivation, involvement, and career development of individuals receiving the unilateral demands.[19]

Objectives Are "Above Standard." Roles in formal organizations are comprised of entire sets of performance criteria, relations, and expectations. This notion of a "role set" is important for organizational participants: it defines the job in terms of prescribed and proscribed behavior and identifies loci of interdependence or interaction over task-related matters.[20]

In any job, standards represent *minimum* levels of acceptable performance. They are defined as the portion of job that, *in toto,* represents the lowest level of performance the organization will tolerate when the role or job is filled. A plant manager's job, for example, is usually defined by standards in a number of areas, including the quantity and quality of goods or materials produced over some period of time. Standards are not necessarily formalized and written down, although job descriptions, contracts, and the like often serve that end.

Objectives are targets or desired future states of affairs that are *above standard;* they represent behavior or performance that transcends the minimum levels defined by standards. This straightforward relation between standards and objectives holds three important theoretical and practical implications for managers. First, the number of objectives should be small (e.g., a range of three to seven). Recent research suggests the cognitive limits of individuals attempting to discern complex patterns and solve many or multifaceted problems simultaneously. Data on decision making and role overload imply that job complexity and stress are positively related to the number of areas or items needing attention within a specified period of time.[21] The point, then, is to limit the number of key result areas in need of attention and action to avoid these negative consequences.

Second, the achievement of an objective with a concomitant violation of some standards is unacceptable; the former must not be attained at the expense of the latter. The plant or production manager who achieves a quality-related objective by drastically reducing quantity below standard is simply not doing an acceptable job.

Third, because objectives represent performance that is above standard, they should never be treated as all-or-nothing criteria. Such binary distinctions as "making it or not" coupled with an assignment of value—"making it" is good performance, but "not making it" is bad—should be avoided because of their devastating effects on motivation and future risk taking. For example, if an objective is to increase something by 15 percent, the attainment of 14.8 percent hardly qualifies as "not making it" or a poor job. If achieving 15 percent is "good" but making 14.8 percent is "bad," the treatment and use of the objective are inappropriate. Such an absolute black-white distinction will create win-lose situations and other dysfunctional consequences. Future risk taking will be avoided if a consequence of setting challenging objectives is always negative reinforcement. Negotiations over time will be characterized by conservatism and "low-balling" as individuals attempt to ensure that they always can make their objectives, thereby avoiding the stigma of constantly falling short.

In brief, the motivational consequences of objectives that are treated as binary, black-white criteria of performance are significant. When control is based on the avoidance of error and bad performance at all costs, the negative impact on such critical areas as innovation, creativity, risk taking, and organizational learning is usually striking and sometimes irreversible.[22] More attention is devoted to these consequences in Chapter 7.

Measurable. Objectives must be measurable. In our opinion, it is impossible to monitor and evaluate performance, achieve needed levels of control, provide feedback, or arrive at sound decisions regarding manpower and related resource requirements if this criterion is not satisfied. The demand for

TABLE 4-4. Operationalizing Measurable Operating Objectives.

Examples of Deficient Operating Objectives	*Examples of Objectives with Measurable Criteria of Performance*
1. To improve morale in the divisions (plant, department, etc)	1. To reduce turnover (absenteeism, number of rejects, etc.) among managers, grades 08–14, by 10%, by October 1, 1982. *Assumption:* Morale is related to measurable outcomes (i.e., high and low morale are associated with different results).
2. To improve support of the sales effort	2. To reduce the time lapse between order date and delivery by 8% (two days) by June 1, 198X. To reduce the cost of goods produced by 6% to support a product price decrease of 2% by December 1, 198X. To increase the rate of before- or on-schedule delivery by 5% by June 1, 198X.
3. To develop a terminal version of SAP (computer program acronym)	3. To develop a terminal version of SAP capable of processing *X* bits of information in time *Y* at cost not to exceed *Z* per 1000 bits by December 1, 198X. *Assumption:* There virtually is an infinite number of "terminal" or operational versions. Greater detail or specificity defines the objective more precisely.
4. To enhance or improve the training effort	4. To increase the number of individuals capable of performing *X* operation in manufacturing by 20% by April 15, 198X. To increase the number of functional heads capable of assuming general management responsibility at the division level by 10% by July 15, 198X. To provide sales training to *X* number of individuals, resulting in an average increase in sales of 4% within a six-month period after the training session.
5. To improve the corporate image	5. To conduct a public opinion poll using random samples in the five largest U.S. cities and determine average scores on ten dimensions of corporate responsibility by May 15, 198X. To increase our score on those ten items by an average of 7.5% by September 30 of the same year.

Examples of Questions to Provide Insights into Performance Areas and Help Identify Measurable Criteria
If this job (unit, department) were eliminated, what would change? What would be the impact on other jobs (units, departments) and how, specifically, would this impact be felt or measured?
If a job (unit, department) were to cease functioning, how soon would the loss be felt? What would change in that period of time?
Given two departments (individuals), assume that one was highly effective and the other highly ineffective. How could you tell the two apart? With no one telling you who was effective and who was not, how could you identify and differentiate between the two departments (individuals)?
Assume that your primary responsibility as staff is to "support" a line function. Assume, too, that others have the same support function. In a given time period, it happens that your support is rated by line managers as "excellent," whereas the support provided by others is considered to be "poor." What did you do, specifically, that is different from that done by the others? What criteria is the line manager using to differentiate excellent from poor performance?

measurability focuses attention on outcomes and results; in the absence of such objective criteria, an inordinate amount of attention is devoted to processes or activities that may or may not be related to desired outcomes.

It is unarguable that certain key result areas and corresponding objectives are easier to measure than others. Many performance indexes or criteria, especially in line or operating positions (e.g., market share, measures of profitability, cost of goods sold, productivity, sales), are easily assessed by clear, quantifiable measures, whereas criteria for the "softer" staff areas are often more difficult to come by. This fact notwithstanding, it does not relieve the staff manager of the responsibility of setting measurable objectives. Expenditures of time and energy to "improve morale," "provide support" for operating areas, or "enhance employee development" are difficult to justify and evaluate if the relevant measurement criteria are not better defined.

Table 4-4 provides partial but practical guidance along these lines by showing some poor objectives and noting the basic operationalizations of some common key result areas that correct the situation. It also notes a number of questions that can be raised to help develop a process or *modus operandi* for the measurement of outcomes. The task is often difficult, as ease of measurability varies, time frames differ by job or area being assessed, and individuals may resist the process of measurement and the evaluation implied by it. Nonetheless, sound short-term operating objectives are necessary for implementing strategy, and a critical component of good objectives is measurability.

As Table 4-4 suggests, useful and practical questions about a position or organizational unit focus on important outcomes. For example, if a unit were eliminated (hypothetically), relevant questions include what the impact would be on other interdependent units and how immediate the effects would be felt. The nature and number of these effects within a given time frame can provide guidance as to measurable aspects of the unit's performance. Similarly, the process of developing criteria to differentiate between two hypothetical units—one assumed to be highly effective and the other highly ineffective—can help to operationalize relevant criteria of effectiveness and increase measurability of performance. In sum, the need to focus on results is paramount; toward that end, various hypothetical questions or scenarios can be directed to develop measures or proxy indicators.

Lest we sound like picky proponents of unnecessary routine and detail, consider the alternative to having measurable objectives. In the absence of clear outcome criteria, it is difficult to assess or experiment with different technologies, processes, means or methods, and action plans. Changing or manipulating independent variables makes little sense if the dependent criterion or outcome variable is not measurable and, hence, differential results cannot be noted. Crystallized outcomes aid and simplify the decision-making process; with unclear measures of results, decision making is more complex and must rely on individual judgments and subjectivity.[23] Similarly, when measurable performance criteria or outcomes are lacking, assessment is based primarily on processes or activities. The senator, personnel manager, and staff consultant are judged not on results achieved, but on such criteria as (1) percentage of meetings or sessions attended, (2) number of training programs provided, or (3) impressions of the "support" provided to other units within the organization. It follows, too, that performance appraisal and review are subjective, at best, and, at worst, political, arbitrary, and capricious due to the lack of objective performance criteria. The point is that the negative consequences of having poor objectives usually far outweigh the costs and efforts directed toward deriving measurable outcomes.

Realistic and Challenging. Objectives must be realistic. If consistently set too high, objectives can be frustrating; if too low, there is no feeling of accomplishment. Objectives that present a challenge are intrinsically satisfying. As indicated, the setting of objectives and the process of evaluating performance against them has definite motivational consequences. To ignore expectations, perceived risks, and the need of individuals to control some portion of the factors or outcomes against which their performance will be assessed can only have negative consequences.

Past performance and the experiences of others can provide a useful guide to determine whether objectives are realistic and challenging. We have argued that planning is a decision process that reflects past performance and prior constraints as well as a look into the future. Comparing future desired criteria of performance to past levels is usually extremely helpful. In fact, one valid and useful measure of effectiveness is the comparison of the organization, unit, or job to itself at some prior time.[24] Such a comparison also facilitates judgments regarding the realities and risks involved in setting the objective. This is not to say that past performance is the only relevant criterion or guide to assess future performance; indeed, excessive reliance on the past can stifle alternative views of the future. The point is that negotiations over objectives should include both a look back and look forward to determine whether the objectives are realistic and challenging.

Consistent. Care must be taken to ensure intraorganizational consistency of objectives. To approve a sales objective when it is questionable that production can manufacture and deliver at the rate required to meet the forecast only results in conflict and inconsistent expectations. Similarly, *care must be taken regarding potential long-term negative consequences of objectives with obvious short-term benefits to the company*. This admittedly is not always an easy task, but it is a critical need. The natural tendency of individuals is to focus on the short term and the rewards that reinforce acceptable behavior. But to achieve short-term results (e.g., increased profits) at the expense of other standards of performance in the longer term (e.g., quality, customer loyalty) is sheer folly and potentially suicidal. Because of the critical need to balance both the short and long term in planning and performance appraisal, additional attention is devoted (in Chapter 7) to how this dual perspective can be achieved.

Benefits Within a Time Frame. An obvious point is that achievement of the objective should result in some utilitarian benefit or outcome. Additionally, it must be recognized that the objectives and expected benefits are time bound. To state that a performance criterion will increase by some amount or degree is not helpful without the introduction of a date for accomplishment. The time frame also relates directly to or determines the progress checkpoints or review dates that are needed to ensure proper feedback and control.

Priorities. The relative importance of objectives must be noted. While all objectives stem from key result areas, some deserve additional attention because of their particular impact on or relation to operating plans or strategy. To avoid conflicting assumptions about the relative importance of objectives, priorities should be discussed and indicated accordingly.

There are a number of methods that can be used to denote priorities. A simple rank ordering often suffices. It must be recognized, however, that a rank order assumes implicitly that the "distance" or difference in importance between ranks is equal. Noting whether an objective is of "top" or "secondary" priority is also common. The assumption now is that all objectives with the same priority weighting are equal in importance. Probably the best approach is to assign percentage weights to the objectives. The sum of the weights is always 1.00, or 100 percent, and the individual weights provide a good insight into the relative importance of the objectives. For example, consider the following, comparing the methods of establishing priorities for three hypothetical objectives:

Objective	*Rank Order*	*Primary (1) or Secondary (2) Importance*	*Percentage Weights*
O_1	1	1	.60
O_2	2	2	.30
O_3	3	2	.10
			1.00

It is clear that the use of percentage weights is more sensitive to differences and provides greater insight into the relative standing of the objectives than do the other two approaches.

Other criteria exist that define workable objectives, but we feel that those discussed serve well. The point, again, is that *it is futile to spend a large amount of time on strategic issues only to have the implementation of strategy and long-term plans fail because of poor short-term operating objectives.* When implementing strategy, the role of objectives in vertical and lateral coordination processes is critical, making it worth the time and effort to ensure that they are sound and do not create any dysfunctional consequences for the organization.

Operating Plans and Budgets

A brief final note on plans of action and budgets is necessary before terminating this discussion of short-term operating-level objectives. While we have implied that objectives require operating plans, it is wise to stress that point formally. The process of planning identifies the key result areas that become candidates for managerial scrutiny and objective setting. When negotiating short-term operating objectives, the attendant action plans are an integral part of the evaluation process. To determine whether objectives are realistic and consistent, for example, it is extremely helpful to examine the intended plans of action, including their assumptions and resource deployments.

It should be stressed that we are using operating or action plan in a general or generic way. The actual title of the plan varies as a function of organizational level, unit type, or organizational tradition (e.g., functional, departmental, business unit, or individual plans). Despite differences in nomenclature, however, action plans for operating objectives typically are marked by some common items or characteristics. Operating plans usually delineate the *tasks* or *activities* that will be employed to achieve the objectives, along with the expected *dates* of accomplishment. Tasks and dates together represent milestones or benchmarks of progress for evaluation of interim performance. In this regard, operating plans usually formalize the times for *review and discussion of progress* against objectives (monthly, quarterly), thereby integrating the operating plan and the control or follow-up system.

Operating plans may detail a great deal more, depending on the nature of the objectives and the salient features or issues involved. Critical path or PERT-type analysis is useful if *sequencing or integration* requirements are important or, similarly, if time and performance constraints are of the essence *Responsibility plotting* (Chapter 6) is a useful technique for noting interdependencies among individuals or units for the accomplishment of tasks. If formal plots or charts of responsibilities are not an integral part of the operating plan, a recognition or notation of interdependence in a "comments" section of the plan often is found. Expected versus actual *cash flows* are occasionally part of the operating or action plan, most notably when it is important to monitor such flows under times of duress or low slack.

In sum, anything of import for the accomplishment of a short-term operating objective is noted on the action plan. Formal notation of this type provides insight into task requirements and resource needs necessary for the attainment of objectives. It also allows for the testing of assumptions and a higher degree of involvement in the process of integrating operating and strategic objectives.

Budgets are critical, for they support the objectives and operating plans. In our experience, there are two observed relations between budgeting and the planning process. One *begins with a budget,* at least an implied one, and then asks what objectives can be achieved given the actual or projected financial resources. The budget here acts primarily as a set of constraints on planning and managerial behavior. It is determined prior to the formalization of operating objectives and action plans and serves to delimit the planning process.

In the alternative approach, *the budget follows from and is justified by* the planning process. Emphasis first is on identifying key result areas and the positive outcomes to be attained by focusing on a given set of objectives and action plans. The benefits of the planning process then are used to justify the budget or the costs involved in achieving the objectives. In the first case considered, budgets constrain the objective-setting process and the operating plan;

in this case, the relative merits and importance of competing outcomes determine budgets and the allocation of resources.

The benefit of determining budgets first is that costs and resources are fixed and known; under the alternative case, budgets and resources remain variable until operating objectives and action plans are virtually complete. The main problem with the prior determination of budgets is that future activities may be too tied in with and dependent upon the past. This can lead to an excessive dependence on previous activities and a myopic approach to planning. Focusing first on objectives and plans emphasizes outcomes and opportunities and militates against myopia and rigid adherence to prior budgets and previously legitimized activities.

We would opt for the prior setting of operating objectives and the identification of outcomes and benefits, which then can be used to justify the resources required. In our opinion, operating budgets should follow, not precede, the planning process. Only under conditions of severe resource scarcity, or when it is purposely and deliberately decided to continue previous budget lines and activities closely, should resource allocation precede the identification of operating objectives and action plans. In essence, budget decisions should follow logically from strategic aims and operating objectives in the implementation process. More is said in Chapter 7 regarding budgets, including the use of strategic budgets to achieve accountability and control over the long-range activities of important functions and organizational activities.

Summary

Creation of an organization's primary structure and prior decisions regarding structure and corporate strategy create a twofold need at the operating level: (1) formulation of strategic objectives for the businesses or major operating units and (2) the setting of objectives that integrate the short and long term and help to ensure the successful implementation of strategy. The first portion of this chapter focused on strategic objectives at the operating level. Similarities and differences between corporate- and business-level strategies were noted and discussed. The general model of strategy formulation developed in Chapter 2 was added to and the specificity of the strategic planning process increased by focusing on the major elements or components of strategy formulation at the operating level.

The remainder of the chapter focused on the integration of long and short term in the implementation of strategy. In our opinion, it is foolish to dedicate a great deal of time and effort to strategic planning, only to render successful implementation unlikely by (1) not integrating the long- and short-term needs of the organization, (2) not integrating plans and objectives vertically and laterally, and (3) relying on poor objectives or measures that create dysfunctional consequences. The differentiation of the organization into parts that represent its primary structure generates the need to integrate objectives and plans so that the whole is served optimally by its major parts.

A portion of the needed integration is provided by focusing on the linking process and developing sound objectives. In implementing strategy, it is necessary to relate short-term operating objectives with long-term strategic issues. Primary design decisions are made to establish structural units within which efficiency and rationality can reasonably be obtained. Operating objectives and plans follow this differentiation process, as more manageable pieces of strategic aims become the foci in the smaller structural units. The need within the units is to integrate objectives and plans, vertically and laterally, to attain the short-term operating objectives that relate logically and practically to strategy.

Because of the centrality and pervasiveness of operating objectives within this integration schema, attention must be devoted to the development of sound objectives. Here we have argued that objectives must meet certain criteria to aid in implementing strategy. At a minimum, operating objectives should not thwart strategic aims and create dysfunctional and costly consequences for the organization.

Finally, this chapter has implied the importance of operating structure for the attainment of operating-level objectives. Recognition of interdependence and the need for coordination to achieve objectives place demands on and otherwise affect the structure of and processes within the operating unit. It is logical and necessary, then, to consider structure as it supports and facilitates performance of the operating unit, and the next two chapters are devoted to this task.

Notes

1. James D. Thompson, *Organizations in Action* (New York: McGraw-Hill Book Company, 1967).
2. Charles Hofer and Dan Schendel, *Strategy Formulation: Analytical Concepts* (St. Paul, Minn.: West Publishing Co., 1978); Peter Lorange, *Corporate Planning* (Englewood Cliffs, N.J.: Prentice-Hall, Inc., 1980).
3. Hofer and Schendel, op. cit., p. 25.
4. Hofer and Schendel, op. cit., pp. 162–177; Michael Porter, *Competitive Strategies* (New York: The Free Press, 1980).
5. D. W. Karger, "Integrated Formal Long-Range Planning and How to Do It," *Long-Range Planning*, 6(4):31–34 (1973).

6. Jay S. Kim and W. C. Hamner, "Effect of Performance Feedback and Goal Setting on Productivity and Satisfaction in an Organizational Setting," *Journal of Applied Psychology,* 61:48–57 (1976).
7. John M. Ivancevich, "Different Goal Setting Treatments and Their Effects on Performance and Job Satisfaction," *Academy of Management Journal,* 20:406–419 (1977).
8. Gary P. Latham and Sydney B. Kinne III, "Improving Job Performance Through Training in Goal Setting," *Journal of Applied Psychology,* 59:187–191 (1974).
9. J. Scott Armstrong, "An Examination of the Value of Strategic Planning," working paper, The Wharton School, February 1981; Robert M. Fulmer and Leslie W. Rue, "The Practice and Profitability of Long-Range Planning," *Managerial Planning,* 22:1–7 (May–June 1974); Charles W. Hofer, "Research on Strategic Planning: A Survey of Past Studies and Suggestions for Future Efforts," *Journal of Economics and Business,* 28:261–286 (Spring–Summer 1976); Gary P. Latham and G. A. Yukl, "A Review of Research on the Application of Goal Setting in Organizations," *Academy of Management Journal,* 18:824–845 (1975); Milton Leontiades and Ahmet Tezel, "Planning Perceptions and Planning Results," *Strategic Management Journal,* 1:65–75 (1980); Paul D. Tolchinsky and Donald C. King, "Do Goals Mediate the Effects of Incentives on Performance?" *Academy of Management Review,* 5:355–376 (1980).
10. Daniel P. Moynihan, "Counselor's Statement," in *Toward Balanced Growth: Quantity with Quality,* report of the National Goals Research Staff (Washington, D.C.: U.S. Government Printing Office, 1970), p. 11.
11. Donald N. Michael, *On Learning to Plan—and Planning to Learn* (San Francisco: Jossey-Bass, 1973), p. 148.
12. James G. March and Herbert A. Simon, *Organizations* (New York: John Wiley & Sons, Inc., 1958).
13. Chris Argyris, "Personality and Organization Theory Revisited," *Administrative Science Quarterly,* 18:141–167 (1973); Louis E. Davis and James C. Taylor, eds., *Design of Jobs* (Baltimore: Penguin Books, 1972); L. G. Hrebiniak, "Effects of Job Level and Participation on Employee Attitudes and Perceptions of Influence," *Academy of Management Journal,* 17:649–662 (1974); L. G. Hrebiniak and Joseph A. Alutto, "Personal and Role-Related Factors in the Development of Organizational Commitment," *Administrative Science Quarterly,* 17:555–573 (1972); Gerald I. Susman, *Autonomy at Work* (New York: Praeger Publishers, 1976); and Martin Patchen, *Participation, Achievement, and Involvement on the Job* (Englewood Cliffs, N.J.: Prentice-Hall, Inc., 1970).
14. March and Simon, *Organizations.*
15. Michael, *On Learning to Plan,* p. 149.
16. Theodore Barry and Associates, "Productivity Decline," *Industrial Engineering,* Nov. 1980; see also Theodore Barry and Associates, *Resource Productivity Management,* (Los Angeles, CA: Theo. Barry & Associates, 1982); Theodore Barry and Associates, "Productivity Has No Easy Answer,"*Engineering News-Record,* May 8, 1980.
17. Michael, *On Learning to Plan.* p. 149.
18. Rensis Likert, *New Patterns of Management* (New York: McGraw-Hill Book

Company, 1961), and *The Human Organization* (New York: McGraw-Hill Book Company, 1967).

19. Robert K. Merton, "Bureaucratic Structure and Personality," in Robert K. Merton, ed., *Social Theory and Social Structure,* rev. ed. (New York: The Free Press, 1957), pp. 195–206; Michael, *On Learning to Plan;* and L. G. Hrebiniak, *Complex Organizations* (St. Paul: West Publishing Company, 1978), Chapter 6.

20. Robert K. Merton, "The Role-Set," *British Journal of Sociology,* 8:106–120 (1957).

21. See, for example, R. L. Kahn, D. M. Wolfe, R. P. Quinn, and J. D. Smock, *Organizational Stress* (New York: John Wiley & Sons, Inc., 1964); James G. March, "Decisions in Organizations and Theories of Choice," in A. H. Van de Ven and William F. Joyce, eds., *Perspectives on Organization Design and Behavior* (New York: John Wiley & Sons, Inc., 1981), pp. 205–244; and Peter Wright, "The Harassed Decision Maker: Time Pressures, Distractions, and the Use of Evidence," *Journal of Applied Psychology,* 59:555–561 (1974).

22. Hrebiniak, *Complex Organizations;* Michael, *On Learning to Plan;* and Merton, "Bureaucratic Structure and Personality."

23. Thompson, *Organizations in Action.*

24. Hrebiniak, *Complex Organizations,* "Organizational Effectiveness, Chapter 8.

5

BASIC OPERATING STRUCTURE

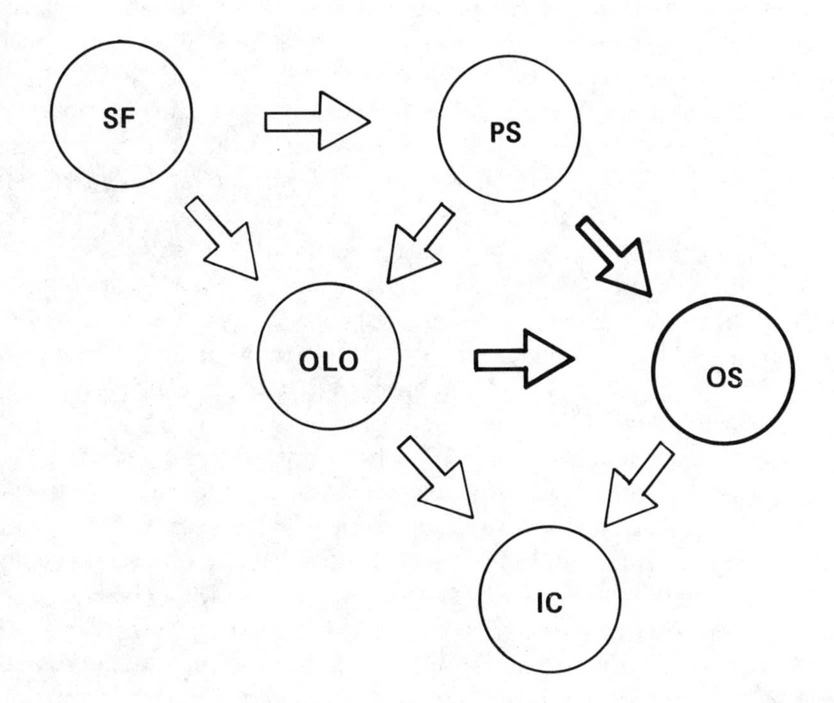

Basic operating structure is contingent upon prior choices of primary structure and operating-level strategies and objectives.

Organizations subject to effectiveness and efficiency criteria seek to develop and implement strategy rationally. To do this, they create strategies that respond, adapt to, and exploit opportunities and threats in their strategic business situations. Because these strategies are often complex, involving portfolios of businesses, multiple technologies, and significant variations in market characteristics, they must be broken down into more manageable components or parts for implementation. When strategy is complex, strategic planning processes alone are not sufficient to accomplish this "factoring" of the strategic mission. Choices of primary structural units must also be made so that within these major organizational segments, rational operating strategies and objectives can be developed. The topic of this chapter, the development of operating structures, follows these choices of primary structure and operating strategies. It is the next logical step in the process of strategy implementation. Primary structures must now be organized internally to facilitate the accomplishment of operating objectives.

Choices of operating structure, therefore, depend upon choices of primary structure and operating strategies. In implementing strategy, these represent the two key points of dependency that both constrain and influence choices of operating structures. The choice of a primary structure represents a first step in organizing that defines the scope of the remaining operating design decisions. This is because choices of primary structure represent decisions to factor the total organization into smaller components. Each of these is charged with accomplishing a portion of the overall mission of the firm. These "portions" of the mission represent the operating strategies and objectives for which the primary structural unit is responsible.

The choice of a primary structure has two consequences for decisions concerning operating structures. First, primary structures determine the size of the major organizational units (divisions, etc.) that require further design; second, they determine the extent of dependence among primary structural units by fixing the degree of self-containment within them. These decisions influence the choice of operating structures in obvious ways. Structures appropriate for large organizations are often different from those appropriate for smaller ones[1]; consequently, the size of primary structural units may become important for further organizing decisions. The degree of self-containment obviously affects operating structure because it determines partially what the decision maker has to organize. Decisions regarding the organization of personnel functions, for example, are irrelevant if there are no personnel functions at the operating level. The point here is that decisions at the primary structural level primarily constrain decisions at the operating structural level by defining the size of the organizing task and the range of functions to be organized.

Operating structures also depend to a considerable degree on choices of strategy. Decisions to serve particular customers, produce certain products, and offer a specific range of services represent answers to the question, "What business are we in?" at an operating as well as overall strategic level. Decisions to serve particular markets and operate specific technologies determine the degree of environmental uncertainty, for example, by requiring the organization to deal with varying levels of demand volatility and technical difficulty. And the types of operating structures appropriate in conditions of low uncertainty are different from those effective when technologies and markets are less well understood,[2] leading to a need to design operating structures consistent with the environment and technical demands of the chosen operating strategy.

In sum, primary structures constrain operating structures by determining the size of operating units and the functions to be organized. Operating-level strategies influence operating structures by determining the business problem that must be solved. Differences in the complexity, interdependence, and understanding of these business problems imply differences in operating structures. We can conclude that primary structure affects operating structure by defining the extent of the *structural problem,* whereas operating strategies and objectives influence operating structure by defining the extent of the *business problem.*

DEVELOPING OPERATING STRUCTURES

Decisions concerning operating structure may be separated into two categories. The first represents decisions regarding creation of *basic operating structures.* These decisions establish the fundamental organization of operating units and often are made in accordance with generally accepted "principles" of management. Departments must be created to accomplish operating objectives, and these departments must then be linked or integrated using rules, procedures, and a formal hierarchy of authority. These integrating mechanisms require additional decisions concerning delegation of authority and appropriate spans of control.

When the operating objectives of a primary structural unit require the organization to engage in nonroutine technologies or serve volatile, heterogeneous, and uncertain markets, the basic operating structure must be supplemented with additional mechanisms to ensure that the decision making and information processing essential to effective task accomplishment can take place.[3] This often involves the creation of additional formal, lateral channels of communications that violate classical principles of management concerning unity of command, delegation of authority, and scalar chains of influence. These nontraditional types of organization are appropriate when the demands of nonroutine activities place decision-making burdens on the organization that cannot be accommodated within the basic operating structure.

We refer to such nontraditional modes of organizing as *complex operating structures* because of their appropriateness to complex decision-making situations and the attendant difficulties required to manage nontraditional organizational arrangements. Complex operating structures are created in addition to, and often are superimposed upon, existing basic operating structures. Basic operating structures are "basic" precisely because they represent the fundamental vehicle by which the organization implements its operating strategies and objectives. Complex operating arrangements amplify the decision-making abilities of these structures in response to uncertain markets and nonroutine, highly interdependent, task activities.

The development of basic and complex operating structures takes place in accordance with the *principle of intended rationality*. Managers choose operating structures to respond to constraints and contingencies posed by previous choices of primary structure and operating strategy. In creating these structures, criteria of logic dictate a progression of design decisions beginning with division of labor and culminating in complex forms of lateral relations. Which of these are used is determined by the *principle of minimum intervention, which requires that complex operating structures be used only when basic operating structures are insufficient or deficient.* When this occurs, basic operating structures are supplemented by more complex integrating devices that provide the requisite levels of decision making.

This and the following chapter correspond to the two topical areas we have just discussed. In this chapter, we develop a model of basic operating structure. Our emphasis here is intentionally basic, as we answer some fundamental, but critical and often overlooked, questions about departmentation, division of labor, rule usage, span of control, role of hierarchy, and delegation in decision making.

Building upon the basics, in Chapter 6, we show how the model must be changed and supplemented to create complex operating structure to respond to complex, uncertain, and interdependent task requirements. The two chapters conclude with a summary of these design decisions and their relationships to components of the strategy implementation model.

ESTABLISHING THE BASIC OPERATING STRUCTURE

Traditional approaches to organizing are critically important in establishing basic operating structures, and managers have used and improved upon them since their early development. Some of the findings of researchers using contingency approaches are directly relevant to basic organizing decisions. Researchers and practitioners from areas other than management have also contributed to a better understanding of organization, as witnessed by the work of industrial psychologists and personnel specialists who have discussed design-related issues. The following sections are intended to integrate the contributions of psychologists, contingency theorists, and others with the essential elements from traditional management theories. Most organizing decisions concern basic operating structure. A useful approach to such decisions is, therefore, not historical or merely interesting; it is essential.

Basic organizing involves decisions about five aspects of organization, as shown in Figure 5-1. Although these decisions are shown in the figure as separate issues, decisions made in one area have implications for decisions in the others. Moreover, there is a basic logic to these decisions that relates them to one another roughly in the sequence shown by the arrows in Figure 5-1. It is important to understand this logical relationship, because it allows us to realize the implications of decisions affecting any one of the basic dimensions for other decisions.

An initial understanding of basic organizing, therefore, depends upon an appreciation of the content and relationships among the dimensions of basic operating structures, as shown in Figure 5-1. However, a deeper understanding is complicated by the fact that specific decisions concerning each dimension are also directly influenced by choices of operating-level strategy and objectives and constrained by choices of primary structure. Primary structure and operating strategy often influence the initial division of labor within the firm, which then in turn *indirectly* influences the choice of appropriate bases of departmentation, rules, hierarchy, and spans of control, as shown in Figure 5-1. But choices of strategy also exert a complicating *direct* influence on each of these organizing decisions as well. For example, assessment of the current strategic position of the firm might indicate a stage of product and/or market evolution in which competition centers on product design features (for example, the development stage). This would impact the firm's division of labor by requiring that appropriate staffing be undertaken to obtain specialized personnel necessary to develop competitive designs and indirectly require

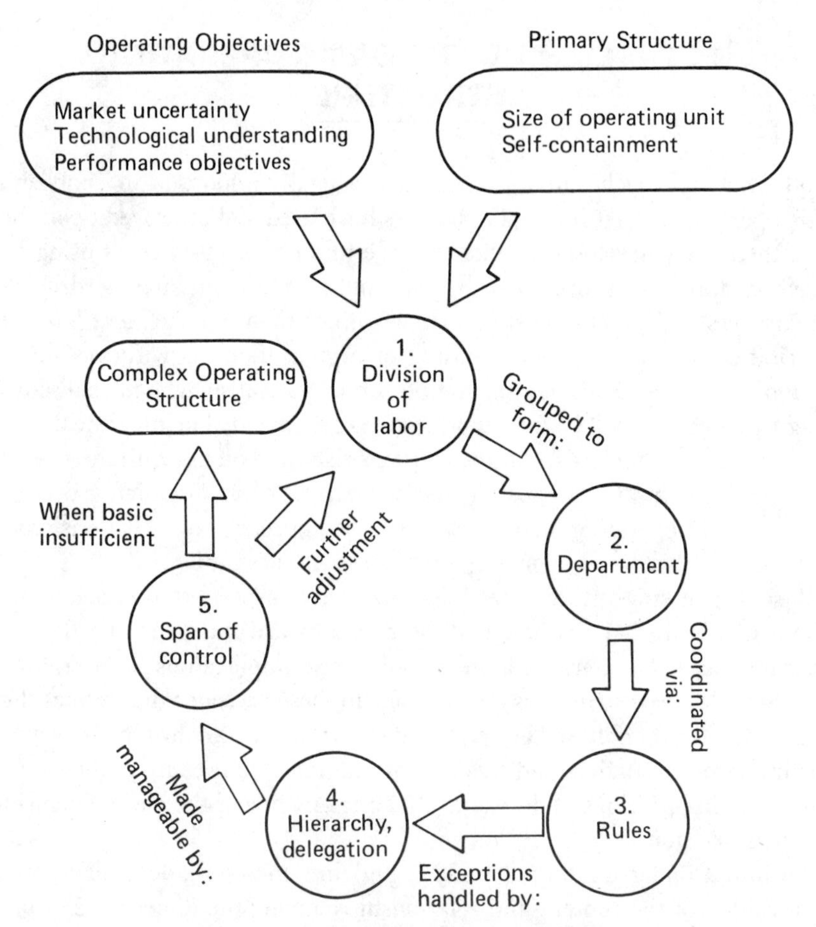

Figure 5-1. Relationships among basic organizing decisions.

these specialists to be coordinated through some form of departmentation. The particular mode of competition undertaken, however, might directly impact the specific basis of departmentation selected by requiring that diverse specialists be grouped together to provide a common focus on a particular new product design, for example, in product departments. Choices of operating strategy and primary structure, therefore, have both direct and indirect effects on basic organizing decisions.

In the following sections, we elaborate on the nature of the relationships among primary structure, operating strategy, and structure and then discuss each of the five basic organizing decisions in turn. We argue that, although the effects of primary structure are mainly *indirect,* operating strategies *directly* influence operating structure. The specific discussion then indicates the logical relationships among the structural decisions as well as the direct effects of key operating strategic choices on these variables.

Strategic Influences on Basic Operating Structure

Basic operating structures are designed to accomplish operating objectives within the constraints imposed by previous choices of primary structure. The previous section argued that there are both indirect and direct effects on basic structural choices due to primary structure and operating-level strategies. Primary structure mainly exerts indirect effects on operating structure by influencing the size and division of labor within the operating unit being designed. Subsequent organizing decisions are, therefore, indirectly influenced by initial choices of division of labor implied by the creation of primary structural units (Figure 5-1).

Some direct effects of primary structure on basic operating structures are, of course, possible and even probable. Corporate personnel policies may directly influence similar policies (rules) developed at the operating level. Similarly, a decision to utilize a particular type of departmentation at the primary structural level (e.g., divisions) will often result in a different type of departmentation being employed at the operating level of the firm (e.g., functional structure), so as to allow the organization the benefits of more than one type of departmentation.

Although such direct effects are clearly observable, we would still argue that primary structure mainly seems to influence operating structure indirectly, as described earlier. Extensive empirical research by Van de Ven and Ferry showed few direct links between primary and operating-level structural variables.[4] Moreover, the indirect effects of primary on operating structure have been implied if not openly discussed in the organization theory literature. What is still lacking is a more systematic discussion of the *direct* effects of operating strategy on basic organizing decisions. This discussion, together with an appreciation of the indirect effects of primary structure and operating objectives shown in Figure 5-1, will yield a more complete understanding of the design of basic operating structures.

Complementarity Between Planning and Design Activities at the Operating Level

A central theme of this book is that planning and organizing decisions must be integrated to implement strategy effectively. The basic model developed in Chapter 1 makes many of these relationships explicit across various levels of

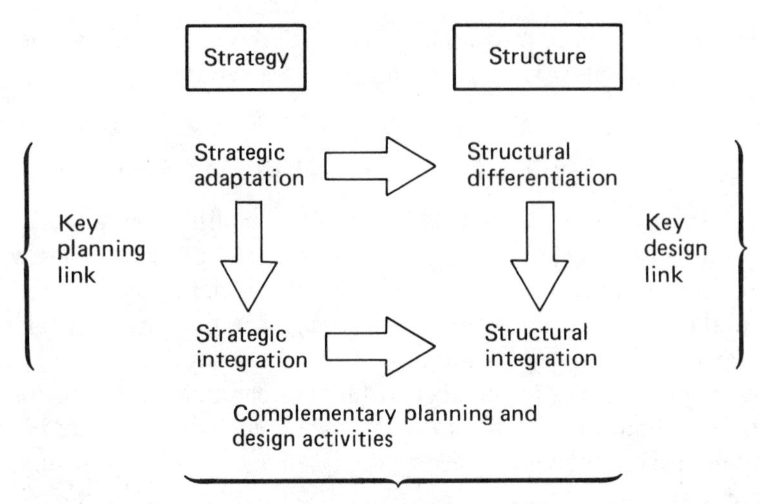

Figure 5-2. Complementary planning and organizing activities at the operating level.

analysis. Figure 5-2 refines and extends the notion of complementary planning and organizing activities for the operating level of the firm. Lorange has proposed that two of the more important functions of strategic planning are *adaptation* and *integration*.[5] Adaptation refers to the development of strategic options, and integration refers to selection from among these alternatives, accompanied by supporting planning activities to facilitate their attainment. In organizing, two key problems are choices of structural *differentiation* and the attainment of levels of requisite *integration*.[6]

Differentiation refers to the division of the organization into appropriate subsystems and the development within these subsystems of work orientations appropriate to the portions of the firm's strategy being addressed by that unit. The firm requires units to perform production, engineering, accounting, marketing, and other tasks, and within these units individuals develop distinct perceptions and orientations appropriate for the accomplishment of those tasks. Integration refers to the processes required to coordinate across these diverse subsystems.

These planning and organizing decisions are complementary, as suggested in Figure 5-2. The development of viable strategic options (adaptation) is supported by a structural choice to facilitate the accomplishment of decided-upon objectives within various product markets (differentiation). Planning processes support the attainment of specific objectives through the development of short-term operating objectives (integration, see Chapter 4), and organizing decisions are made to facilitate the coordination of diverse subgroups (structural integration). Strategic adaptation and structural differentiation represent complementary planning and organizing decisions, both responding to and exploiting environmental opportunities and threats. Strategic and structural integration are complementary and similar in that both seek to coordinate internal resources to accomplish operating-level strategic objectives.

There are two important conclusions to be drawn from this discussion of the relationships between planning and organizing at the operating strategic level: first, planning and organizing are complementary managerial activities in implementing strategy, and (consequently), second, *problems of strategic adaptation are most often associated with decisions concerning structural differentiation, whereas problems of strategic integration are most often associated with problems of structural integration and coordination.*

The previous sections have outlined relationships among primary structure, operating strategies, and objectives, arguing that the direct effects of strategic operating decisions on organization design have received too little attention and that there is a basic complementarity between planning and organizing decisions. In the following discussion, we present each of the basic organizing decisions in turn, showing the logical relationships among components of the basic model in Figure 5-1 and thereby illustrating the indirect effects of primary structure and operating objectives just discussed. In addition, hypothesized direct effects of strategic choices on each component of the model will also be presented. These relationships are summarized in Table 5-1, which should prove a useful reference as the discussion proceeds.

Basic Organizing Decisions

Division of Labor. The first basic organizing decision concerns *division of labor.* This decision is basic because it arises from the very nature of organizations. Organizations exist to solve problems and carry out tasks that individuals acting alone cannot accomplish. Consequently, when we organize, more than one person is required to execute tasks, raising the first basic organizing decisions: What skills are necessary in this organization, and who should perform what portions of the overall task? Should each person carry out a "whole" task from beginning to end, or should the work be specialized, with each person contributing only a small portion of the task? These are problems of division of labor.

Traditional approaches to organizing generally advocated division of labor based upon function or process, a choice expounded upon by early writers, most notably, Adam Smith.[7] His now-classic example of the benefits of specialization of labor was derived from a pin manufacturing plant. Smith observed that one worker in charge of the entire pin assembly could manufacture only about 20 pins per day. However, when the pin-making job was broken down into parts, and workers specialized in only one of the component operations, productivity improved dramatically. A work group of 10 workers produced as many as 48,000 pins per day, for a 240-fold increase in productivity!

Selection of workers is one of the basic activities in implementing a division of labor, particularly for new organizations and those that are growing rapidly. Such organizations must hire workers who have the requisite skills, training, and abilities to meet strategic and operating objectives. In such situations, the division of labor is dictated partly by the disciplines, trades, and professions available, and the manager's job is to select workers who best match the objectives of the firm or unit within it. The selection of workers to create an appropriate division of labor is usually guided by the "task specialization" process. French[8] defines this process, specifically, as the flow of events that allow the task of an organization to be broken into manageable proportions. The "manageable proportions" are the jobs of the firm that constitute its division of labor. Briefly, the steps in this process are as follows:

1. Establishing organizational objectives.
2. Organization planning and design decisions to establish the major components of the firm.
3. Developing position descriptions for the jobs required by the various units or segments.
4. Determining the qualifications necessary to hold one of these jobs.
5. Developing performance standards for each job.
6. Elaborating work rules relating to several jobs or groups of workers.

It is important to note that, although we begin discussing basic organizing actions with decisions about division of labor, these decisions are not made in isolation. As the first steps in the task specialization process imply, decisions about the appropriate division of labor are made with definite reference to strategic and operating-level objectives as well as to the primary structure of the organization, to avoid hiring workers who cannot contribute to the purposes of the organization. This process, therefore, implicitly recognizes the effects of primary structure on basic operating structures, as discussed in previous sections.

The division of labor within an operating unit is also directly affected by choices of operating strategies and objectives, as shown in Table 5-1. Assessment of the firm's *current situation*—for example, its strategic position—might indicate that its products fall primarily in a stage of product/market evolution termed the development stage. In this stage, research and development activities are critical, and, consequently, the firm's division of labor

TABLE 5-1. Strategic Variables Impacting on Basic Operating Structures.

Structural Variables / *Strategic Variable/ Analysis*	Adaptive		Integrative		
	Division of Labor	*Departmentation*	*Rules*	*Hierarchy/ Delegation*	*Span of Control*
Analysis of current strategic position					
Product and market evolution	X	X	X	X	X
Competitive position	X		X	X	
Generic strategies	X	X	X	X	X
Environmental analysis					
Market analysis					
Size and growth			X	X	
Segmentation	X	X			
Buyer needs	X				
Industry analysis					
Rivalry			X	X	
Seller concentration			X	X	
Barriers to entry			X	X	
Barrier to exit	X	X			
Capital intensity			X	X	
Retained value added			X	X	
Economies of scale		X	X	X	
Technical change	X	X	X	X	X
Product differentiation		X	X		
Supplier analysis					
Input dependencies	X				
Threat of vertical integration			X (contracts)		
Competitor analysis	X	X	X	X	X
Resource/capability analysis					
Flexibility	X	X	X	X	X
Distinctive competence	X	X	X	X	X

reflects the need for appropriate scientific and technical skills. Similarly, *environmental* analysis could influence choices of division of labor by suggesting a segmentation of the market, which, in turn, requires changes in the division of labor to provide the necessary skills to compete effectively in newly defined market segments. Finally, *resource/capability* analysis might suggest a distinctive competence accruing to the firm as a consequence of its changed, specialized work force, which has been expanded and strengthened, thereby affecting the existing division of labor.

Division of labor, therefore, is the answer to the question of what skills are necessary in the firm and to the question of who should perform what portions of the overall tasks. Figure 5-3 summarizes the discussion by showing schematically this basic element of organizing and the consequent specialization to accomplish a task that one person acting alone cannot accomplish as quickly or as efficiently. But in answering this first basic question, we have

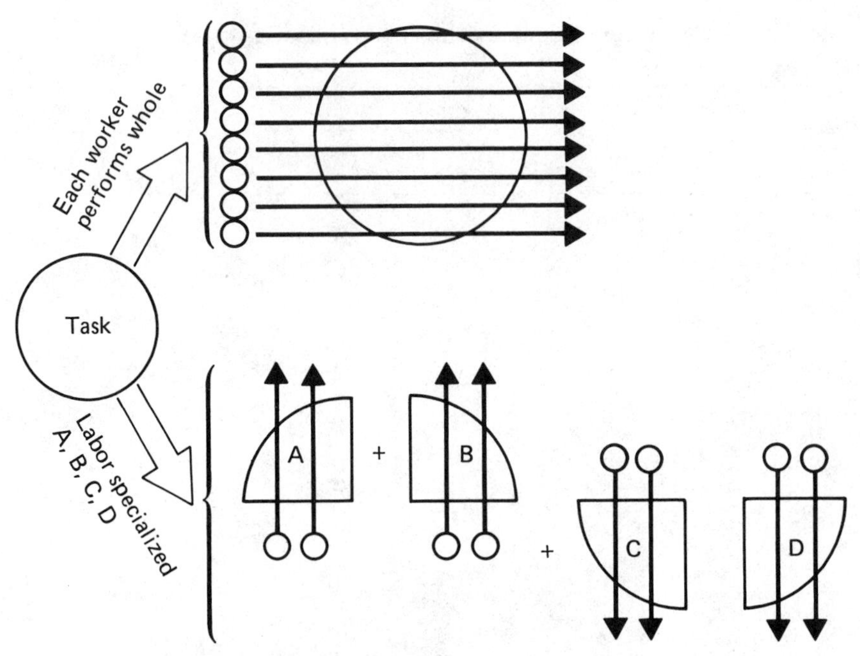

Figure 5-3. Choice of division of labor.

posed yet another: "How shall we coordinate the activities of workers in the many jobs making up the firm's division of labor?" The first response to this question is to group jobs that are interdependent into common work groups to facilitate the close coordination required to integrate specialized tasks. This is called *departmentalization,* the second of the five basic organizing decisions.

Departmentalization. Managers create departments of workers to help accomplish the operating objectives of the firm by coordinating the division of labor. Establishing a division of labor generates a diverse group of workers whose skills are necessary to accomplish the basic task or mission of the firm. However, by choosing to divide the work of the organization into many jobs, we have made each of these jobs dependent on others. In performing tasks, workers will frequently find that they need information, help, or resources from others or that their jobs are interdependent. Because each worker's job performance often depends upon how well co-workers are performing, managers must be concerned with coordination. To achieve the necessary integration, managers create departments of workers whose jobs are complementary. By placing workers who depend on one another in the same work group, face-to-face cooperation is facilitated, resulting in efficient coordination of the com-

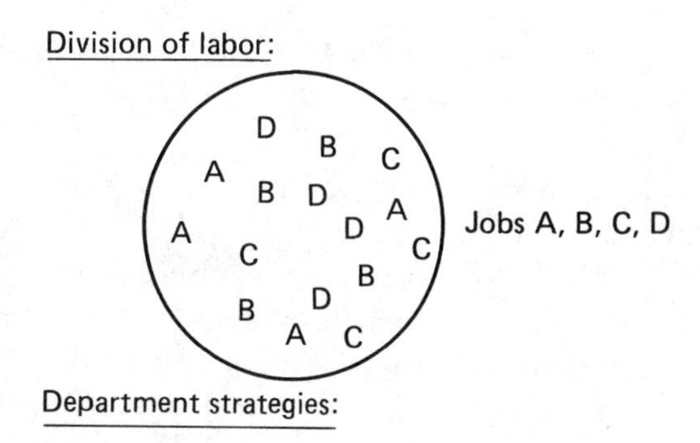

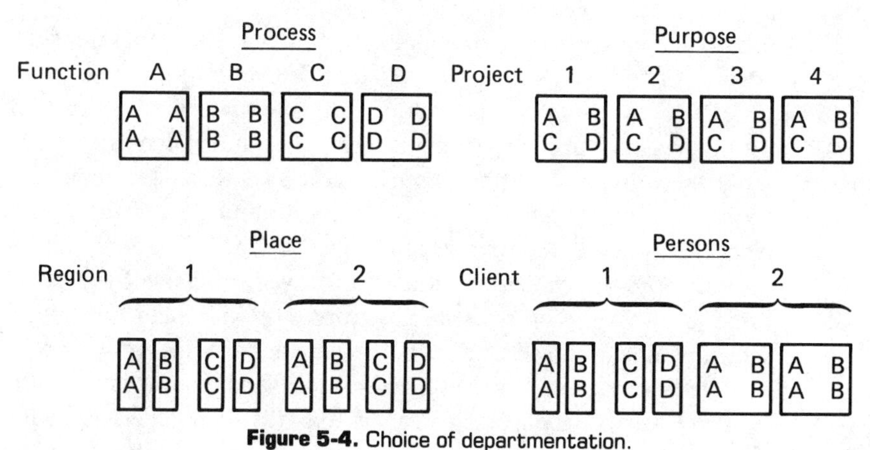

Figure 5-4. Choice of departmentation.

plex division of labor. Departmentalization is a decision about how to group jobs in an organization, as shown in Figure 5-4.

Davis and Lawrence[9] state that a decision to utilize a particular type of departmentalization is a decision to "focus" the energy of the organization on particular problems. Subject to criteria of intended rationality, managers choose the type of departmentalization that focuses the energy of the unit on its most important strategic problem or its dominant competitive issue. The choices of focus that can be made were first presented by Gulick,[10] who proposed four principal bases of departmentalization.

According to Gulick "It will be found that each worker in each position must be characterized by"

1. *The major* purpose *he is serving, such as furnishing water, controlling crime, or conducting education.*
2. *The* process *he is using, such as engineering, medicine, carpentry, stenography, statistics, and accounting.*
3. *The* persons or things *dealt with or served, such as immigrants, veterans, Indians, forests, mines, parks, orphans, farmers, automobiles, or the poor.*

4. *The* place *where he renders his service, such as Hawaii, Boston, Washington, the Dust Bowl, Alabama, or Central High School.*

Basic organizing decisions generally involve an "either-or" approach to departmentalization, although use of types 3 and 4 usually requires further departmentation by purpose or process (this type of *stratified* departmentation will be discussed further). Each of the four bases have relative advantages and disadvantages, and the manager responsible for basic organizing decisions chooses one based upon an analysis of these costs and benefits in relation to his or her specific situation.

The primary advantage of departmentalization by purpose is that it results in a high degree of self-containment, as Chapter 3 notes. Essential activities within purpose departments can be carried out without close coordination with other similarly organized departments. Self-containment denotes the fact that the department contains all the resources necessary for task completion, including human resources (having all necessary technical specialists) and material resources (having the necessary machines, financing, and raw materials). Generally, purpose departmentalization is very effective for accomplishing projects and tasks on time or in accordance with plan. However, purpose departmentalization sometimes is less efficient or effective in a technical sense. This is because a "critical mass" of technical experts is required so that specialists have an opportunity to share expertise and experience with other similarly trained experts. This face-to-face interaction is often missing from purpose departments because size often requires that only one specialist be assigned to particular departments, and in the long run, technical issues are slighted. In some cases, purpose departmentation results in duplication of effort, leading to an inefficient use of scarce resources.

The weakness of purpose departmentalization is the strength of the second type of department discussed by Gulick, process departmentalization. Early management theorists believed that grouping jobs on the basis of similarity in the functions performed by the workers was the most effective way in which to departmentalize because it encouraged specialization and allowed significant economies of scale. By grouping workers on the basis of process, managers would ensure that there would be enough "work of a given technical sort to permit efficient sub-division"[11] and, consequently, that the workers could achieve high levels of technical proficiency through specialization. Therefore, when managers choose process departmentalization, they are choosing to focus the energy of their firm on efficiency and technical issues related to specialization.

This emphasis under process departmentalization, however, can lead to or result in an unintended weakness. Process departmentation focuses on processes or inputs with the consequence that workers sometimes lose sight of the objectives toward which they toil. In these circumstances, workers may focus on the technical or process elements of their work to the detriment of the overall objectives of the firm. Examples are commonplace of process specialization resulting in budget and schedule overruns, although quality and technical issues are seldom compromised.

Process and purpose specialization are clearly the most important forms of departmentation. However, the remaining two, *persons or objects* dealt with and *place,* are sometimes important as well. The advantages of each of these are more straightforward than are those of purpose and process departments. Choosing departments on the basis of the persons dealt with, or by clientele, allows workers to develop specialized knowledge of the needs and characteristics of the persons being served by the organization. Marketing groups are often departmentalized by client so that they can focus on the unique characteristics of particular clients or market segments to serve them better. In health care, managers organize by clients to provide better services unique to classes of users or client groups. Hospitals create departments such as ambulatory care, intensive care, or cardiac care units and commonly distinguish between in- and outpatient services. In both examples, the purpose is to allow specialization by clients to meet consumer needs more effectively.

Departmentalizing by *place* is also called geographic departmentalization, and it is relevant at the operating as well as primary structural level (Chapter 3). Managers choose geographic departmentation when clients or customers from an area have needs or characteristics different from those of other regions; in this case, client and place departmentation are the same. Sometimes workers must be located close to natural resources to avoid excessive costs of transporting raw materials to manufacturing sites, so managers use departmentalization based upon geographic location near the needed resources. In other cases, geographic departmentalization is required when managers must be able to respond quickly to customer requests or service problems that require the physical presence of a representative of the firm. In all these examples, departmentation by place has obvious advantages.

Occasionally, managers may find that they require the advantages of more than one type of departmentalization. For simple tasks, departmentation schemes may be stratified hierarchically (that is, one type of department may be "nested" within another different type) to provide more than one focus for decision making. For very complex tasks, it is usually necessary to use more than one type of departmentalization at the same time. This is what is called simultaneous or *matrix* departmentalization. The gains of simultaneous structures, however, are not without costs, because using more than one basis of departmentalization results in violations of many of the traditional principles of management such as unity of command, scalar chain of authority, and the idea that authority and responsibility should always be equal. Because using more than one basis of departmentalization violates these basic principles, we reserve further discussion of the several varieties, costs, and benefits of matrix organization until the next chapter, on complex operating structures, in which we present an integrated five-stage model of basic and complex departmentation.

Choices of departmentation are directly affected by operating objectives, as implied earlier and as shown explicitly in Table 5-1. The firm's *current situation,* for example, may require a focus on process rather than on product innovation due to a mature stage of product or market evolution. This condition would favor functional departmentation consistent with the arguments just advanced. *Environmental* analysis could indicate industry characteristics showing that effective competition requires obtaining significant economies of scale, say, in manufacturing activities. This would again directly indicate the choice of a functional form of departmentation; the need is the sharing of critical resources across many activities as opposed to creating self-containment (e.g., distinct product departments) that excludes such sharing and incurs losses of economies of scale (particularly for smaller organizations). *Resource/capability* analysis may require departmentation by function to afford key technical specialists the "critical mass" necessary to develop a distinctive competence in process innovation.

In sum, bringing together more than one person to solve a problem or execute a task causes us to decide who should do what in our organization. This is the question of division of labor. In answering this question, we pose a new problem: How should the actions of diverse specialists be coordinated or recombined to accomplish the objectives of the firm? As we have just indicated, the manager's first response to this problem is to group jobs that are dependent upon one another into departments that focus the activities of workers on the firm's dominant competitive issue, as shown in Figure 5-4. Unfortunately, departmentalization alone is not enough to coordinate complex, interdependent jobs. Once having established departments, the manager must still coordinate relationships between or among the departments, and so the third basic organizing decision noted in Figure 5-1, the establishment of *rules and operating procedures,* becomes important.

Rules and Operating Procedures. Departmentalization facilitates coordination among interdependent jobs or positions by grouping, thereby allowing face-to-face interaction and encouraging quick, direct communication. Regardless of the basis of departmentation chosen, some interdependence usually remains, because, as Thompson notes, the components of organizations "employ several processes, . . . frequently serve more than one clientele, and for the most part . . . are geographically extended." The departments initially formed to facilitate coordination among interdependent positions, therefore, are not totally autonomous, for if they were they "would not be or remain a part of the organization."[12] It remains for the manager to coordinate the relatively independent contributions of basic departments through the establishment of rules and operating procedures.

The development of rules and operating procedures is, therefore, indirectly affected by previous choices of primary structure and operating objectives because these decisions require a division of labor and subsequent choices of departmentation for coordination purposes. These decisions indirectly require rules because departments now must coordinate their activities to achieve organizational objectives.

However, rules and procedures are also directly influenced by strategic choices as well. Assessment of the firm's *current situation,* for example, its competitive position, may indicate low levels of slack resources and a weak position. In such situations, decision making becomes more centralized, with a greater reliance on rules and procedures. *Environmental* analysis of industry characteristics might indicate a low degree of seller concentration, implying a roughly equal size of firms and a highly competitive situation. Such conditions are associated with high levels of interfirm rivalry and pressures for efficiency. Rules facilitate the attainment of such outcomes. Similar effects could be hypothesized as a result of *resource/capability* analysis, as shown in Table 5-1.

For departments performing relatively routine tasks where information is clear, cause-effect relationships are well understood, and the time between the making of a decision and the realization of its consequences is short, rules and operating procedures are usually sufficient to provide task coordination. However, such routinized coordinating devices are not sufficient to provide the requisite integration implied by more sophisticated technologies. As decision making becomes more and more nonroutine, exceptions to rules and operating procedures are more frequently encountered. Some mechanism is required to resolve such exceptions. The *creation of a hierarchy* by delegating authority from top- to lower-level managers to act in linking capacities is effective for this purpose. Consequently, this represents the next element in the creation of a basic operating structure.

The Creation of a Hierarchy: Delegation of Authority. Decisions about division of labor and departmentalization determine the major components of the organization that must be coordinated. According to the principle of minimum intervention, rules and procedures are initially used to achieve this integration and, for relatively simple, well-understood tasks, may be sufficient. Generally, however, more powerful integrating devices are needed to resolve exceptions to rules and procedures encountered as decision making becomes more and more uncertain and nonroutine.

As Figure 5-1 indicates, a *hierarchy of authority* is created for this purpose, representing "a combination of interdependent groups, to handle those aspects of coordination which are beyond the scope of any of its components."[13] The hierarchy is created as top managers delegate authority to subordinates to act as coordinators of the various departments chosen on the basis of the criteria developed. One of the key functions of a manager is to act as a linking pin, and we can clearly see how this function emerges from problems of organizing. Figure 5-5 illustrates how hierarchy and rules combine to provide integration necessitated by previous decisions concerning division of labor and departmentalization.

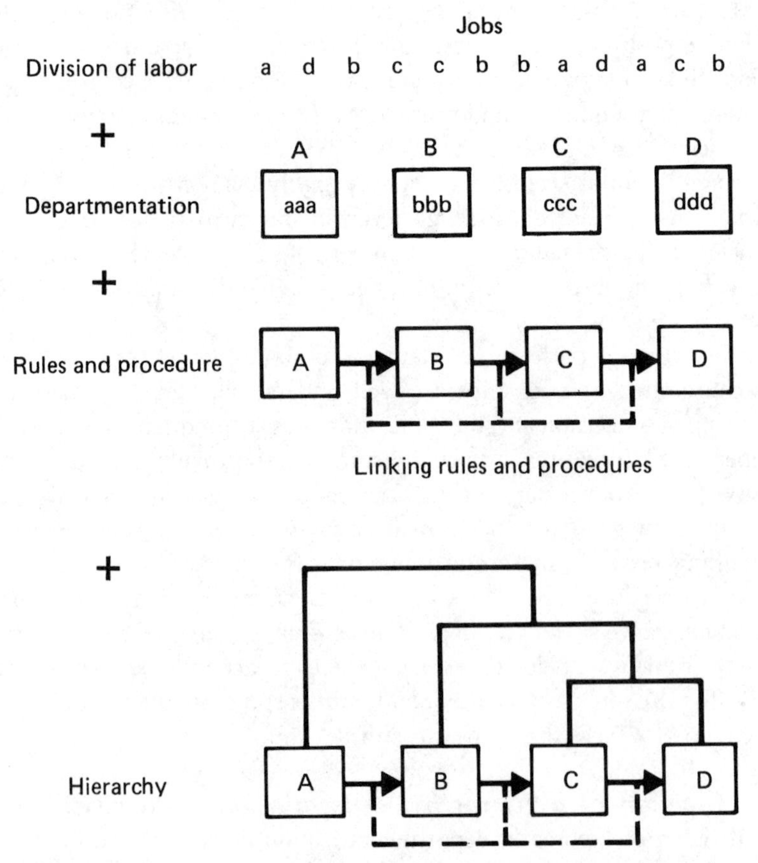

Figure 5-5. Integrating decisions in basic organizing: rules and hierarchy.

Delegation is also influenced by choices of operating objectives, as shown in Figure 5-1. For example, stages of product/market evolution *(current situation)* requiring product innovation demand and result in more delegation than do stages in which efficiency issues are paramount. Similar arguments are appropriate when industry analysis *(environmental analysis)* indicates high rates of technological change. Under these conditions, organic or "flat" structures are typically much more effective than centralized structures in creating an ability to respond to a changing and problematic environment.[14]

Practically, decisions about delegation of authority are made by determining the appropriate responsibilities of a position in the organization and then assigning authority equal to these responsibilities in accordance with classical principles of management. With respect to coordinating responsibilities, this would involve determining which departments are most dependent upon one another in carrying out their tasks and then assigning responsibility for the coordination of these departments to a new manager appointed to act in this linking and integrating role. Following the principles of management, authority is delegated to this person in proportion to the responsibilities assigned to him or her.

As an example, consider an aerospace corporation in which departments are formed to perform wind tunnel testing, wing design, and stability and control analyses. Although each of these departments represents a particular technical specialty, they are extremely interdependent. An engineering decision to utilize a particular size and geometry of wing affects stability and control, and both must rely on wind tunnel information. Because these functions are interdependent, they are usually placed beneath a manager who is responsible for coordinating them. This person—the chief of aerodynamics—is delegated the authority to direct the activities of the departments that he supervises in proportion to the responsibilities of his position. Delegation, then, is a decision to create subordinate managerial positions with coordinating responsibilities and then to assign authority to carry out this task.

Lawrence and Lorsch[15] provide some guidelines that aid in this process. Responsibility should be assigned to managers and workers depending upon their knowledge of the problems being considered. In some organizations, as problems become more difficult, complex, or uncertain, persons with relevant skills and knowledge are frequently found at lower hierarchical levels. This is due to the fact that, as one moves lower in these organizations, specialization increases, whereas as one moves to higher levels, generalized knowledge increases. Therefore, when specialized knowledge is required to solve a nonroutine problem, it may be located at lower levels of the firm. By assessing the complexity of the problems being considered, managers should assign responsibility to positions where the knowledge required to produce solutions to these problems exists.

Once appropriate responsibility has been assigned in accordance with task uncertainty, authority should be delegated that is equal to these responsibilities. Lawrence and Lorsch showed that authority should reinforce responsibility for basic organizing functions. Simply assigning responsibility appropriately is not enough; managers must also have authority to take action based upon their responsibilities.

These prescriptions apply directly to basic organizing decisions and provide an excellent example of how the work of contingency researchers has contributed to managerial practice in delegation. They have provided contingent guidelines for making difficult delegation decisions that traditional researchers did not. For basic organizing, the principle remains the same: authority and responsibility should be equal, but responsibilities between positions are seldom so, and therefore authority must be delegated accordingly.

In certain situations in complex operating structures, it is not always true that formal authority is commensurate with role responsibilities. We defer this issue and discussion of similar problems and characteristics of complex structure to the next chapter.

Span of Control. Delegation arises from the organization's need to coordinate groups of workers formed by previous decisions concerning division of labor and departmentalization. Managerial positions are created and assigned integrating responsibilities, and authority is delegated to carry out these responsibilities. As in our other decisions, the creation of linking roles has raised a new problem. How many workers should report to each of these new linking managers? Should it be three, or five, or even seven? This, the fifth issue noted in Figure 5-1, is the problem of *span of control.*

The problem of span of control is a natural consequence of delegation of authority. Once we have established subordinate managers with linking responsibilities, the next logical question that we face is how many workers should report to them.

Table 5-1 shows some direct effects of strategy on span of control, but its main determinants appear to be the cumulative indirect effects of previous basic organizing decisions. Industry analysis may indicate rates of technological change requiring specific spans of control, but generally these decisions are more complex than simple industry analysis would indicate. Approaches to this complex problem can be classified roughly under three headings.

Traditional researchers *first* searched for an optimal span of control. It was once suggested that a span of six subordinates for every manager represents traditional thinking.[16] This principle was very easy to apply because it was noncontingent; the same span should be chosen in all cases. However, more recently, researchers have observed that spans of control in organizations range widely. For some organizations, wide spans seem appropriate, whereas for others narrower spans seem most effective. The *second* answer to the span-of-control problem was provided by researchers who were attempting to explain these apparent discrepancies.

The most important work on spans from this perspective was done by Joan Woodward.[17] She found that appropriate spans of control varied with the technology that the firm utilized to produce its outputs. Woodward developed a scale for measuring technology based upon production continuity. Three main types of technology can be discussed. In order of increasing production complexity and continuity, these are the unit or small-batch, the mass-production, and continuous-process technologies. The *unit* or *small-batch* technology is one in which small amounts of output are produced to specific customer requirements, as in prototypes and other made-to-order products. The *mass-production* technology involves production of large batches on assembly lines. A *continuous-process* technology involves the continuous-flow production of liquids, gases, or solids, as in chemical manufacture or oil refining.

Woodward found that appropriate spans of control varied as a function of the technology as well as the level in the hierarchy at which spans are being designed, as shown in Figure 5-6. A supervisory span of control is the number of production workers reporting to a first-line foreman, or the lowest managerial level in the firm. An executive span is the number of subordinate managers reporting to their immediate superiors at higher levels. Figure 5-6 illustrates that appropriate supervisory spans were related to technology, but not in a linear fashion. Supervisory spans were found to be higher for mass-production technologies than for unit-small-batch and continuous-process technologies.

Executive span varied directly with production continuity. The more sophisticated the technology, the larger the allowable executive span. This is because, as the technology becomes more integrated, a portion of top managers' coordinating responsibilities is handled by the technology itself. Consequently, managers can provide coordination for a larger number of departments, and larger spans appear appropriate. In Woodward's research, the closer the firm's executive and supervisory span to the modal spans for their respective technologies, the higher the economic performance of the firm.

A *third* contingency approach to spans of control was provided by Barkdull,[18] who argued that seven factors affect appropriate spans of control at middle-management levels. These factors are:

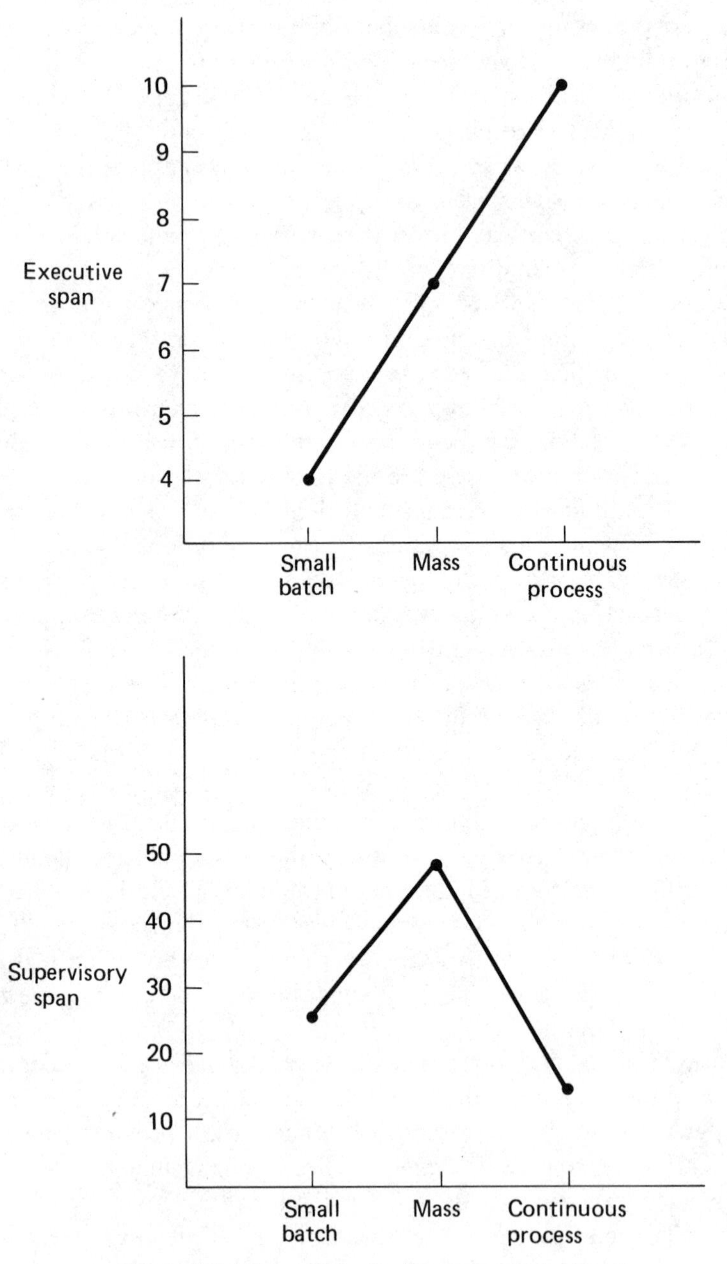

Figure 5-6. Effects of technology on span of control.

1. Similarity of functions being supervised
2. Geographic contiguity of functions
3. Complexity of functions
4. Direction and control required by personnel
5. Coordination required
6. Planning required
7. Staff assistance available

Figure 5-7 shows how these factors impact on managerial spans of control. Similarity of function, geographic contiguity, and the availability of staff assistance combine to allow *wider* spans of control. As task complexity and the requirements for coordination and planning increase, allowable spans *decrease*. Similarly, as supervisors must provide more direction and exercise more control, allowable spans decrease so that managers may have sufficient time to devote to such activities.

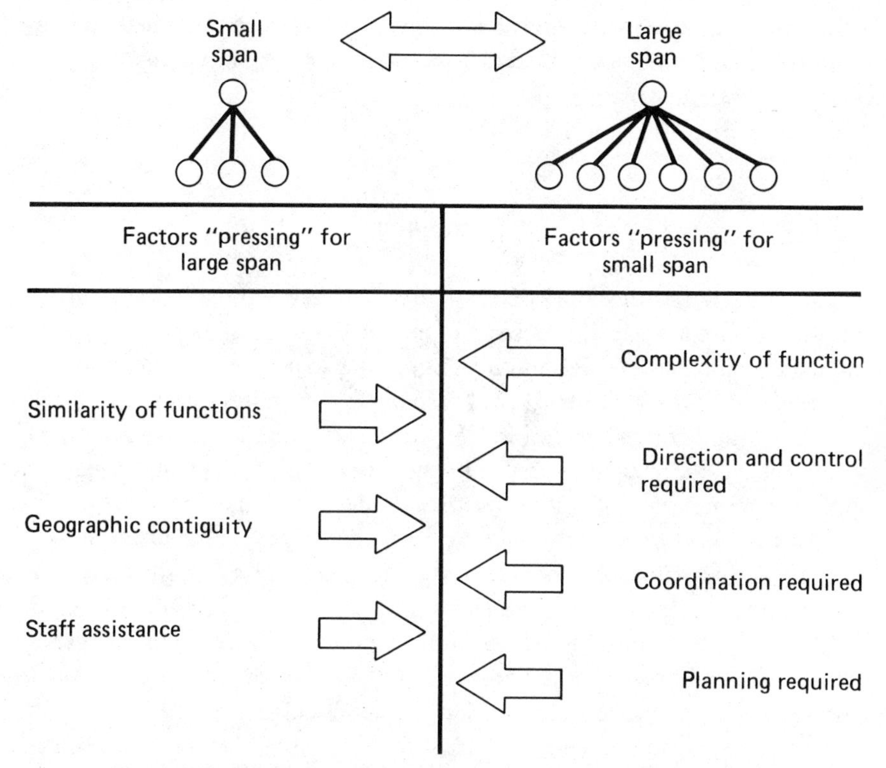

Figure 5-7. Effects of various situational factors on span of control.

The impact of these various factors on spans of control is a reflection of what March and Simon referred to as "bounded rationality." Simply stated, we are not as smart as we would like to be; our information processing capabilities are limited, forcing us to "satisfice" rather than optimize in decision making. Other things being equal, managers would prefer wide spans of control. This would encourage "flat" organizations with quick, accurate, information handling characteristics due to a truncated hierarchical communication network. However, there are limits to how wide such spans can be that are imposed by our limited information processing capabilities. By grouping similar functions in common locations and providing staff assistance, we allow wider spans of control. But task complexity and requirements for planning, coordination, and control place upper bounds on the effects of such activities by imposing demands on the limited decision capabilities of managers.

Final spans of control are chosen by considering, evaluating, and balancing factors such as those proposed and discussed by Woodward and Barkdull. Task demands, interdependence, physical setting, and management judgments combine to provide alternative perspectives for refining classical prescriptions concerning span of control, the final element in our consideration of basic operating structure.

Summary

This chapter has proposed that organizations develop operating structures to respond to contingencies posed by previous choices of primary structure and operating objectives. In designing operating structures, primary structure defines the *extent of the structural problem* by determining the size of operating units and the range of functions to be organized (the degree of self-containment), thereby indirectly influencing operating structure. Operating objectives define the *extent of the business problem* by engaging strategies that imply differences in the complexity, interdependence, and uncertainty of business decisions and that both directly and indirectly affect structure.

When choices of primary structure and operating objectives do not require high levels of decision making and information processing, basic operating structures are appropriate. The creation of a basic operating structure requires decisions concerning division of labor, departmentalization, development of rules and procedures, delegation of authority, and span of control. Decisions in each of these areas impact on subsequent decisions in basic organizing. Basic organizing relies most heavily on traditional principles of management, but these principles should be modified by findings of contingency theorists.

As the scope of structural and business problems becomes more complex, eventually basic operating structures become inadequate to provide the requisite decision and information processing capabilities. Complex operating structures must be developed to provide such capacity. The nature of such structures, specific factors requiring their utilization, and their potential problems in application are examined in the next chapter.

Notes

1. Roy Payne and Derek S. Pugh, "Organizational Structure and Climate," in Martin Dunnette, ed., *Handbook of Industrial and Organizational Psychology* (Chicago: Rand McNally & Company, 1976).
2. Paul R. Lawrence and Jay Lorsch, *Organization and Environment* (Boston: Division of Research, Division of Business Administration, Harvard Business School, 1967).
3. Jay R. Galbraith and W. F. Joyce, *Organization Design* (Reading, Mass.: Addison-Wesley Publishing Co., forthcoming).
4. Andrew H. Van de Ven and Diane Ferry, *Measuring and Assessing Organizations* (New York: Wiley-Interscience, 1980), p. 185.
5. Peter Lovange, *Corporate Planning: An Executive Viewpoint* (Englewood Cliffs, N.J.: Prentice-Hall, Inc., 1980).
6. Lawrence and Lorsch, *Organization and Environment.*
7. Adam Smith, *The Wealth of Nations* (New York: Random House, Inc., 1937).
8. Wendell French, *The Personnel Management Process* (Boston: Houghton Mifflin Company, 1970).
9. Stanley Davis and Paul Lawrence, *Matrix* (Reading, Mass.: Addison-Wesley Publishing Company, 1977).
10. Luther Gulick, "Notes on the Theory of Organization," in I. L. Gulick and L. Urwick, eds., *Papers on the Science of Administration* (New York: Institute of Public Administration, 1937), pp. 3–45.
11. Ibid., p. 15.
12. James D. Thompson, *Organizations in Action* (New York: McGraw-Hill Book Company, 1967), pp. 57–58.
13. Ibid., p. 59.
14. T. Burns and G. M. Stalker, *The Management of Innovation* (London: Tavistock Press, 1961).
15. Lawrence and Lorsch, *Organization and Environment.*
16. Herbert Simon, *Administrative Behavior.* 2nd ed. (New York: Macmillan Publishing Co., 1957).
17. Joan Woodward, *Industrial Organization: Theory and Practice* (London: Oxford University Press, 1965).
18. C. W. Barkdull, "Span of Control—A Method of Evaluation," *Michigan Business Review,* 15:25–32 (1963).

6 COMPLEX OPERATING STRUCTURE

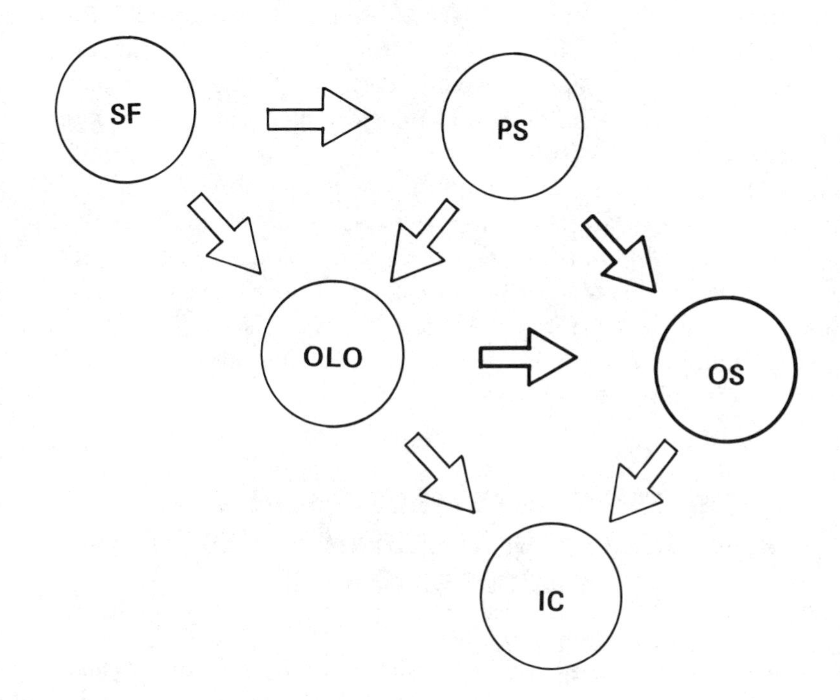

Complex operating structures are employed when basic operating structures are insufficient to meet demands imposed by increasing strategic complexity, uncertainty, and interdependence.

Basic operating structure is created to accomplish operating objectives within the constraints of previous choices of primary organization. For relatively simple tasks, routine technologies, and stable business situations, these simple structures are adequate. Decisions can be made routinely in accordance with rules and procedures and communicated through formal hierarchical channels with little delay or distortion. When operating strategies and primary structures engage more problematic tasks, environments, and technologies, decision-making requirements may increase to the point that the basic operating structures become inadequate. The quality of decisions suffers, individuals who need to be involved in key decisions are excluded unintentionally, and people who should be informed concerning decision outcomes frequently are not. These are commonly encountered signals that the basic operating structure is not adequate to meet the decision-making burdens imposed by choices of operating objectives and primary structure.

Operating structure depends upon the decision-making requirements of the operating unit being considered.[1] Complexity of decision making requires complex operating structures. While it is obvious that all organizations require decision making to accomplish operating objectives and that they, therefore, require a basic operating structure, it is not obvious that all require high levels of decision-making capability and, therefore, complex operating structures. Before we proceed to a discussion of the choices made in creating complex operating structures, it is appropriate to discuss the factors generating decision-making requirements and the relationships of these factors to choices of operating objectives and primary structure.

DETERMINANTS OF DECISION-MAKING REQUIREMENTS: ASSESSING INFORMATION PROCESSING NEEDS

Contingency views of organization design have argued that in choosing an organization structure "it all depends." One of the criteria used for the development of the approach to implementing strategy presented in this book, the criterion of *contingent prescription,* argues that simply knowing that "it all depends" is not enough. Managers must also know, first, what it all depends upon and, then, what to do about it.

Many answers have been given to the first of these dual requirements for contingent prescription. Researchers and practitioners have argued that choices of structure are influenced by characteristics of business environments,[2] technology,[3] the size or organizational components,[4] and industry differences.[5] Each of these variables has been conceptualized and measured in various fashions, often using a single aspect or component of one of these major contingency variables. Business environments have been described in terms of their uncertainty,[6] their turbulence,[7] their homogeneity,[8] and their complexity,[9] as well more conventional economic concepts. The effects of technology have been studied using measures based upon technological understanding,[10] rates of product innovation,[11] work flow continuity,[12] and input-output[13] boundary transaction uncertainty. Although specific research findings have sometimes produced conflicting results, contingency views have become generally accepted.

It is also important to note that although many organization design approaches take variables such as those just mentioned as a "starting point" or reference for further choices of organization design, these contingency variables are themselves products of previous strategic choices as well as choices of primary structure. Strategic analyses concerning stage of product/market evolution, market segmentation, and industry characteristics such as firm size and rivalry obviously bear on the characteristics of what organization designers have simply termed "environment." Strategic choices also may imply the use of specific technologies, or index rates of technological change, which also serve as inputs for choices of organization design. This suggests that strategy and primary structure may impact on complex operating structures indirectly by determining the levels of decision making and information processing that must be accomplished, as discussed next (see Table 6-1).

The various contingency variables just outlined are useful for researchers and academics trying to understand and extend knowledge about organiza-

TABLE 6-1. Examples of the Impact of Choice of Primary Structure and Operating Objectives on Decision Uncertainty, Complexity, and Interdependence.

	Uncertainty	*Complexity*	*Interdependence*
Primary structure		Size of operating unit (no inputs)	Dependence on other primary units
		Range of human inputs	
		Self-containment: range of functions to be integrated	
Operating objectives	Exposure to contingencies of particular environment	Number of products	Technologically required interdependence
	Market understanding	Efficiency goals	Boundary transaction uncertainty
	Technological understanding of cause-effect relations		Task interdependence

tions. They are less attractive to managers because each aspect becomes somewhat "sterile" and unidimensional when removed from the complex and confusing network of relationships among variables that is encountered in implementing strategy. In this book, we want to suggest that all these aspects of technology, environment, and industry are involved in selecting an appropriate operating structure. What is important presently is finding a way of thinking about how choices of primary structure and operating strategy and objectives influence decision requirements and how these decision requirements affect choices of operating structure. The remaining portion of this chapter is devoted to this purpose.

Three factors combine to determine the level of decision-making requirements facing the organization. These are the levels of *decision uncertainty, decision complexity,* and the *interdependence of task-related activities.* Although these factors clearly are not totally independent, we will treat them separately in the discussion to show their relationship to choices of structure and operating objectives more clearly.

Uncertainty. Uncertainty refers to a situation in which the individual finds it difficult to decide because of a lack of relevant information concerning important contingencies faced by the organization. For organizing purposes, two key sources of contingency are business environments and technology. A business environment is composed of consumers, suppliers, competitors, and regulatory agencies.[14] Each of these can pose problems for an organization, for example, by withdrawing services, introducing new products or service-related innovations, changing regulations, or terminating contractual arrangements. Technology also poses important contingencies as new methods and scientific understanding are developed, threatening existing product lines and distinctive competence. At the core of this type of contingency is the firm's understanding of cause-effect linkages related to its technology (see Chapter 2). Some organizations face problems for which no known solutions exist, thereby requiring that information processing and decision making produce such solutions.

Uncertainty requires information processing to manage important contingencies posed by environment and technology and to develop new understanding of cause-effect linkages. Data concerning competitors' actions must be developed to aid in the selection of new projects, and managers must understand the dynamics of the market to choose appropriate competitive responses and launch new programs. Research and development activities are required to implement new technologies so that an uncertain, unclear, and untried technique can become economically feasible. Burns and Stalker, for example, described such activities as the "institutional process of technology." They argued that flexible, decentralized operating structures are required to provide the necessary information processing capabilities when new technologies make understanding of cause-effect linkages problematic.[15] The selection of "organic" structures to facilitate decision making illustrates how operating structures respond to uncertainty posed by technology as well as environment.

Complexity. Complexity requires information processing as a consequence of the number of inputs and outputs that must be dealt with by the firm as well as the amount of "slack" resources available in transforming these inputs to required outputs. As the number of inputs and outputs of the operating unit increases, so does the complexity of the decision situation. The amount of slack resources available also influences decision complexity because, as less and less slack is available, operations must be performed more efficiently to achieve equivalent production levels. Consequently, more decision factors must be considered under conditions of low slack, generating increased complexity. Simply, the argument is that it is harder to be more efficient than less efficient and that higher efficiency levels (less consumption of slack) require increasingly sophisticated and complex decision-making approaches.

Complexity also increases as the division of labor of the operating unit being structured increases. More technical specialties represent more "inputs" to operating decisions whose "outputs" must be coordinated. As the number or diversity of these human inputs and outputs increases, so does the complexity of decision making, requiring adjustments in operating structure.

Interdependence. The interdependence of task activities also affects the requisite level of decision making and impacts on choices of operating structure. Various levels of interdependence, such as sequential interdependence in which the outputs of one worker become inputs for another, can be managed by basic operating structures in conjunction with operating plans. This is the familiar assembly-line situation. More complex types of interdependence, such as reciprocal task interdependence in which everyone depends upon everyone else, require coordination by "mutual adjustment." High levels of information processing are required to manage such complex dependencies because there is no natural ordering of problem-solving activities dictated by the task, and each situation must be approached as a "new" problem to be solved.

The levels of decision making required by uncertainty, complexity, and interdependence result from previous choices of primary structure and operating objectives, as shown in Table 6-1. The table relates the factors discussed to these choices and shows that both primary structure and operating objectives affect decision requirements. Operating objectives impact on uncertainty, complexity, and interdependence, whereas primary structure affects mainly the last two variables.

In sum, primary structure and operating objectives affect operating structure by defining the scope of the structural and the business problem, respectively, as suggested in Chapter 5. This section has indicated that this occurs because choices of primary structure and operating objectives affect levels of uncertainty, complexity, and interdependence and that increases in these variables require increased levels of decision-making and information processing capability. Operating structure is designed to facilitate such decision making, consistent with the principle of intended rationality.

As decision requirements increase beyond levels that can be coped with by the basic operating structure, a more complex operating structure must be developed and utilized to avoid the unintentional consumption of excessive amounts of resources. When slack is available in the form of excess human, financial, or material resources, it is possible to achieve requisite levels of decision making and coordination by applying these resources to the tasks at hand. Often, however, this consumption of slack resources represents a prohibitively expensive "organizing" mode. When this occurs, complex operating structures are created by establishing formal lateral channels of communication and decision that supplement existing hierarchical channels. These structures represent varying degrees of *lateral inclusion* in decision making, beginning with simple direct contact relationships between managers from different functional groups and culminating in what we call complex departmentalization schemes. The next section discusses the variety of complex operating structures and the relationship of these structures to decision-making requirements.

COMPLEX DEPARTMENTALIZATION: LATERAL INCLUSION IN DECISION MAKING

Complex operating structures are created to supplement the decision-making capabilities of basic operating structures. This is done by creating new formal channels of communication that are overlaid on the existing basic organization. These channels afford the additional information processing capabilities required to deal with uncertain, complex, interdependent decision requirements. As we progress from basic to complex operating structure, the role of the lateral manager becomes increasingly important, more formalized, and imbued with more authority, until the overlay structure becomes in a sense "equal" to the original basic organization. We refer to this situation as complex departmentalization because, in these schemes, workers are simultaneously members of more than one department, and multiple basic structures co-exist within a single operating unit. Such arrangements violate many principles of management, with the consequence of making both organizational design and the managers' job more complex.

These lateral structures can be viewed as a series of steps separating two qualitatively different stages in the evolution of departmentalization schemes. Organizations can be described in terms of a five-stage model of departmentalization as shown in Figure 6-1. These stages are called (I) implicit departments, (II) simple departmentation, (III) stratified departmentation, (IV) simultaneous departmentation, and (V) coordinate hierarchies. Stages I through III are encountered in basic operating structures, whereas stages IV and V occur only in complex operating structures. Stratified departments (stage III) are separated from simultaneous departments (stage IV) by a series of steps representing increased lateral inclusion in decision making, as described next.

Before we discuss complex departmentation, however, it is appropriate to describe briefly the first three stages shown in Figure 6-1 to provide a point of departure for discussion of the more complex alternatives. Actually, the first three stages are appropriately considered aspects of basic organizing. We have delayed discussing them to present the five-stage model in its entirety. The next sections present the first three stages of departmentation. Three "steps" in lateral decision mechanisms are then shown to separate basic operating structures (stages I–III) and complex operating structures (stages IV and V). Following a discussion of these steps, we conclude our discussion of complex operating structures with an examination of simultaneous departments and coordinate hierarchies.

BASIC DEPARTMENTATION: IMPLICIT, SIMPLE, AND STRATIFIED DEPARTMENTS

Implicit, simple, and stratified departments are illustrated in Figure 6-1. They can be distinguished in terms of the number of explicit bases for departmentation utilized and the manner in which they are given priority.

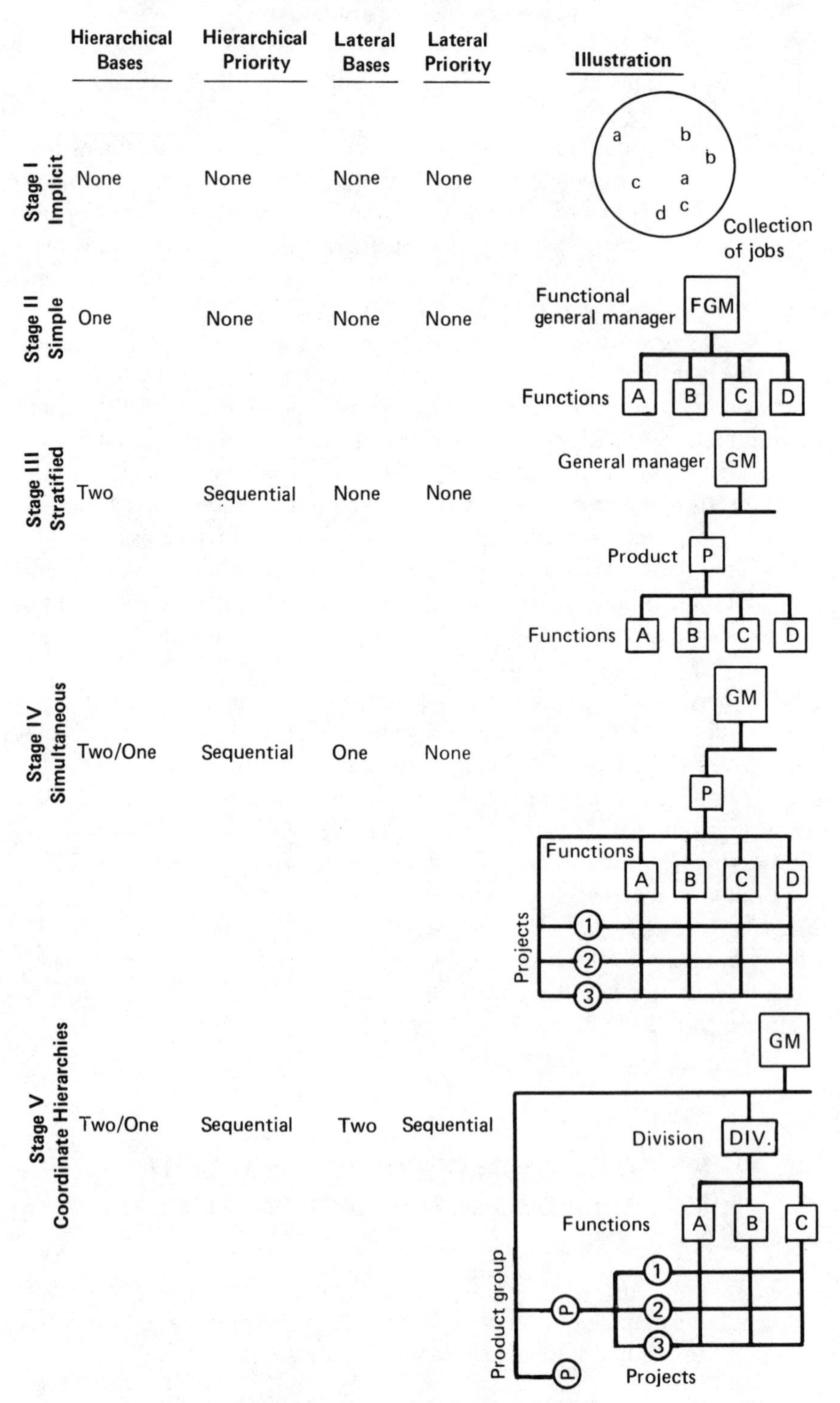

Figure 6-1. Stages of departmentation.

Implicit Departments (Stage I)

Implicit departments are schemes in which there are no formal departments. Naturally, since there are no explicit departments, no one variety of department using Gulick's classification has been given priority (Chapter 5). Firms that are "unorganized" in this sense are usually small; coordination is not problematic because workers produce relatively "whole" pieces of work in the absence of formal specialization and division of labor. The term "implicit" is not used to imply that this form of structure is inappropriate; it is used to point to the absence of formal explicit bases of departmentalization. Examples of this stage of departmentalization include sole proprietorships, independent consulting firms,[16] and what Thompson[17] has called "synthetic organizations." In the synthetic type of organization, previously designated types of departments are ignored in favor of control structures determined by the coincidence of resources and knowledge of how best to apply them.

Simple Departments (Stage II)

Simple departments are formed when one and only one basis of departmentalization is used, for example, in the purely functional organization. Since only one basis is utilized, it is obviously the one given priority. As noted in Chapter 5, the choice of a basis of departmentalization is a decision to focus the energies of the firm on particular issues. In simple departmentalization, one basis, generally either process or purpose, is chosen to the exclusion of others. Departments are formed to facilitate face-to-face coordination of tasks among workers who are interdependent as a consequence of specializing labor to achieve operating economies. Simple departmentation schemes occur when the complexity of operations (usually as a function of size) preclude implict structure by requiring formal mechanisms for coordination, as discussed in Chapter 5.

Stratified Departments (Stage III)

Stratified departments occur when more than one basis for departmentalization is used within a single operating unit and the priority among these bases is sequential. Such organizations are common, the divisional firm being a frequently encountered example. In such structures, the core departments are often specialized by process (functionally), and these departments are then nested hierarchically, within divisions specialized by purpose (products or projects, for example). This example represents what we have called primary structure earlier, but it is equally relevant at the operating level. Stratified departmentation is appropriate when operating objectives require that more than one "focus" be included in decision making but clearly indicate that a particular focus should predominate.

The level and type of information processing allows for the interdependence among these foci or bases to be managed sequentially, usually by plan. Operating objectives for product groups are established during strategic planning activities, and functional groups then coordinate their activities to accomplish these objectives. This "coordination by plan" around product group objectives is sufficient to ensure the appropriate relative emphasis on both product and functional objectives. This could occur, for example, in a situation in which many of the firm's products were entering the "maturity" stage of product/market evolution. Process innovation (and thus functional departmentation) would be important for competition, but further growth might require the development of new products to extend the firm's mix of products across different stages of product-market evolution. *Creating an operating structure with process departments nested within product groups could provide this type of dual focus.*

Product plans could be developed for these groups to ensure the necessary development of new products, with these plans being executed by the functional departments. Product planning and functional activities would therefore be "sequential" to one another in a logical and, to a lesser extent, temporal way. Product planning in this firm represents an emerging but currently less important activity than successful competition in the organization's major line of business, at least in the short run. As a result, process innovation and efficiency should take priority. Should product innovation assume greater importance in the future, it would require explicit design choices to support an increased role in the firm's operations. More powerful integrating devices would have to be found in the form of new channels of communication and lateral decision. Such steps in lateral relations would culminate in the remaining complex departmentalization schemes, which are discussed next.

ELABORATING COMPLEX DEPARTMENTATION SCHEMES: LATERAL RELATIONS STRATEGIES

Stratified departmentation (Stage III) and *Simultaneous* departmentation (Stage IV) are separated by a series of "steps" in lateral relations that successively transform a Basic Operating Structure into a Complex Operating

Structure. Each of these steps represents an increase in the degree of lateral inclusion in decision making. Lateral inclusion is defined in terms of formalization of the lateral decision role and authority in decision making. Galbraith has identified several varieties of lateral relations which can conveniently be grouped into the following three levels or types of lateral inclusion: (1) Natural approaches, (2) Group forms of lateral inclusion, and (3) Formal Influence strategies. Each of the six varieties is discussed separately in ascending order of lateral inclusion.

Natural Forms

Natural approaches to lateral relations arise simply in response to increased demands for information processing that cannot be satisfied within basic operating structures. Additional lateral channels of communication are required to supplement formal hierarchical structures.

The simplest natural strategy is what Galbraith has termed a *direct contact role* (lateral strategy 1).[18] Establishing a direct contact role amounts to legitimization of a violation of the classical principle of management that calls for adherence to a scalar chain of command. Rather than processing information and communicating through formal hierarchical channels, individuals from different groups or functions simply contact one another directly, thereby shortening the path or distance that information must follow if the scalar chain principle is adhered to, as shown in Figure 6-2.

Although direct contact roles are simple and straightforward, they require managerial action to ensure their effectiveness. This is so because departmentalization results in the development of unique perspectives or orientations within different groups. Marketing develops a "marketing" viewpoint, engineering an "engineering" one, and so on. These distinctive orientations among workers in different subgroups are part of and help to define what Lawrence and Lorsch termed differentiation.[19] Differentiation is usually quite important in organizations, as noted previously, but it does cause an additional problem. Once appropriate orientations have been established *within* departments, it becomes more difficult to facilitate cooperative behavior among individuals differentiated *across* departments. For direct contact roles, the implication is that the greater the extent of differentiation, the harder productive collaboration will be to achieve. Generally, such techniques as job rotation and management training coupled with normal hierarchical interventions are sufficient to overcome these problems for simple direct contact roles.

Liaison roles (lateral strategy 2) represent an increase in inclusion in deci-

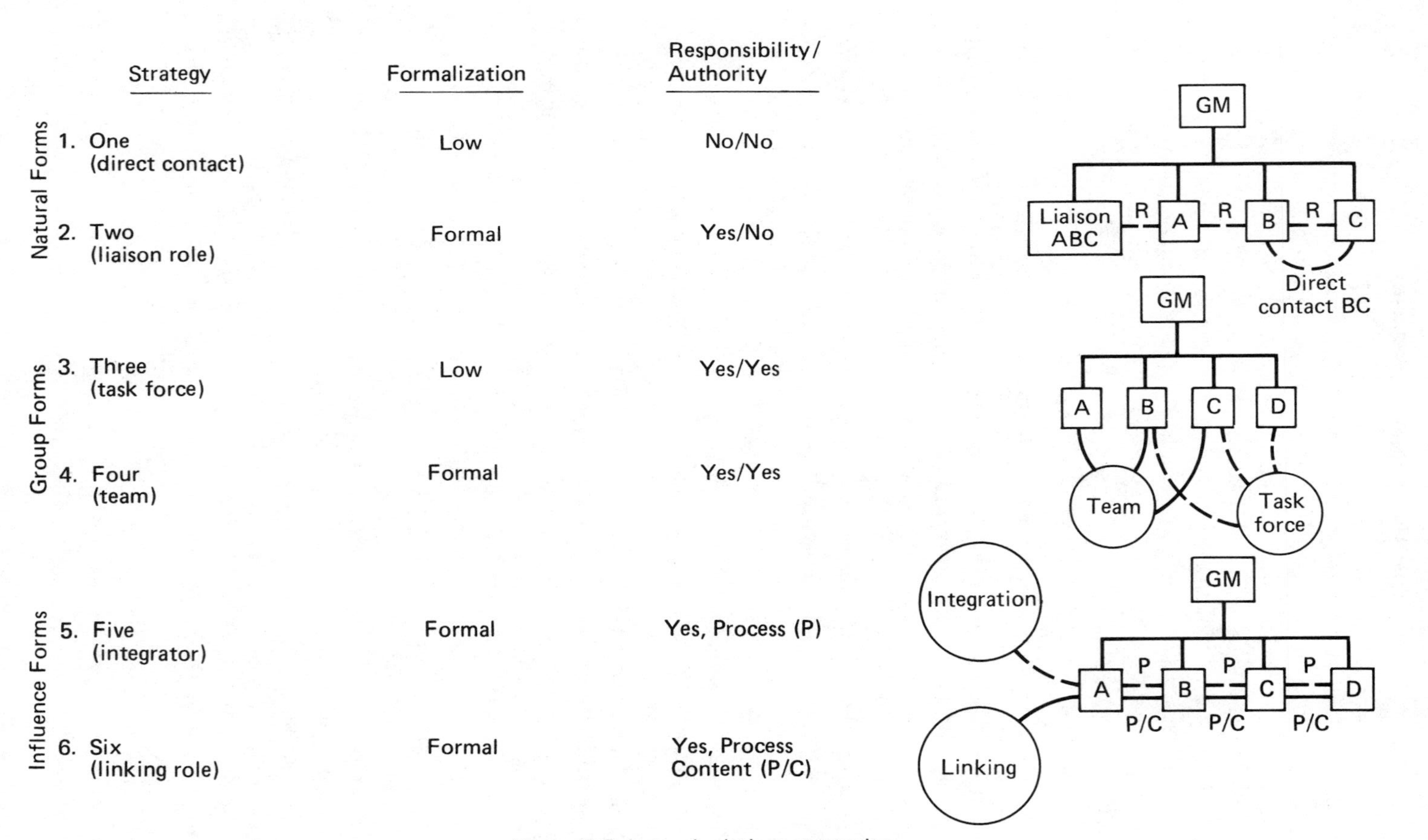

Figure 6-2. Lateral relations strategies.

sion making through formalization. At the operating level, there are two principal varieties of liaison roles. The first is the formalization of the direct contact role. This is appropriate when the frequency of lateral contact between groups justifies that a portion of someone's time within a particular work group be formally allocated to lateral coordinating activities.

As the frequency of lateral contact increases, it usually becomes necessary to utilize full-time liaison roles. Because of the differences in task orientation among different groups, full-time liaison roles are usually not located within a particular group. This could result, among other things, in an unbalanced perspective on the part of the liaison manager and suspicion on the part of the individuals in other groups or functions. Liaison roles, thus, represent a separate function that must be staffed consistently with the efficiency and effectiveness criteria that guide the staffing of all areas.

Because liaison positions are formally recognized, responsibility for coordinating or expediting activities requiring the involvement of more than one work group can be assigned. However, little authority is given to support this responsibility. Liaison managers depend heavily upon knowledge and charisma to accomplish their objectives. Because of this emphasis on "local" problems and the importance of becoming influential based upon informal sources of power, liaison managers usually cannot be hired from the outside. Instead, the organization must "grow" them within the organization by rotating them through several functions so that they obtain the necessary social acceptance and the "intermediate" orientation necessary in their role. Lawrence and Lorsch have shown that this intermediate orientation is necessary to achieve requisite levels of coordination in highly differentiated firms.[20]

Group Forms

Group approaches to lateral relations are utilized when information processing demands exceed the capabilities of a single liaison role or when the uncertainty of business decisions requires group rather than individual decision making. Group approaches amplify the information processing capabilities of the organization by providing an additional point of decision in the form of an artificial "manager" (the group). There are two varieties of group approaches, task forces and teams.

A *task force* (lateral strategy 3) is less formal than a team. It typically is an ad hoc group that is created to deal with a nonrecurring problem or situation and is disbanded after the problem has been solved or the situation resolved. Consequently, responsibility for task force activities is usually somewhat unstructured because adjustment in formal job description is not justified for "one-time only" projects.

A *team* (lateral strategy 4) is a more permanent group created to solve recurring problems. This increased formality is the principal difference between the two group-related lateral structures. A team represents a greater degree of lateral inclusion in decision making than does a task force because of its more formal and lasting role. Typically, formal permanent adjustments in responsibility are warranted when teams are established, possibly including designation of full-time team members.

Teams and task forces are often ineffective due to violation of a few simple rules for utilizing lateral relations effectively. Extensive productive discussions of these factors have been presented by Galbraith and by Lawrence and Lorsch, but we would be remiss not to mention and summarize the more important ones at this point.[21] These factors are

1. *Relevant Knowledge and Skills.* Team members must possess requisite understanding of the problems being faced, as well as the implications of alternative courses of action. Generally, this requires that interdisciplinary teams be composed of individuals from differing hierarchical levels. As uncertainty in a particular area goes up, individuals with requisite levels of technical understanding are found at lower levels. This is partially because skill specialization is necessary to provide insight to highly uncertain activities.
2. *Authority to Commit Resources.* Teams are created to make decisions and solve problems to augment the information processing capabilities of an overloaded hierarchical communication network. Obviously, if such teams are not allowed to commit resources, they do little more than complicate decision making in an already overburdened situation. It is very important that the authority to commit resources only be assigned after individuals with the relevant skills and knowledge have been identified. This will ensure that power drives knowledge. If individuals are selected for teams on the basis of their formal power, it is possible that this influence will be used to enact inappropriate decisions when the team requires decisions for which the individual is unqualified.
3. *Tie-in with Formal Structure.* Teams and task forces create new lateral channels of communication to supplement existing hierarchical channels. If these channels are not integrated with existing channels, they do little to reduce the burden on these systems and may actually create new problems in the form of an alternative costly information system which is inconsistent with the established hierarchical mechanism.

4. *Reward System.* This is really an element of control that will be discussed further in Chapter 7. It is so important to the functioning of teams that we mention it briefly now. Behavior that is reinforced tends to be repeated. This psychological fact is often ignored when teams are established. Commitment to teams is difficult when the cost of such commitment is a lower performance appraisal, poorer compensation, or denial of a promotion from the manager of the employees primary work group. Rewards should reinforce team behavior if teams are to work.
5. *Importance of Team Participation.* The perceived importance of being a team member influences team performance. Occasionally, teams are populated with low performers. This is because managers are asked to send someone to team meetings whom they can "spare." When the basic operating structure is overloaded, it is only natural for managers to designate team members whom they can spare the most. Unfortunately, most employees know who the poor performers are and assignment to such a task force becomes a punishment rather than an important assignment. Herbert Simon, the 1979 Nobel laureate in economics, is reputed to have said that there is nothing so satisfying in one's career as to look around and find oneself surrounded by only good people. The converse is also true; it is therefore important to encourage effective team performance through assignment of high rather than low performers.

Several other factors such as leadership, conflict handling, and team building also influence the successful utilization of teams and task forces. Although they are beyond the scope of the present volume, they must be considered important aspects of effective team implementation.

Teams and task forces as discussed thus far rely upon group decision making without formal leadership roles. As decisions become more uncertain, complex, and interdependent, formal lateral authority roles are required. These roles often are used in conjunction with the group approaches.

Influence Forms

Influence approaches to lateral relations are used when a formal lateral leadership role is required. Increasingly uncertain tasks may result in one or more members of a team obtaining disproportionate amounts of influence in decision making as a consequence of access to information required by other team members. Formal leadership roles may be required to manage decision making in such situations. Two lateral influence strategies are common: the use of integrators and linking roles.

An *integrator* (lateral strategy 5) is delegated formal influence, but it is influence of a special kind. An integrator has authority over the *process* of decision making but not its *content*. An integrator chairs a team or task force, calls meetings, and devises the agenda for such meetings but cannot decide for the group. As in liaison roles, integrators usually must be developed within the organization. They acquire influence through informal processes and the assignment of formal authority for decision processes.

Unlike the integrator, the *linking manager* (lateral strategy 6) can decide for the group. Linking managers have formal lateral authority similar to managers in the hierarchy of the basic operating structure. This increased influence is used to obtain decisions in situations where more egalitarian, group-centered methods have failed to obtain consensus on a course of action. The effectiveness of linking managers is encouraged by assigning approval power in decision processes and by making sure that these individuals are included early in the planning process, at least at the level of operating objectives. Their effectiveness is also increased by assigning them control of budgets (see Chapter 7). Linking managers are therefore often said to manage dollars not people. Although they have considerable discretion and influence, their control generally does not extend to the day-to-day supervision of personnel. This authority constitutes a final step in lateral influence as the organization completes the transition from basic to complex operating structures by adopting what has been termed a matrix organization.

Although organizations using linking managers resemble matrix organizations and often are described as such, technically, matrix is the next step in the series of lateral relation strategies. This step represents a fundamentally different approach to departmentalization. It involves the creation and maintenance of more than one basis of departmentation *simultaneously*—a radical departure from traditional organizing principles.

COMPLEX DEPARTMENTATION: SIMULTANEOUS DEPARTMENTATION AND COORDINATE HIERARCHIES

Complex departmentation occurs when two or more bases of departmentation are used concurrently, as shown in Figure 6-1. The first variety of complex departmentation is *simultaneous departmentation.* This is often called "matrix" organization and is represented by stage IV in our model of departmentation. Simultaneous departmentation is usually limited to two dimensions (two bases of departmentation) because of the significant management difficulties involved when more than two bases of departmentation are used concurrently. Complex departmentation schemes often employ a third or fourth basis of departmentation in a stratified sense as shown in Figure 6-1. When this stratification occurs on the lateral dimension, a type of organization that we call a *coordinate hierarchy* (stage V) results. The next sections discuss these two varieties of complex departmentalization.

Simultaneous Departmentation

Simultaneous departmentation (stage IV) is the final step in the transition from basic to complex operating structure. Two bases of departmentation exist concurrently, and workers are simultaneously members of more than one department. As the model of departmentation suggests, complex departmentation schemes evolve from basic operating structures. Most basic operating structures are functionally organized (by process); consequently, simultaneous departmentation most often involves a functional structure with an overlay utilizing a different basis of departmentation, such as purpose or clientele. This overlay produces a grid appearance and the common designation of such arrangements as "matrix" structures as shown in Figure 6-1.

Simultaneous departmentation arrangements are defined by the use of concurrent multiple bases of departmentation resulting in the formation of what Davis and Lawrence call the "matrix diamond," as shown in Figure 6-3.[22] Four key roles define the matrix diamond. The top of the diamond is occupied by the *top manager* whose functions are power balancing, standard setting, and managing the decision context. The top manager controls who listens to whom in matrix arrangements and "balances" the relative influence of the two dimensions of the matrix. To do this, he or she uses a variety of procedures that we discuss at the end of this section. The operating objectives of the matrix unit are administered by the top manager, who is responsible for establishing a productive, problem-solving culture in the organization.

The second key role is that of the *functional manager.* In matrix, the functional manager's role is primarily changed in three ways. First, some of the decision responsibility previously held by functional managers is assigned to another role in the matrix diamond, the program or business manager. This results in the functional manager's job becoming more "stafflike." That is,

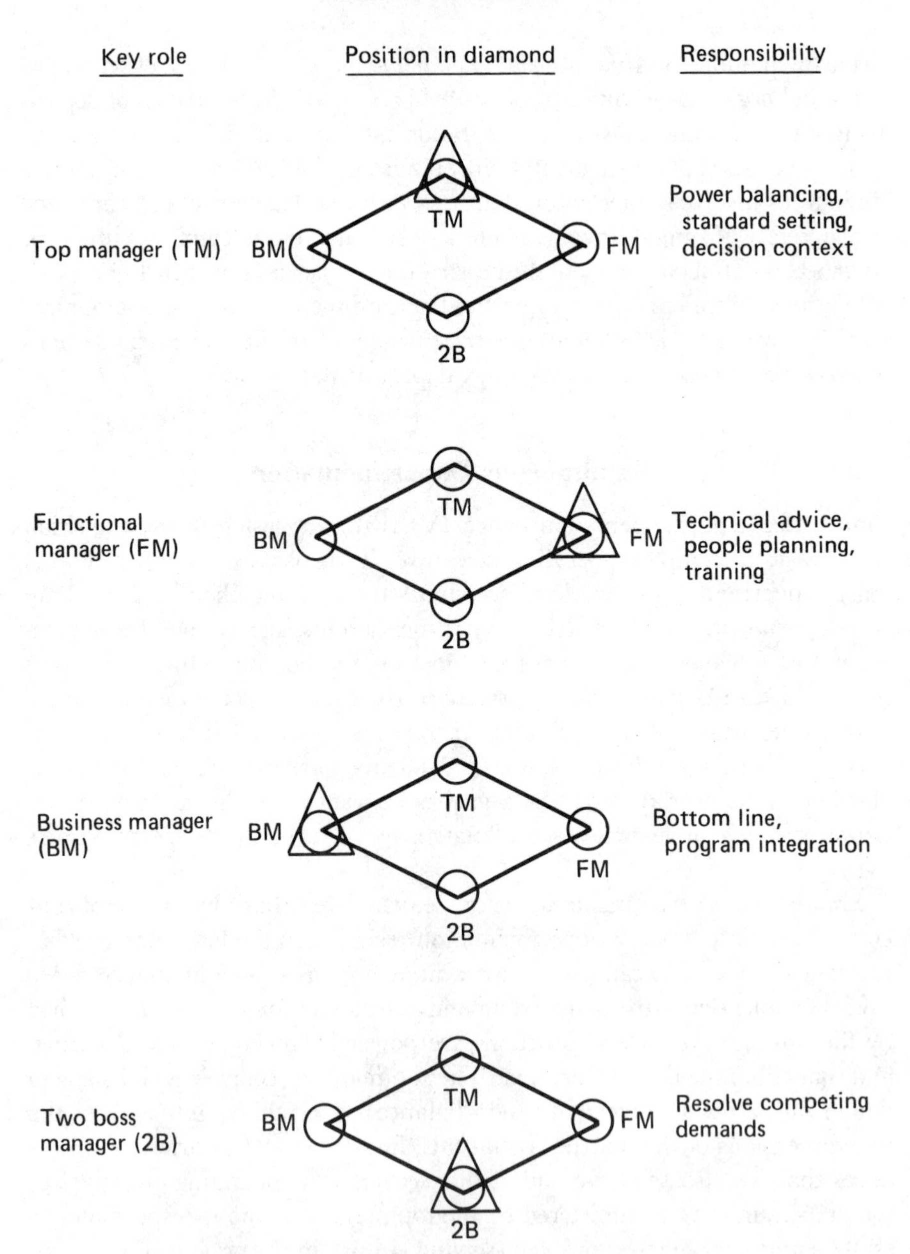

Figure 6-3. The matrix diamond in simultaneous structures.

functional managers find themselves in the position of providing technical "advice," training, and performing people planning functions. Thus, they may begin to derive their satisfaction partially as a function of facilitating the activities of business managers. Although this is very challenging, it allows functional managers less opportunity to satisfy "effect needs," which are the needs to see the effects of one's actions on the work setting. At Canadian Marconi corporation, top management referred to such problems as teaching functional managers "how to get their satisfaction sideways!"

A second consequence of matrix arrangements is that functional managers perceive a loss of status or power when a second basis of departmentation is added. Poor implementation often complicates this problem, for example, when functional managers are made to seem like second-class citizens through inappropriate manipulation of symbols of status and influence. Although business managers acquire influence in matrix, it does not mean that functional managers necessarily have less. In fact, maintaining the functional managers' influence should be given priority because, as Lawrence and Lorsch have shown, the higher the average power of functional managers in the firm, the greater the effectiveness of the organization.[23]

One last problem confronts the functional manager, and that is the need to be a more effective conflict manager. With only one form of departmentation, functional managers have a number of bases of influence available to them, including reward, coercive, legitimate, expert, and charismatic power. In simultaneous departmentation, the first three of these bases of influence, often favored by functional managers, must be shared with business managers. Reliance on these "command" types of influence is therefore less appropriate in matrix systems and complex behavioral adjustments in the direction of more "negotiated" conflict resolution are required for the handling of disagreements.

Business managers have the responsibilities of general managers, although on a smaller scale. They often are responsible for the "bottom line" of businesses that they manage or for integration in project or product varieties of matrix. Business managers often report that they have more responsibility than authority and that, consequently, they find their jobs very difficult to execute. This situation occurs as a result of power balancing decisions made by the top manager and do not always occur in matrix arrangements.

The *two-boss manager* is the final role in the matrix diamond. The two-boss manager is responsible for resolving the often intentionally conflicting demands imposed by functional and business managers. The person occupying this bottom role in the matrix diamond can be a manager of others lower in the organization who report in a traditional scalar sense.

The two-boss manager finds his or her job difficult because of a violation of the unity-of-command principle. This results in high levels of role ambiguity and intersender role conflict, which represent two varieties of role stress. Role ambiguity occurs when the job occupant does not have sufficient information to execute the task properly. Intersender role conflict occurs when one boss "sends" one message to the two-boss manager and the other sends another, conflicting one. These varieties of role stress can impact negatively on job performance and satisfaction if they are not managed properly. One way in which to accomplish this is through what we call complex delegation or role negotiations, which we discuss along with other approaches to problems of complex departmentation at the conclusion of this section of the chapter.

The "costs" of matrix or simultaneous departmentation include the human costs just described. The financial costs of complex departmentation are also significant, and these two categories of costs are, of course, not mutually exclusive. The introduction of complex departmentation schemes usually represents a significant step in implementing strategy, for it requires changes in more than one component of the strategy implementation model outlined in this book. Incentive and control systems are required to manage complex departmentation schemes. Reward systems must facilitate dual performance appraisal and review by functional business managers, and budgeting and formal information systems must support both dimensions of the structure. These changes often represent significant financial and human costs to the organization.

Given these significant costs, one might speculate as to why such complex operating structures are ever chosen. We have argued that they represent a choice influenced by decision-making requirements in the context of the principle of minimum intervention. If simpler forms of lateral relations have proven insufficient to deal with the information processing imposed by uncertainty, complexity, and interdependence, then the minimum-cost solution to the effectiveness or performance problem at hand will be complex departmentation. The situation calling for such a complex operating structure is typically marked by three characteristics identified by Davis and Lawrence and discussed briefly in Chapter 3 on primary structure.[24] These conditions result from qualitative as well as quantitative decision-making requirements imposed by previous choices of operating objectives and primary structure. Specifically, they are

1. High need for information processing and decision making (frequent decision occasions due to uncertainty, complexity, and interdependence).
2. Need to share resources (as, for example, when decisions are complex, due to a lack of slack resources, or interdependent, due to choices of technology requiring use of common equipment, or when vital resources are extremely scarce).

3. Pressure for dual focus (as when operating objectives require both technical excellence and cost effectiveness, imposing an interdependence between functional and project tasks).

When these conditions obtain, simultaneous departmentation must be used. However, these conditions should be assessed carefully and used in conjunction with the principle of minimum intervention. As Davis and Lawrence state,

> *The move to a matrix should be a serious decision, made by the top level of management, signalling a major commitment, and thoroughly implemented through many layers of the organization. It is too difficult to undertake superficially, too costly in human terms to attempt haphazardly, and too encompassing to experiment with unnecessarily.*[25]

Simultaneous departmentation is costly and difficult. Occasionally, however, even more demanding varieties of complex departmentalization are required. The next section discusses the final stage in the model of departmentation, coordinate hierarchies (stage V).

Coordinate Hierarchies

In the previous discussion, it was argued that simultaneous structures occur when two qualitatively distinct bases of departmentation are required concurrently at the operating structure level. Coordinate or dual, equal hierarchies are found when *a third basis of departmentation is added to a simultaneous structure (stage IV) by stratifying on the horizontal, rather than the vertical, dimension of the matrix.*

Coordinate hierarchies essentially amount to the creation of an additional *lateral* hierarchical structure that overlays the basic operating structure of the firm. Coordinate hierarchies can also be viewed as the combination of various stages of departmentation within the hierarchical and lateral dimensions of a simultaneous structure, as shown in Figure 6-1. Coordinate hierarchies represent the combination of a simple (stage II) or stratified (stage III) hierarchical structure and a stratified (stage III) lateral structure. A simultaneous structure (stage IV) would only utilize *simple* departments (stage II) laterally. Both simultaneous departments and coordinate hierarchies, therefore, represent combinations of previous stages of departmentalization executed on hierarchical and lateral dimensions of the operating structure.

Coordinate hierarchies become a structural option in the following way. Usually, a change in strategy requires that an *additional* "focus" for decision making be included in an organization that already is marked by simultaneous (stage IV) departmentation. Given this need, two alternatives quickly present themselves: stratify the hierarchical structure or stratify the lateral dimension of the organization. The choice is determined by the possibility of further self-containment within the operating unit. In the strategy implementation model, choices of primary structure establish the nature and size of the operating unit being designed. If further self-containment within the operating unit is not an option, for example, due to losses of economies of scale or potential duplication of effort, then stratification *must* take place along the lateral dimension to allow critical resources to be shared. Two criteria for the elaboration of coordinate hierarchies from simpler simultaneous structures must therefore be met. First, there must be a pressure for an additional, third, focus for decision making, and second, further self-containment on the hierarchical dimension of the structure must not be an option, forcing stratification to take place laterally.

In addition, costs of coordination and the minimum intervention principle also encourage the use of coordinate hierarchies. Given that there is a need for an additional focus for problem solving, an alternative to coordinate hierarchies would be to utilize a three-dimensional simultaneous matrix structure in which workers report to three separate bosses. Experience with two-dimensional simultaneous structures and the limited knowledge of "higher-order" three-dimensional forms suggests that this alternative is extremely costly, disorderly, and confusing. The principle of minimum intervention applied to costs of coordination suggests that the use of coordinate hierarchies and lateral stratification is the preferred step. Higher-order, n-dimensional simultaneous matrix forms may represent a sixth stage in our model of departmentation. However, we have chosen not to pursue them further in this volume due to their lack of occurrence in practice.

Coordinate hierarchies, in sum, represent organizations in which two qualitatively different bases of departmentation are utilized on the lateral dimension of the matrix. An example that will help to illustrate the conditions under which such structures are appropriate is shown in Figure 6-4. Assume that an organization is pursuing a number of complex projects. These projects are technologically sophisticated and require high levels of information processing for their successful completion. To ensure that the projects are completed using the most appropriate and up-to-date methods, it is required that members of project teams also simultaneously focus on functional skills and methods. Furthermore, individuals with requisite skills and knowledge to staff these projects are in short supply, requiring that technical specialists be shared across projects. These three conditions—a high need for information processing, an outside pressure for dual focus, and a need to share resources—

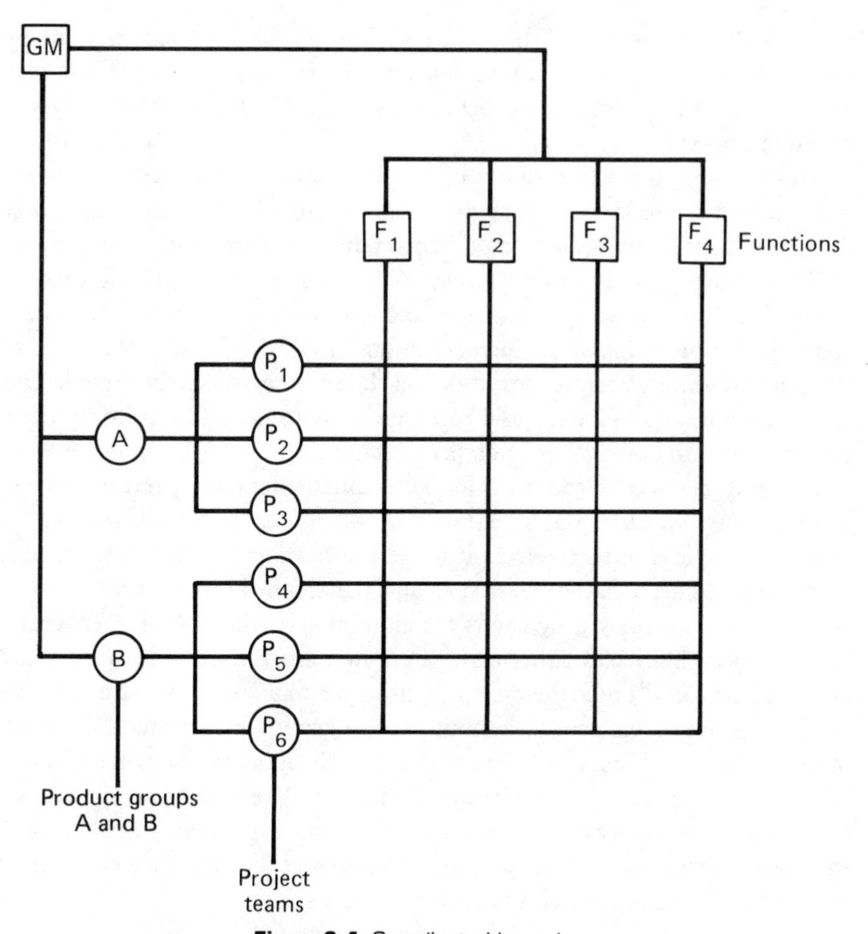

Figure 6-4. Coordinate hierarchy.

combine to require stage IV simultaneous departmentation or a matrix arrangement, as discussed. This situation is typical of many industries (e.g., aerospace, electronics, chemicals) characterized by sophisticated technical demands in combination with pressures for self-containment and dedication of resources to specific programs and projects.

A coordinate hierarchy can be seen as the next step in departmentation, as we impose additional requirements on the operating structure. As indicated, coordinate hierarchies are appropriate when an additional "focus" in decision making is demanded, as, for example, when an organization is required to emphasize products or product areas while still maintaining the dual focus on projects and functions. In terms of Figure 6-4, the organization has a need to focus on self-contained product groups, within which members of various project teams must focus simultaneously on project requirements and functional skills and methods. That is, in addition to the requirements imposed by simultaneous departmentation, our hypothetical organization must worry about *n* number of distinct product groups, each of which is characterized by multiple projects.

This pressure for a *third* focus in decision making is the first criterion for use of a coordinate hierarchy, as discussed. In our example, this might occur as market conditions become more uncertain, requiring the organization to dedicate more managerial resources to sensing market opportunities and developing and selecting products and projects consistent with market research. One alternative in such situations would be to form separate self-contained divisions around products and then to create matrix organizations within each division. This would represent a choice of both a primary (product divisions) and operating (matrix) structure.

However, the second condition for a coordinate hierarchy prevents this possibility. *This condition states that further self-containment is not an option.* In our example, the scarce technical specialists represent a critical resource that *must* be shared. Either these specialists cannot be hired in sufficient number to staff all proposed divisions or, alternatively, the cost of such staffing would be prohibitive. In this case, these human resources must be shared across all projects. Thus, the only way in which to achieve the required product focus is by nesting projects within product groups on the lateral dimension of the matrix. As Figure 6-4 shows, this gives form to an operating structure characterized by dual or coordinate hierarchies. The simultaneous structure of the stage IV matrix organization is effectively expanded into the stage V structure, coordinate hierarchies, characterized by the existence of stratification on both hierarchical and lateral dimensions.

PROBLEMS OF COMPLEX OPERATING STRUCTURES

Complex operating structures pose problems that simpler organizations do not. Some of these are just more complicated versions of traditional organizing problems, whereas others are completely new. The next sections summarize some of the more important problems encountered. Undoubtedly, this list will grow as more organizations utilize complex operating structures to provide the decision-making capability necessitated by change in primary structure and operating objectives.

Balancing Hierarchical and Lateral Dimensions of Complex Operating Structures

When lateral structures are created through the use of stage IV and stage V departmentation schemes, some choice must be made concerning the *relative influence* of hierarchical and lateral dimensions of the organization. In some matrix organizations, for example, the choice is to let project managers predominate when considerations of cost require relatively more "focus" on these issues than on technical matters. Alternatively, ultra-high-technology users of matrix such as the National Bureau of Standards or the Los Alamos Scientific Laboratory often find that their structures must favor functional groups, although a project emphasis is required for cost-effectiveness or technological focus. This relative emphasis is determined by the operating objectives of the unit being structured, and ultimately it must be enacted by the top manager of the matrix diamond. This problem is new to organizations utilizing complex departmentation schemes and does not occur (except implicitly) in basic operating structures.

The mechanisms available to effect a balance are shown in Figure 6-5 as either key or secondary balancing factors. The key factors are designated as such because of their strong effect on the relative influence of lateral and hierarchical managers. Either dimension of the complex operating structure can be strengthened by assignment of budget responsibility, by reward and performance appraisal power, or by locating workers with managers representing the "favored" dimension. Sometimes, however, the key factors cannot be manipulated, for example, due to sunk costs in existing performance appraisal and reward systems. When this occurs, other methods must be used. Although not as powerful as the key factors, these secondary factors have a significant influence on who listens to whom in complex organizations.

Level of pay affects the perceived influence of managers, regardless of whether the firm practices pay secrecy. Perhaps the worst kept secret in organizations is pay information. The grapevine is very quick in communicating such information (as well as other "interesting" rumors), and it affects the standing and status of managers. Other secondary balancing factors shown in Figure 6-5 include symbols of rank, status, or influence. The use of symbols in organizations is more than simply interesting; it is a widely used practice to affect the distribution of influence. Some firms have "manuals of symbolism" that prescribe what symbols individuals of particular rank may have. Common symbols include office size and location, furnishings, parking locations, "perks," and so on, which can have powerful effects on behavior.

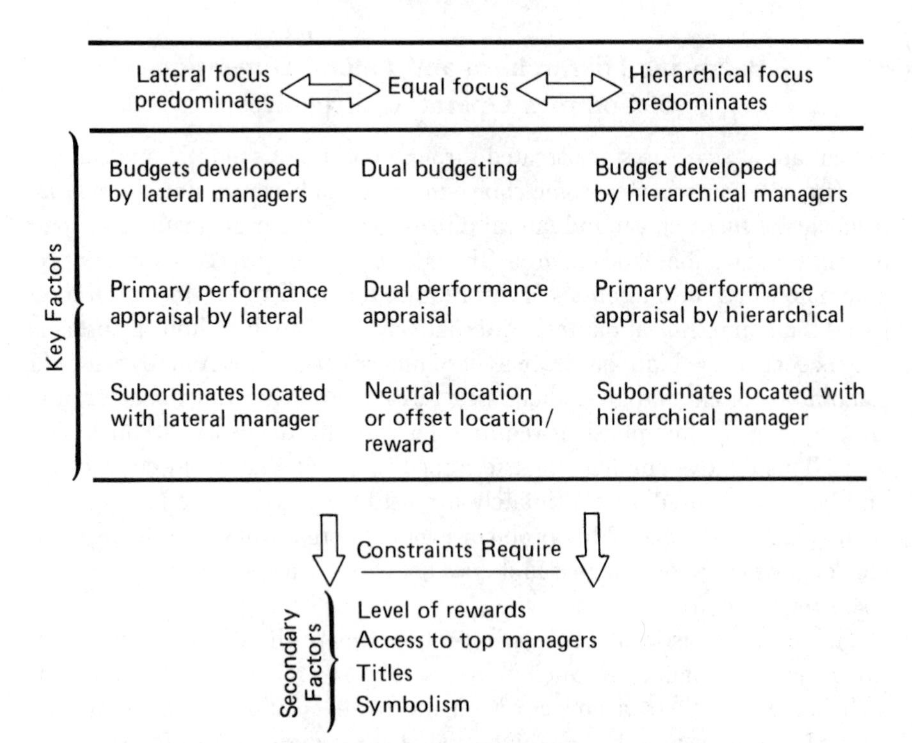

Figure 6-5. Balancing decision focus in simultaneous structures.

Functional Exclusion in Decision Making

This is primarily a problem of coordinate hierarchies. When stratified departmentation is utilized on both hierarchical and lateral dimensions of the structure, the simple matrix diamond of simultaneous stage IV structures is disturbed. A chain of command exits on both sides of the organization, as shown in Figure 6-4. When problems arise, top lateral managers communicate with top hierarchical managers. Similarly, those at the bottoms of the dual authority structure communicate. However, members of the middle level often feel "left out" because they are not actively involved in dual focus decision making.

This is more problematic for functional than for lateral managers because (1) typically functional chains of command are longer than lateral chains and, therefore, there are usually more middle-level functional managers, and (2) the functional hierarchy or basic operating structure performs more tasks than simply interacting with lateral decision makers. The functional hierarchical structure is necessitated by basic as well as by complex operating problems. Therefore, a portion of their work does not require interaction with lateral managers. These units may represent key linkages between the top and bottom of coordinate hierarchies but play primarily a communication rather than a decision role. Thus, midlevel functional managers are "left out" because they *should be* left out of interdisciplinary decision making. This is less true for lateral managers because a lateral hierarchy has no function of its own in the absence of the basic operating structure upon which the lateral dimension is superimposed.

Functional managers occasionally report less inclusion in decision making simply because lateral managers tend to be more effective communicators. This is because, in the transition to coordinate hierarchies, lateral managers often have little formal influence, so they must consciously develop skills that provide them with the requisite power to execute their tasks. One of these influence bases is expert power, which is gained partially through effective information gathering and communication. Functional managers may rely more on reward, coercive, and legitimate power within their hierarchical structures, leaving such communications skills less developed.

The problem of functional exclusion may be minimized by avoiding excessive stratification on the hierarchical dimension of the structure and creating realistic role expectations for functional managers. Generally, when stratification on hierarchical dimensions takes place, it should occur *outside* the matrix diamond.

Overloading Two Hierarchies

Complex departmentation schemes are created when the information processing demands imposed by uncertain, complex, and interdependent tasks overload the limited decision capacity of basic operating structures. Additional lateral channels of communication are created and, in the case of coordinate hierarchies, constitute a supplementary hierarchy of communication that overlays the basic operating structure.

In coordinate hierarchies, increased information processing capability requires that decisions be made *jointly* by managers representing both the lateral and hierarchical dimensions of the structure. This is so because the information that must be processed would overwhelm the basic operating structure if the new lateral channels were not utilized. However, it frequently occurs that decisions are not made jointly in coordinate hierarchies, perhaps because the very existence of lateral and basic operating hierarchies suggests that coordination may be achieved using simple "management-by-exception" principles appropriate in less complex structures. When this occurs, decisions that should be made jointly are referred upward in both the lateral and basic operating hierarchies, further overloading the (already overloaded) basic operating structure and the simpler lateral structure as well.

In Figure 6-4, this would occur when a conflict between a project and functional manager is referred to their respective immediate superiors for resolution rather than being resolved by these managers directly. The project manager refers the problem "upward" to the product manager to whom he or she is responsible, and the functional manager similarly refers the *same* problem upward to the director of functions. The result is two overloaded hierarchies instead of one. The problem requires control systems that reinforce face-to-face conflict resolution as well as minimize the use of excessive stratification on the lateral dimension of the structure.

Complex Delegation: Role Negotiations

The previous chapter discussing basic operating structure argued that appropriate assignment of authority was a matter of first determining the extent of responsibility associated with a particular role or job and then delegating authority sufficient to execute this responsibility. For complex departmentalization schemes, however, this process becomes problematic.

Consider, once again, the structure of a coordinate hierarchy shown in Figure 6-4. If we view the structure from the "top-down," product managers are apparently equivalent in responsibility to functional managers since they are located at the same level in the organization. Yet, if we view the same structure from the "bottom-up," from the perspective of the two-boss managers, project and functional managers are apparently equivalent. The point is that responsibility is seen less clearly and authority is more difficult to delegate in complex departmentation schemes involving simultaneous structures and coordinate hierarchies.

The complexity of such situations mitigates against the possibility of a single individual delegating authority appropriately. In such situations more complex, group-based techniques must be used to produce effective allocations of authority. We refer to such problems as problems of *complex delegation*. They are marked by considerable ambiguity and lack of role clarity and are found with some frequency in complex operating structures.

Role negotiation is a technique useful for problems of complex delegation. Role negotiations (or responsibility charting as it is sometimes called) is a technique for resolving role ambiguity and clarifying responsibility. After responsibilities have been made clear, various degrees of authority or decision involvement can be associated with particular issues and roles. Role negotiation is appropriate when simple delegation processes are impossible due to the complexity of the situation.

There are several "phases" to a role negotiation session. The first involves construction of the responsibility matrix, an example of which is shown as

Figure 6-6. This involves identifying decision issues about which there is some confusion as well as the roles potentially associated with the making of those decisions. The decisions comprise the vertical axis of the matrix and the participants' roles comprise the horizontal. While the decisions about which there is ambiguity are occasionally easy to determine, it is more often the case that the vertical axis of the matrix is very hard to construct. Users should be prepared to commit considerable time to this effort.

The second phase is a balloting to determine the current division of responsibility. Before this takes place, it is usually useful to provide a framework for discussing how the term "responsibility" will be used. Usually, four degrees of responsibility are sufficient for analysis. These are signified on the chart using the following symbols and definitions:

1. R – this role is responsible for initiating a decision.
2. A – this role approves a decision made by another.
3. C – this role is consulted prior to the making of a decision.
4. I – this role is informed following a decision.

The chart may be completed either privately or publicly. Once it has been filled out with perceptions of the current situation, the final phase can be started.

The last phase is analysis and adjustment of roles. In this phase, individuals analyze (1) their roles as seen by themselves and others, (2) responsibility assignments across decisions by roles, and (3) responsibilities across roles by decision issue. Adjustments are made on the basis of problems identified in this stage, and a commitment is made to utilize the "final" responsibility matrix and consequent authority structure for a period of three to six months. After this time, roles will be renegotiated and authority reassigned, a process particularly germane to the uncertain business situations necessitating complex departmentalization schemes.

Summary

Complex operating structures are developed when the information processing demands created by decision uncertainty, complexity, and interdependence exceeds the capacity of basic operating structures. These information processing requirements are imposed by previous choices of primary structure and operating objectives.

Complex operating structures are elaborated from simpler basic operating structures. Five stages of departmentation may be identified. These are (I)

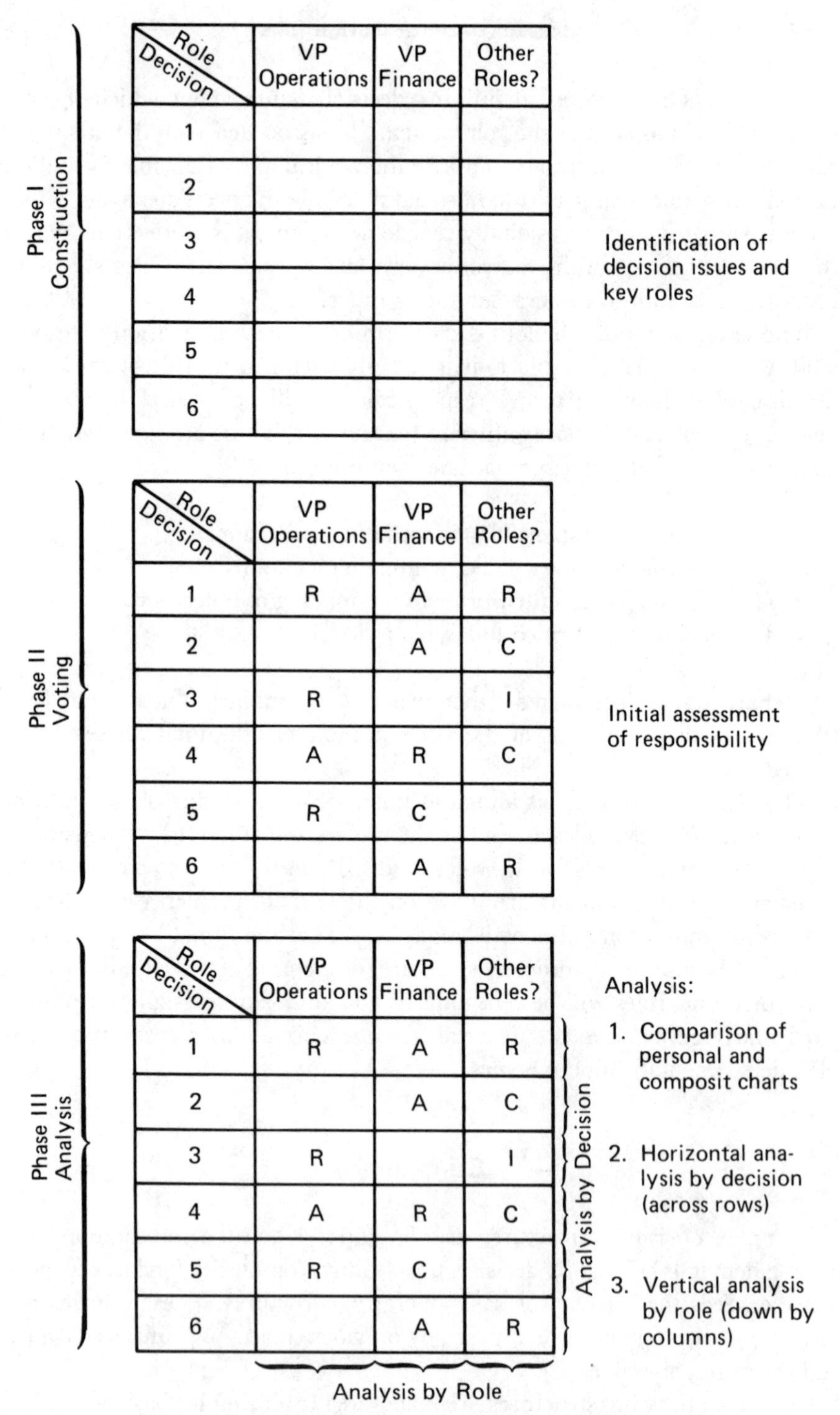

Decision \ Role	VP Operations	VP Finance	Other Roles?
1			
2			
3			
4			
5			
6			

Decision \ Role	VP Operations	VP Finance	Other Roles?
1	R	A	R
2		A	C
3	R		I
4	A	R	C
5	R	C	
6		A	R

Decision \ Role	VP Operations	VP Finance	Other Roles?
1	R	A	R
2		A	C
3	R		I
4	A	R	C
5	R	C	
6		A	R

Figure 6-6. Complex delegation: phases in role negotiations.

implicit departments, (II) simple departments, (III) stratified departments, (IV) simultaneous departments, and (V) coordinate hierarchies. The first three of these stages occur in basic operating structures, whereas the latter two occur in complex operating structures. Stages III and IV are separated by a series of "steps" in lateral relations that successively transform basic operating structures into complex operating structures. These "natural," "group," and "influence" strategies of lateral relations may be distinguished in terms of formality, responsibility, and authority in decision making.

Complex operating structures are costly and difficult to administer because they result in the violation of several "principles" of management. In addition to the recurring problems involved in using teams and task forces, complex operating structures pose several new problems. Some of these are balancing hierarchical and lateral dimensions of simultaneous structures, functional exclusion from decision making, overloading multiple hierarchies, and complex delegation. The costs of dealing with such problems are justified only when basic operating structures are inadequate, and more complex structures are required consistent with the principle of minimum intervention.

Operating structures create frameworks of relationships within which the actions of individual workers can be combined to accomplish operating objectives consistent with both the primary structure and strategic mission of the firm. However, individuals' goals, aspirations, and priorities are often at odds with those of formal organizations, requiring some mechanism to ensure that actions taken in consonance with such goals are consistent with role behaviors required to accomplish strategic and operating objectives. This requires the development of formal incentive and control systems, a topic to which we turn in Chapter 7.

Notes

1. Jay Galbraith, *Designing Complex Organizations* (Reading, Mass.: Addison-Wesley Publishing Company, 1973).
2. Paul R. Lawrence and Jay W. Lorsch, *Organization and Environment: Managing Differentiation and Integration* (Homewood, Ill.: Richard D. Irwin, Inc., 1967).
3. Charles Perrow, "A Framework for the Comparative Analysis of Organizations," *American Sociological Review,* 32:194–208 (1967).
4. Derek Pugh, "The Aston Program of Research: Retrospect and Prospect," in Andrew H. Van de Ven and William F. Joyce, eds., *Perspectives on Organization Design and Behavior* (New York: Wiley-Interscience, 1981), pp. 135–166.
5. Paul R. Lawrence, "The Harvard Organization and Environmental Research Program," in *Perspectives on Organization Design and Behavior,* pp. 311–337.

6. Lawrence and Lorsch, *Organization and Environment.*
7. F. E. Emery and E. L. Trist, "The Causal Texture of Organizational Environments," *Human Relations,* 18:21–32 (1965).
8. James D. Thompson, *Organizations in Action* (New York: McGraw-Hill Book Company, 1967).
9. Tom Burns and G. M. Stalker, *The Management of Innovation* (London: Tavistock, 1961).
10. Perrow, "A Framework for the Comparative Analysis of Organizations."
11. Burns and Stalker, *The Management of Innovation.*
12. Joan Woodward, *Industrial Organization: Theory and Practice* (London: Oxford University Press, 1965).
13. Gerald Susman, *Autonomy at Work* (New York: Praeger Publishers, 1977).
14. Thompson, *Organizations in Action.*
15. Burns and Stalker, *The Management of Innovation.*
16. Robert H. Miles, *Macro Organizational Behavior* (Santa Monica, Calif.: Goodyear Publishing Company, 1980).
17. Thompson, *Organizations in Action.*
18. Galbraith, *Designing Complex Organizations.*
19. Lawrence and Lorsch, *Organization and Environment.*
20. Ibid.
21. Galbraith, *Designing Complex Organizations.*
22. Stanley M. Davis and Paul R. Lawrence, *Matrix* (Reading, Mass.: Addison-Wesley Publishing Company, 1977).
23. Lawrence and Lorsch, *Organization and Environment.*
24. Davis and Lawrence, *Matrix,* pp. 11–24.
25. Ibid., p. 19.

7

INCENTIVES AND CONTROL

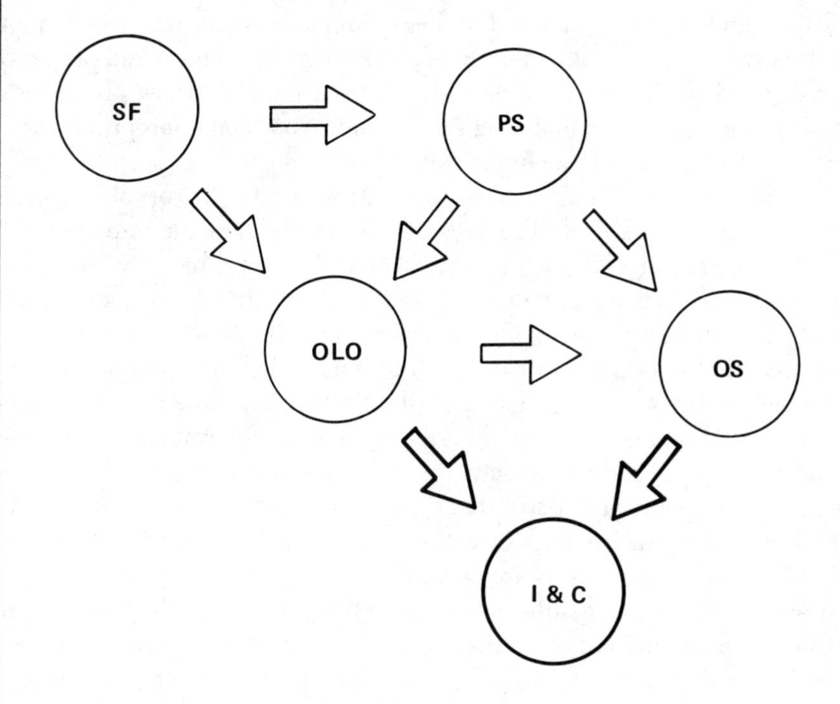

Appropriate incentives are critical to the successful implementation of strategy. Given norms of rationality, it is imperative to reward performance that is consistent with strategic aims. Controlling the implementation process and integrating the short and long term are also central managerial concerns.

To this point we have attempted to proceed logically through the various steps involved in the formulation and implementation of strategy. Attention has been paid to the planning and design decisions underlying that process as well as to the interactions between or among these two decision areas. In terms of the model in Chapter 1, we have presented our arguments and ideas beginning with strategy formulation and ending in the previous chapter with the discussion of complex operating structures.

In our analysis thus far, we have made several important assumptions regarding the actors involved in the various strategic and operating decisions. This is evidenced, for example, by the assumption of intended rationality and our discussion of the centrality of values and personal preferences in the formulation and implementation of strategy. Implicit, too, in our presentation has been the contention that incentives and controls are central and pervasive in organizations. Their importance, it has been implied, derives from their ability to motivate individuals and ensure consistency and appropriateness of performance against desired organizational outcomes.

It is now necessary to make our arguments regarding the role of incentives and controls more explicit. The present chapter discusses the importance of incentives and controls in the implementation of strategy. In our view, incentive plans and controls are so inextricably related that we subsume them under the heading of "planning decisions." Our intention is to show that incentive schemes or plans provide a stimulus for action, while controls ensure the appropriateness of the actions and the effectiveness of the presented stimuli. We argue that good incentives are critical to the motivation of organizational participants and, conversely, that poor incentives clearly have a negative impact on individual performance and the achievement of desired ends. The factors that underly poor incentives and contribute to the breakdown of effective control mechanisms are also discussed in this chapter.

We contend, too, that sufficient attention must be paid to the long term in the development and use of incentives and controls. Our concern is that perceived rewards or sanctions may force attention to short-run performance to the neglect of long-run or strategic performance. The short-term consequences of poor incentives and controls are discussed in this chapter as is the need to include an assessment of strategic contribution in the performance appraisal and review process.

Another introductory point is worth a brief mention. We realize that there is no paucity of theoretical and empirical literature on individual motivation and the role of incentives and controls in complex organizations. On the contrary, myriad conceptual frameworks and empirical data exist on these critical topics, especially in the area of motivation. Our purpose presently is not to add to the existing quantity of thought and data that exist. Rather, *the purpose of this chapter is to distill and derive a few concepts and arguments from the existing literature that are significant for the successful implementation of strategy.* The choice and development of propositions and points clearly reflect our bias and view of the implementation process. We do wish, however, to be selective and focus only on a few significant points that can affect the achievement of desired organizational and individual outcomes.

Finally, we feel that insufficient attention has been paid to the *integration* of previous work on incentives and controls in the organizational behavior and strategy literatures. Motivations at the *individual* level, especially in middle-management positions, rarely have been related to strategy implementation and performance at the *organizational* level of analysis. In our view, this lack of integration is unfortunate. As we shall argue, individual motivations and decisions, including those made in the short term, can result in a negative impact on the strategy implementation process. Inappropriate incentives and controls can produce an organizational climate geared toward risk aversion or extreme conservatism, which militates against creativity and innovation. In this chapter, we shall argue that individuals concerned with the successful implementation of strategy should focus on short-term as well as long-term incentives and controls. Motivation and performance in both time frames are important and inextricably related. The need is to integrate views and the disparate literatures in an attempt to explicate how the implementation process relates short- and long-term effects on organizational performance.

INCENTIVES AND MOTIVATION

A helpful first step is to describe the setting within which incentives and controls are directed toward the attainment of strategic and short-term operating objectives. In our view, a basic assumption can be made that follows logically from the works of Barnard,[1] Etzioni, March and Simon, and others: namely, that the implementation of strategy occurs primarily in organizations that are *utilitarian* in nature. We believe that the assessment and calculation of inducements versus contributions lie at the core of individuals' motivations and decisions regarding behavior or performance. Because of the importance of this assumption, it would be helpful to explicate our reasoning further.

Etzioni focuses on *compliance* in organizations.[2] Compliance refers to both (1) the relationship in which an individual behaves in accordance with a stimulus (e.g., a directive) supported by another's authority, and (2) the orientation of the former individual to the influence applied. Thus, there are two important aspects of the compliance relationship: the influence or power of one person and the reaction or response of another who is subject to it. If the response of individuals is analyzed in terms of involvement—both positive and negative—the compliance relationship can be used as an analytical basis for the study of incentives and motivations in organizations.

Etzioni distinguishes three types of influence or power that can be used in a supervisor-subordinate relationship. These may be viewed roughly as physical, material, or symbolic types. They are (1) pure *coercive* power; (2) *utilitarian* power, based on control over resources and rewards; and (3) *normative* power, which rests on the allocation of symbolic rewards and ritualistic acceptance (e.g., as religious organizations). Involvement is also differentiated into three types: (1) *alienation,* indicating a strong negative orientation of the subordinate; (2) *calculative,* based on the weighing of rewards and costs or inducements to contributions; and (3) *moral,* which suggests a positive, highly intense, psychological orientation or commitment. The argument simply is that the motivation, involvement, or commitment of individuals depends on the type of power, influence, or incentives used in the organization. Where coercion is used, alienation is the typical response of the individuals being coerced; where utilitarian influence is most prevalent, a calculative involvement based on perceptions of rewards received to work performed is most typical; and where normative power exists, a moral involvement characterized by full acceptance of norms and identification with the organization most often results.

Our contention, again, is that the formulation and implementation of strategy occur most often in settings characterized by utilitarian influence and calculative involvement. This is not to say that coercion or normative influence never appear in these settings; clearly, coercive power is used by individuals, and organizations are seen occasionally as embodying normative influence, resulting, respectively, in the alienation of subordinates or intense identification with the organization. Rather, it is to say that the typical organization is characterized primarily by (1) utilitarian benefits and, occasionally, symbolic rewards that co-vary with and imply the utilitarian (e.g., salary, bonuses, promotions, titles, impressive trappings), and (2) the primarily calculative response of individuals who weigh the rewards against the work or costs involved.

This view closely parallels that of Barnard as well as March and Simon who discuss the notion of organizational "equilibrium."[3] Participants in organizations, they argue, work for the inducements they receive. As long as inducements outweigh contributions in the minds of participants, they remain in the organization. If contributions are seen to outweigh inducements, the employment contract is imbalanced and in jeopardy. The individual feels a heightened desire to seek options elsewhere, and the situation is one of disequilibrium. *Organizational survival and growth, then, reflect success in arranging payments to individuals sufficient to motivate their continuing involvement and performance.*

The utility of this view of motivation and behavior in organizations is that it enables us to approach the issue of incentives and controls logically and realistically. The complexities of the "human variable" notwithstanding, most individuals who seek managerial careers in organizations are attracted to and remain in their positions largely because of the utilitarian and concomitant symbolic benefits that accrue to them based on performance and seniority. While it would be ideal to apply and rely on other approaches to motivation in the work setting, that task often is not feasible. It is extremely difficult and problematic, for example, to measure accurately individual needs, libidinal drives, satisfactions, valences, and expectancies and to design incentives and controls to individual specifications.

Basic Stimulus-Response-Reinforcement Model

Our view of motivation and the employment contract enables us to develop a straightforward stimulus-response-reinforcement model of the application and use of incentives and controls in organizations. Figure 7-1 shows such a model and indicates some of the key variables or conditions affecting the implementation of strategy. Using the model, we outline broadly the role of incentives and the factors affecting the motivation to perform. We then apply the general model to the implementation of strategy by focusing on specific stimuli and their effects on individuals responsible for the implementation process. In a later section of this chapter, we devote considerable space and time to the relationship between control and the implementation process.

Stimulus for Action. Figure 7-1 begins with a stimulus for action. "Stimulus" would include, for example, a request from a supervisor; normal task or job demands; a formal objective and action plan that require attention due to the brevity of the time frame for completion; or information regarding an external crisis situation that may require a decision or reaction. A stimulus, then, can be viewed simply as an environmental or situational element whose salience or importance for action must be interpreted, evaluated, and weighed by the individuals receiving it.

Clearly, one could argue that the salience of any stimulus depends on such preconditions or precursors as memory and prior experience. It also can be argued that the typical case involves many different stimuli that compete for the individual's attention at any point in time. While these points are certainly valid, it is useful to start with a situation that has a given stimulus for

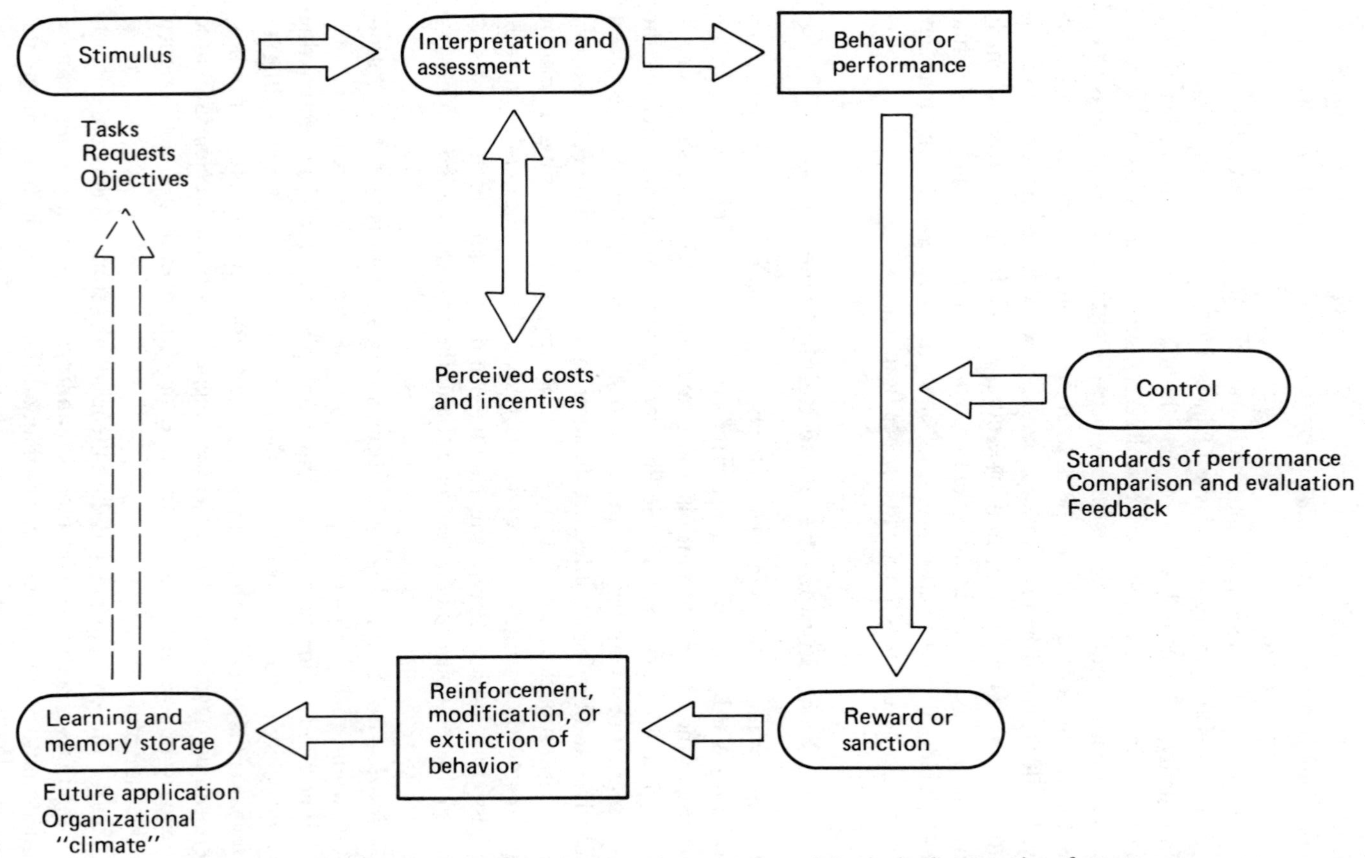

Figure 7-1. Reinforcement model: use of incentives and controls in the implementation of strategy.

action. In this way, we can begin to assess the impact on the individuals involved. Specifically, we can discuss relations to the stimulus condition as the individual perceives and weighs the pro's and con's of competing responses.

Interpretation of Stimulus and Assessment of Costs and Benefits. An important first event obviously is the perception and interpretation of the stimulus. A request for cooperation or an influence attempt can be judged in terms of its legitimacy or perceived necessity. An order from a higher-level manager is supported by formal power or legitimized influence and is more likely to be followed than a request from a peer in a different functional area. Similarly, requests for action that are seen to be within the domain and scope of influence of the person making the requests are judged differently from demands not within legitimate bounds.[4]

Another issue is whether the stimulus evokes many different options or just a few for the individual. The larger the set of options seen by the individual, the more complex the assessment process typically will be. Similarly, the greater the number of options generated by a given stimulus, the greater is the probability of consequences or results that are *unanticipated* by the actors who provided or defined the stimulus in the first place. As we show momentarily, for example, poor short-term operating objectives often create reactions or dysfunctions not anticipated by those who defined and designated them as performance measures for others to achieve.

A critical aspect of the interpretation and assessment process, of course, is the weighing of costs and benefits implied by different responses to the stimulus. In utilitarian organizations, the anticipated relation between behavior and rewards is central to an understanding of motivation. It is imperative to realize that behavior or performance that is not reinforced, or that is punished, will disappear. To have a stimulus taken seriously, it is necessary to reinforce the behavior seen as most appropriate for or consistent with intended outcomes. In the vernacular, it indeed is true that "you get what you pay for." In a related view, it makes little sense to plan for one outcome but unintentionally reward another. If an intended positive outcome for the organization is seen as resulting in a negative outcome for the individual, the stimulus for action may not generate the desired results.

Control: Feedback and Reinforcement. The assurance of performance that is consistent with intended outcomes is one important aspect of the control function. As will be indicated, control involves the (1) comparison of actual performance or behavior to measures of desired performance, (2) evaluation of any aberrations from those norms, and (3) feedback to individuals based on performance. An integral and critical aspect of feedback is the use of rewards or incentives to reinforce desired behavior. This relation between performance and rewards appears straightforward and obvious. In our opinion, however, the misuse of rewards and, at times, blatant disregard of the performance-feedback relation are often core factors or reasons for the poor implementation of strategy.

Figure 7-1 shows, finally, that any feedback of information or reward to reinforce or modify behavior becomes part of the "memory" of the individual. Indeed, continued reinforcement and use of rewards and sanctions over time become part of a collective memory or organizational "climate" that affects future performance and risk taking immensely.[5] The appropriate application of controls and use of rewards, then, assume a fair amount of importance in the strategy implementation process.

A Brief Illustration: The Reinforcement Model and the Implementation of Strategy

To understand better the general model of Figure 7-1, especially the unanticipated negative effects on strategy implementation that result from poor objectives, it would be helpful to consider an actual case. By providing the brief illustration, we are attempting to emphasize the central, if occasionally overlooked, role of incentives on the strategy implementation process.

The company involved is a small manufacturer selling its goods primarily to a well-defined regional market. Its strategic long-term aims at the time focused primarily on increased market penetration and were expressed, accordingly, in terms of changes in market share over a targeted five-year period. The translation of long-term market share goals into short-term operating objectives was straightforward, resulting in clear sales and market penetration objectives for any given year. The company had a small but aggressive sales force whose relatively long average tenure was seen as an organizational asset. Despite this and other strengths, however, top management was not at all satisfied with company performance. Market share objectives were not being met; indeed, the company over the most recent three years had actually lost a small percentage of market share, despite what top management labeled an all-out sales and marketing effort. Talking with managers and a sample of sales personnel, we were able to identify some interesting and formidable obstacles to the strategy implementation process. For purposes of illustration, we focus on one of these—performance against sales objectives.

The Stimulus. In terms of Figure 7-1, the sales objective was an important stimulus for action. It was based heavily on past performance, with "planning" being primarily an extrapolation of past performance trends onto the future. The sales objective was derived by adding on a fixed percentage increase across the board to the previous year's performance. For all sales personnel, last year's actual performance was increased by X percent, with the percentage increase determined by top management upon review of total sales and market penetration objectives.

To emphasize the importance of the sales objective, a bonus was attached to its achievement. While commissions were paid on all items delivered, sales-representatives became eligible for what was described as a "nice" bonus only when the objective was actually achieved. Performance below objective—regardless of how close the individual's actual output was—did not qualify one for the additional compensation. The underlying rationale, of course, was that the salience of the stimulus—the importance of the sales objective—could be heightened only by attaching a large reward to "making it." It was clearly performance against objective that counted. To ensure a commitment to the short-term operating objective, thereby facilitating the attainment of strategic market penetration objectives, top management felt that a proper incentive had to be provided to motivate superior performance.

Interpretation, Assessment, and Outcome. Figure 7-1 indicates that behavior or performance obtains only after the individual interprets the stimulus and evaluates the relevant costs and benefits of potential reactions. The intended result in this case was a superior sales effort, leading to a sizable bonus for good performance. Actual results, however, proved to be quite different and disappointing. The crux of the issue was that the sales representatives' assessments of inducements and contributions culminated in dysfunctional consequences for the organization but logical or rational results for the individual. The incentives provided did not motivate superior performance against sales objectives; rather, incentives negatively affected sales results, which clearly boded poorly for the achievement of strategic aims.

Observations of performance trends and discussions with key personnel uncovered some basic but debilitating characteristics of the assessment process and evaluation of the inducements-contributions ratio. For example, yearly operating objectives were sometimes seen as unrealistic; the X percent add-on to last year's performance resulted in an unattainable target or, at least, one whose prior probability of achievement was seen to be significantly less than 1.00. Because of the all-or-nothing aspect of the sales objective (recall that the bonus was paid only if the objective was reached), this perception of unrealistic objectives was important. Hard work and the resultant achievement of 99 percent of a difficult goal resulted in no additional compensation. In fact, coming so close to an extremely difficult objective would be foolish and suicidal, given the automatic add-on to actual performance; next year's objective, that is, would be completely unattainable.

The result of the assessment of costs and benefits was clear and logical upon scrutiny and anyalysis. If the probability of achieving the objective were judged to be 100 percent, the individual would strive for the bonus and meet the sales objective. He or she clearly would not surpass the objective by much, however. The bonus would not increase as a function of performance over objective, and, given the automatic addition to actual performance to determine next year's target, the motivation was clearly one of barely meeting or beating the sales goal.

If assessment of the probability of success was less than 100 percent, the result typically was one of "holding back." If the feedback was going to be negative (i.e, no bonus), it made eminently more sense to achieve 70 percent of objective rather than 95 percent because of the effect on next year's figure. In both cases, the individual did not "make it," so it was only logical to minimize the negative consequences of substandard performance. Results included a decreased sales effort; holding back on year-end orders to credit them toward next year's results; and occasionally, if a good number of sales representatives were "sandbagging" simultaneously, negative consequences on production, including layoffs in slow periods and high overtime expense after the first of the year when orders began to pour in.

Other negative consequences were uncovered as a result or our analysis, but we feel that the ones noted are sufficient to emphasize the point. Figure 7-1 argues that *short-term incentives used inappropriately, even if unknowingly, surely can have negative, if unintended, consequences for the process of strategy implementation.* In utilitarian organizations, individuals weigh the costs and benefits of behavioral options open to them. Performance that is rewarded is reinforced, despite its potential negative impact on superordinate ends. In the case presented, market penetration and sales results clearly suffered because of the type of operating objective and the logical or rational individual behavior it motivated. Sales representatives judged that it was better to receive a bonus every two years than none at all (i.e., purposely poor performance ⟶ lower objective next year ⟶ bonus, but barely "making it" ⟶ higher objective with low probability of success ⟶ purposely poor performance). The stimulus for action and assessment of inducements and contributions, in sum, motivated actions inconsistent with the strategic aims of market penetration and growth. *What was logical and rational at the individual level was debilitating and arational at the organization level.*

Two final points must be emphasized. First, many of the negative consequences observed resulted from a poor short-term objective. Chapter 4 has noted the defining characteristics of objectives, so the reader presently is referred back to that discussion. Second, Figure 7-1 shows aptly that the reward and reinforcement of performance is an integral part of the control process. Because of the centrality and importance of controls, it is necessary to cover that topic in greater detail. Accordingly, the next section discusses the nature of the control process. More important, the discussion emphasizes where control systems can fail and lead to negative consequences for the implementation of strategy.

THE CONTROL PROCESS

Control in organizations follows logically from the planning process. Its underlying rationale or purpose is to ensure that the organization is achieving what it intends to accomplish. Planning involves the setting of objectives or determination of some future desired state of affairs; the control process tracks performance against desired ends and provides the feedback necessary to gauge or evaluate results and take corrective action, as needed.

Control: Following Up on Planning Decisions

Figure 7-2 shows a simplified version of the control process that has been distilled and derived from a number of more complete and in-depth treatments of the subject.[6] The figure also suggests five common problems that detract from or negatively affect the implementation of strategy in organizations. Focusing, first, on the basic elements of the control process, Figure 7-2 assumes the existence of operating objectives and budgets. The assumption is that planning has occurred, and both long- and short-term objectives exist.

We feel that this assumption is a logical one. We have already argued that strategic objectives must be reduced to smaller, more manageable proportions and that therein lies the rationale and need for smaller structural units within the organization and operating objectives to guide them. For the sake of illustration and discussion, and to show the importance of control in strategy implementation, our focus begins with a hypothetical set of short-term operating objectives that has resulted from this reduction process and that represents the future desired state of affairs that the organization or subunit wishes to achieve.

The same arguments hold to explain the existence of budgets. It can be assumed that the same negotiation process that resulted in operating objectives for the hypothetical organizational unit also resulted in the development

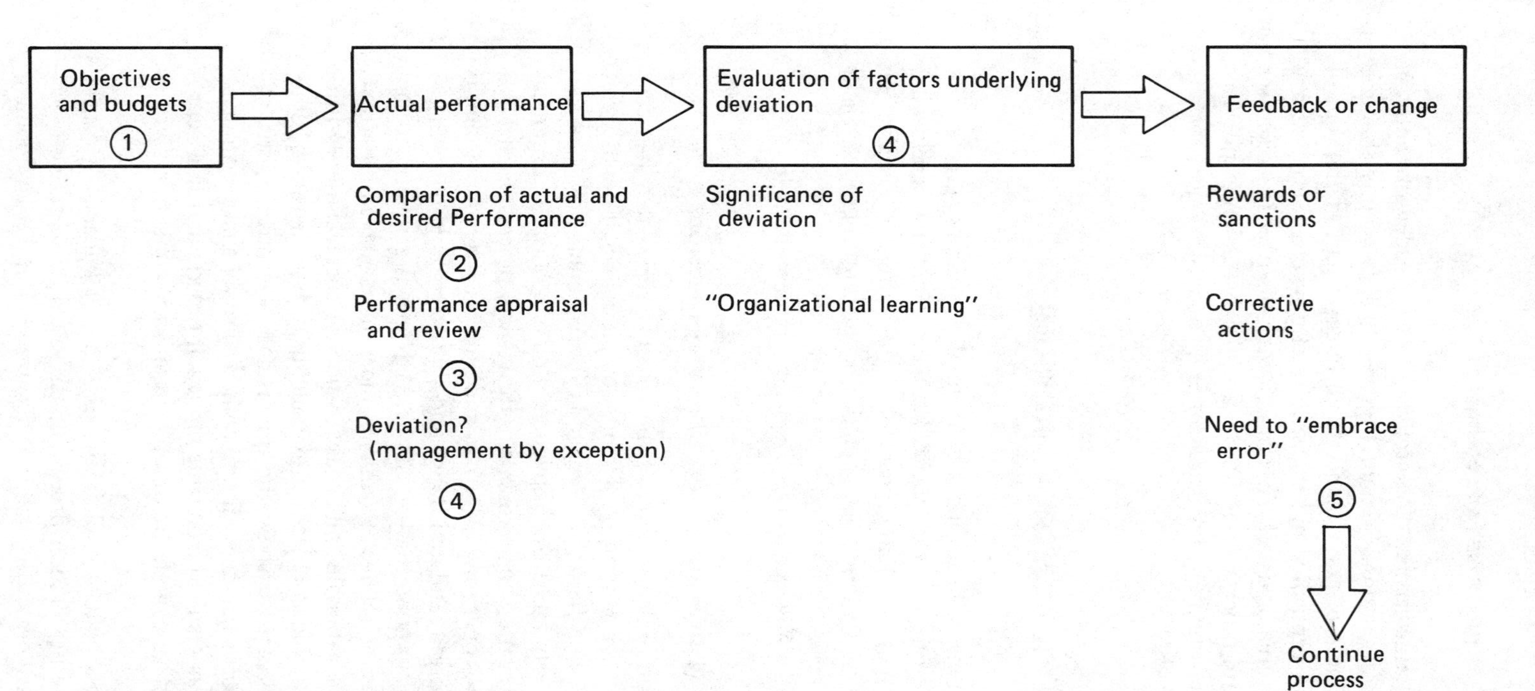

Some reasons why control fails (see text):

1. Poor objectives.
2. Insufficient or faulty information processing capabilities.
3. No or poor performance appraisal and review.
4. Management by "negative" exception and poor evaluation techniques resulting in little organizational learning.
5. Emphasis on avoidance of error; need to embrace error.

Figure 7-2. The control process in the implementation of strategy and reasons why control works or fails.

of appropriate budgets. Taken together, the objectives and budgets represent standards of performance and stimuli for action. Objectives are intended to motivate superior performance, and budgets exist to provide guidelines, constraints, and a definition of the appropriate arena for individual action.

The first necessary step in the process of control shown in Figure 7-2 is the *comparison of actual and desired performance.* The initiation of control is dependent on this comparison. Objectives or shorter-term performance milestones based on them represent future desired levels of achievement; tracking performance against objectives or milestones initiates the control process by inquiring whether there is a deviation between what is being aimed at and what is being accomplished. Responding to deviations between actual and desired levels of achievement or between budgeted and actual levels of cash flows represents what is commonly referred to as "management by exception."

The identification of and follow-up on exceptions or deviations between actual and desired performance implies an important evaluative aspect of the control process. There are performance aberrations and then there are performance aberrations; additional concerns include the *significance* of the deviations and the causal or contributing factors or variables underlying and explicating them. Explaining and understanding the reasons for past performance affects positively organizational learning and the ability to plan in the future.[7] This process of evaluation and learning is critical for continued success in the implementation of strategy. Because of the centrality and impact of this aspect of control, more attention is devoted below to both the consequences of poor evaluation and the factors that militate against learning in organizations.

Figure 7-2 also indicates that *formal performance appraisal and review is part of control* and that appraisal procedures in organizations must include and build on performance against objectives. Formal review mechanisms, that is, should contain comparison of actual and desired levels of achievement, with formal feedback and rewards dependent to some degree on the results of this review. This type of evaluation and feedback is central to the control process and is critically important for the reinforcement of behavior that is consistent with the successful implementation of strategy.

The figure indicates, finally, that *something of consequence must result* from the process of control and the comparisons, analysis, and evaluation it implies. Included in these outcomes or consequences are rewards for outstanding performance, as already indicated; changes in objectives or plans and other corrective actions; and development of alternative, more timely sources of information to facilitate the tracking and evaluation of performance in the organization. Another critical outcome is to ensure that the process of evaluation and follow-up does not contribute to an unhealthy emphasis on avoiding risks and errors at all costs. Rigid and uncompromising control systems that do not tolerate error, and, thus, breed an overly conservative emphasis on maintaining the status quo and being safe, have debilitating effects on motivation as well as on the formulation and achievement of intended plans of action.

This last point and others mentioned in this discussion imply that controls are critical to the successful implementation of strategy but that mistakes in control, even if unintended, can have negative consequences for organizational performance. Figure 7-2 numbers and summarizes what we believe are five common control-related problems that usually result in dysfunctional consequences, including a poor or unsuccessful implementation of strategy. In essence, the problems provide at least a partial answer to the question of why control systems go awry or fall apart, thereby creating major problems for the organization.

Common Control Problems

1. Poor Objectives. The first and very pervasive reason for poor controls and consequent problems in implementation of plans is the existence of poor objectives. Objectives represent outputs of the planning process and necessary inputs to the control system. To a great extent, objectives represent the standards of performance against which actual results are compared. If, for example, objectives are not measurable, forcing descriptions of results or outcomes to be totally subjective, any comparison of desired and actual performance is problematic. If there exist competing definitions or subjective measures of objectives and behavior, a sound control system becomes increasingly improbable. The differences in opinon that are often created by unmeasurable objectives also typically result in perceptions of inequality and capriciousness on the part of individuals whose performance is being monitored and evaluated over time. These negative feelings are exacerbated only further and are reinforced by other aspects or characteristics of poor objectives, such as those requiring "all-or-nothing" or "black-white" assessments of performance, as has been indicated.

The first requirement of a sound control system as well as the successful implementation of strategy, then, is the definition and use of sound strategic and short-term objectives. The criteria or characteristics that we regard as crucial to the development and deployment of good objectives were presented in detail in Chapter 4; the reader, accordingly, is referred back to that discussion.

2. Insufficient or Faulty Information-Processing Capabilities. If the first step in the process of control is comparison of desired and actual performance levels, it is obvious that organizations require sufficient information processing capabilities. Failure to provide timely and valid information, or the inability to locate and collect data that are appropriate for the measurement of task performance, clearly represents a severe liability that detracts from the implementation of short-term and strategic objectives.

There are at least three reasons or factors that explain this problem of control and, ultimately, poor implementation of strategy. The first refers to the preceding section where the argument for measurable objectives was presented. To reiterate a point, collecting information and tracking performance accurately become increasingly difficult or impossible if the data needed to assess performance are not available. Use of subjective information or data in the evaluation of performance is problematic, as already discussed. The quality of information used in control, then, often reflects the quality of objectives or standards of performance that result from the planning process.

The second explanation of poor or incomplete information processing derives from insufficient attention to the specific needs of the organization's *strategic control system*. Thus far we have treated control as a general generic process. We do believe, however, that control at the strategic level creates a few additional demands on the organization. Strategic control is often more problematic and difficult than is the short-term process of control. Because of the importance of information processing and other aspects of strategic controls, a separate discussion is dedicated to this topic in this chapter.

The third reason for untimely, inaccurate, or incomplete information is a poor operating structure. Basic operating structures become overloaded, for example, thwarting the flows of task-related information to the appropriate levels or positions for decision making. Or the relevant information for task completion or problem solving becomes short-circuited because of inappropriate or insufficient reporting relationships, such as those attributable to insufficient communications.

These types of problems and other structural issues that affect information processing capabilities in organizations were considered in Chapters 5 and 6, where operating structure was discussed extensively. The relation between structure and information processing capabilities has also been treated by other theorists and practitioners concerned with the impact of alternative structures on decision making.[8] For present purposes, it is only necessary to reiterate the importance of sound information gathering and processing techniques for control and, ultimately, the implementation of strategy.

3. Management by "Negative" Exception and Poor Evaluation of Performance. Figure 7-2 indicates that control-related problems can result from an inappropriate emphasis and use of "management by exception" and the evaluation of performance that logically ensues. A management-by-exception approach emphasizes that significant deviations from targeted performance deserve managerial attention; the absence of such aberrations implies that all is proceeding well and that personal follow-up and evaluation are not required. Emphasis when managing by exception, then, focuses on performance that deviates significantly from some predetermined norm or agreed-upon standard of outcome.

A problem arises when follow-up occurs *only when the deviation is negative,* significantly below the desired level of performance. Managers concerned with the implementation of short-term and strategic objectives respond only to problems, not to aberrations *above* the predetermined standards of performance. The underlying logic seems to be one of leaving well enough alone and concentrating only on poor performance and deleterious consequences.

This type of response to exceptions over time has a decidedly negative impact on control, evaluation, and the implementation process. Feedback is negative, with little if any attention systematically or routinely devoted to positive aberrations from plan. Communication between subordinates and supervisors is usually negatively affected or distorted as managers avoid interactions that typically are associated with negative feedback and that, over time, have become extremely distasteful. A natural reluctance develops to approach supervisors, even with information regarding better controls and implementation procedures, because of the prevailing negative emphasis on avoiding mistakes and the resultant wrath of supervisors at all costs.[9] Motivation to innovate diminishes, and the emphasis or prevailing climate instead becomes one of conservatism, avoiding attention, and doing primarily what one is told to do because of the perfect defensibility of behavior that such action affords.[10]

The point is that successful implementation of operating-level objectives and related organizational strategies depends on a *learning process* that is premised on sound communication, confrontation of task-related problems, and evaluation of the reasons or factors underlying significant deviations from expected performance. To facilitate such communication and evaluation, management by exception must include follow-up and analysis of significant positive deviations in performance, as well as negative ones. Organizational and managerial learning occur only if the factors underlying both good and substandard performance are identified and fully explicated. Future planning and implementation attempts benefit by exploring relationships among specific actions, decisions, or methods and significant deviations from plan. Feedback for performance above standard, finally, is clearly consistent with the reinforcement model of motivation discussed earlier.

*4. **Poor Performance Appraisal.*** Avoidance of this implementation problem has been mentioned or alluded to consistently. The need, simply, is to include performance against objectives in a formal appraisal or review process. The importance of performance against short-term operating objectives and, ultimately, strategic ends is underscored by its inclusion in the review process and its contribution to the receipt of inducements or rewards in a utilitarian organization. Seeking good performance and ensuring sufficient attention to the integration of short- and long-term needs of the organization depend in large part on the reinforcement of behavior consistent with those ends.

This last point raises a terribly important but problematic aspect of the reinforcement model: namely, to ensure that attention is devoted to *both* short- and long-term objectives in the implementation process. Because of the importance of this topic for the implementation of strategy, a separate discussion is devoted to the problem of including assessments of strategic contributions in the performance appraisal and review process.

*5. **Avoiding and Embracing Error.*** The cumulative result of various control techniques or actions can have a major impact on organizational climate and the strategy implementation process. Michael emphasizes, for example, that the net impact or consequence of poor control systems can include what he labels an overemphasis on "avoiding" error or insufficient concern with "embracing" error.[11] While these conditions have been implied, their importance makes them worthy of additional attention presently.

At one extreme, the effects of control may include a strict avoidance of error. Individuals are preoccupied with not making mistakes, for previous reactions to errors by superiors have effectively reinforced the position that being wrong, uncertain, or confused is inappropriate. Making mistakes carries with it an aura of failure or managerial incompetence. The avoidance of error at all costs breeds a climate that is often mean-spirited and unfair but one that can easily be justified by individuals concerned with "covering themselves" and maintaining a strong defensibility of behavior when their actions are scrutinized by others. Individuals may even learn to keep out of trouble by getting others in trouble, thereby effectively blaming or implicating others while diverting attention away from their own mistakes or problematic performance.

At the other extreme, Michael describes the importance of control systems that "embrace error." Making mistakes is treated as a necessary consequence of a planning and control system that seeks innovation and risk taking. While being wrong, uncertain, or confused clearly is not encouraged, organizations that embrace error exhibit a relatively greater tolerance of experimentation and more novel, less tried approaches to problem solving and decision making.

Table 7-1 summarizes some of the differences between control systems that emphasize avoiding or embracing error. The events listed and the typical responses to them under the two types of control borrow from Michael, Merton, Hrebiniak, Tannenbaum, and others concerned with the effects of control on creativity, motivation, and decision making and the formulation and implementation of plans of action.[12] The table suggests, for instance, that top-down unilateral control is more often associated with avoiding errors than is self-control or negotiation of control standards. Strict enforcement of rules under top-down control constrains behavior and ensures formal accountability. This tends to result in a strong concern with defensibility of action and, in the extreme, breeds conservatism and rigidity of behavior among organizational members subject to control. In organizations that embrace error,

TABLE 7-1. Examples of Responses to Events, Actions, or Situations in Control Systems That Avoid or Embrace Error.

Events, Actions, or Situations	*Avoiding Error*	*Embracing Error*
Control process or techniques	Primarily top-down or unilateral; reactive or constraining; emphasis on predictability and correctness	More self-control; negotiation of job standards; less constraining; emphasis on learning
If alleging a mistake or accusing of an error	No error occurred; it was unimportant or someone else's fault	Admit the error; examine the causes and learn for future
Emphasis on	Being right; defensibility of action	Risk taking; innovation
Acceptance of responsibility	Ritualistic	Realistic; shared
Setting objectives	Top-down; monocratic; little involvement or negotiation	Shared with greater participation; norm that goals reflect conditions that are changing and, thus, are not immutable, all-or-nothing criteria of performance
Faced with uncertainty	Avoidance; seek out controllable situation	Confrontation; seek out uncertainty
Attitude toward change	Resistance	Embracing change as necessary
Interpersonal orientation	Guarded; low trust; alienation	Open; higher levels of trust and cooperative attitude

defensibility of action is less important. Emphasis is on innovation and assuming risk, even if this results in making mistakes.

To see the differences between organizations that avoid or embrace error, it is only necessary to consider what happens when someone is accused of making a mistake. In the error-avoiding situation, it is important to be correct. In fact, it is so important that, when supposedly there is an error, "it is considered within the bounds of the ethic which sets the highest priority on organizational survival to assert that no error occurred, or that if it did it was unimportant, or that if it was important it was someone else's fault."[13] In the error-embracing situation, mistakes are more likely to be acknowledged as necessary ingredients of the learning process and unavoidable by-products of the organizations's attempts to cope with uncertainty or plan for change. The argument is that mistakes are not unnatural but, rather, a natural correlate of individual and organizational learning.

Table 7-1 suggests that planning and the process of setting objectives differ substantially in the two control systems. In the error-avoiding organization, objective setting is likely to be the privilege of a few—the higher echelons. Objectives are likely to represent inviolate standards against which errors are judged. Where error is embraced, planning reflects an attitude that objectives are motivators and the process of deciding on them is so important that widerspread participation and involvement are encouraged. Mistakes or aberrations in performance are more likely to be seen as normal and unavoidable and, thus, easily confronted, which facilitates decision making, the acceptance of responsibility, and organizational learning. Attitudes toward change and interpersonal orientations support planning and agreement on objectives in the error-embracing situation, while restraining those processes or rendering them useless in the avoidance situation.

The point here and in this entire section of the chapter is simply to emphasize that *control and the inherent methods of responding to, evaluating, and reinforcing performance have profound effects on behavior*. The forced conservatism and severe avoidance of risk under some control methods clearly effect the planning process and the number and difficulty of objectives that individuals seriously attempt to attain. Failure to reinforce desired behavior sufficiently surely affects its occurrence in the future. The negative consequences of poor controls, even if unintended, impact greatly on individual performance and the motivation to attain objectives, which clearly has import for the organization's ability to achieve strategic aims. Poor controls in the short-term can bode disaster for the long-term, suggesting that care must be taken to thwart or eliminate any of the control-related deficiences noted in this discussion.

STRATEGIC CONTROL ISSUES

Discussion of control thus far has focused on it as a generic concept and process, with elements equally applicable to both the short and the long term. Clearly, this is true; the measurement, evaluation, and feedback aspects of Figure 7-2 obtain for all control systems, regardless of time frame.

We also feel, however, that while the control elements are applicable for all discussions of control, it also must be recognized that strategic control places a slightly different type of burden on the organization than do short-term operational controls. The same general control elements or variables obtain, regardless of time frame, but the specific questions or issues that are salient or problematic under a generic heading such as "measurement" can vary for strategic and operational controls. The remainder of this section adds to the general model of control of Figure 7-2 by highlighting some special issues, needs, or problems that characterize strategic control.

Information Processing and the Measurement of Performance

The first step in the control process is the gathering of performance data and the comparison of actual and desired performance to detect significant deviations from plan. Examining the work of various authors suggests some differences in the process of information gathering, processing, and analysis and decision for the short or long term.[14] For example, among other things Hurst argues that[15]

1. *Strategic control requires data from more sources, and more data from external sources, than does short-term control. In the latter case, the "operation" itself (e.g., machine performance, flow of work, and output data regarding quantity and quality) generates the only data used for control purposes.*
2. *Strategic control is less precise than is operational control, making analysis more difficult. The former aggregates approximations from a complex environment or a "large world," while the latter focuses on more precise representations of a much smaller world.*
3. *Alternative actions or decisions are more difficult to choose in advance under strategic control than in short-term, operational control models. This has many consequences, including heightening the effect of errors of omission under strategic control (e.g., not uncovering, moving into, and taking advantage of a new business opportunity in a timely manner).*
4. *Strategic control data are less accurate and their receipt more sporadic than those derived from operational monitoring.*

Taking these few examples and relating back to our discussion of planning as a decision process in Chapter 2, we can argue that, under strategic control, the relation between means and ends is less precise than it is under short-term control conditions. Similarly, the clarity or certainty of cause-effect relations is likely to be lower under strategic control conditions, which increases the difficulty of the planning decision. Because of the needs or characteristics of strategic control raised by Hurst and others, we would again emphasize, consistent with our arguments in Chapter 2, that effective strategic planning and control depend heavily on (1) increasing the certainty of cause-effect or means-ends relations and (2) obtaining agreement on goals or objectives among managers responsible for those strategic activities. Any resultant decrease in uncertainty will positively affect the strategic control process.

Integrating Short-Run and Long-Run Performance in the Control Process

We feel that the issue of short- versus long-term performance is an extremely salient one for strategic control and the successful implementation of strategy. Even a cursory examination of the literature reveals countless arguments that American organizations have been overly preoccupied with the short run to the neglect of the long term. Managers in the United States are increasingly being accused of myopia and indicted for preferring a zealous and aggressive quest for short-run profits rather than research and development activities that will help to ensure long-term profitability and organizational survival. Short-term profits denote rapid feedback in terms of bonuses and related perquisites, making performance over the long haul less salient and less deserving of management's attention. This decreased importance and attention, it is argued, have resulted in poor strategic planning and control and a severe erosion in competitive position over time as others (e.g., Japanese firms), whose planning horizons have been longer, fare increasingly well in the marketplace.

While clearly there are dangers in decidedly short-run thinking and neglect of the longer term, we believe that there also is a real danger in a too hasty condemnation of short-term ends. It is easy to argue that managers must be concerned with long-run performance; it also may be too easy to make the mistake of concluding that short-term concerns are not important or that they are necessarily contraproductive to the strategic needs of the organization. Such a simplistic and quick conclusion, indeed, is dangerous, for we argue that just the opposite is true: *namely, that short-term objectives or aims support and are critical to the achievement of long-term strategic ends. The prob-*

lem is not the short-versus long-term concerns of management; it is the lack of integration of and consistency between long- and short-term plans and objectives in the control system that is vital to the successful implementation of strategy. To elucidate and emphasize this argument, two points consistently made in this book must be reiterated.

Individual Rationality. Problems of overemphasis of the short term to the neglect or detriment of the long term do not arise because managers are evil, impatient, or stupid. On the contrary, such myopia exists primarily because individuals in utilitarian organizations are *rational* and calculative in their weighing of inducements and contributions. In most instances of exclusive attention to short-term horizons, managers are behaving in a rational way, doing precisely what the organization is asking them to do.

Consider just two cases we have encountered to see how easily one may be beguiled by short-term concerns. The first involves a well-known multidivisional corporation that employs fairly consistent performance criteria across divisions to maintain control and guarantee comparability of performance. Within divisions, there is greater flexibility in performance criteria to reflect local concerns and ways of doing business. A number of years ago, after acquisition of a major company that became an important operating division, the company had to confront a number of problems, including some attributable to poor short-term objectives and controls.

The acquired division employed a profit plan and budget to control and evaluate the performance of its major departments. It was clear to all that meeting the plan and staying under budget were critical to a good appraisal. Given this emphasis, it became obvious to us why department heads would routinely, if unobtrusively, do such things as (1) defer or postpone hiring of individuals with needed technical skills because of the effects on budget; (2) eliminate critical advertising and related marketing expenses, again to stay within budget; (3) eliminate or reduce inventories to accentuate return on assets (a measure of performance on the profit plan), despite stock outs and consequent customer dissatisfactions; and (4) not approve overtime, even when needed to allow sales to meet a delivery commitment, because of the adverse effects on the overtime-to-direct-labor-cost ratio. Despite long-term repercussions that would surely ensue, the emphasis was solely on meeting plan and budget requirements. Quite simply, it was individually rational and logical to do so.

The second case is one of an oil refinery that had long been under federal, state, and local indictment for not eliminating effluents that were contributing to the pollution of a river. Despite monetary penalties, the refinery did not make the required investments in appropriate pollution control devices. Were the managers involved so heartless, completely unmindful and uncaring of the environment and delicate balance of nature in the affected body of water?

Again, the answer is not one of intended evil or neglect but, rather, one of individual rationality. The refinery in question was a high-turnover situation, but in a positive sense: a good performance by top management usually led to promotion or lateral move to a larger refinery or more desirable work location within the company. The criteria of performance included, among other things, a ratio that we can label a measure of return on investment. In simple terms, the purchase and installation of pollution equipment would have resulted in some drain on current earnings as well as an enlargement of the plant's investment base. Thus, achievement of a socially desired end would have necessitated a reduction in the numerator and an increase in the denominator of an important criterion of performance, which could affect promotion or mobility.

In light of this desire for achievement and subjective assessment of the performance ratio, it was more logical and less risky to avoid the installation as long as possible and continue paying fines that were not directly attributable or detrimental to individual measures of performance. Despite potentially negative effects on the company in both the short and longer term, it was easier for a given individual to avoid the issue and rationalize the decision in terms of career mobility and the fact that, someday, someone would take the necessary action.

These cases may represent extreme examples of the negative impact of individual behavior on organizational performance, but we view their point as being critical and worthy of emphasis. Managers are not foolish or evil; in utilitarian organizations, individuals usually behave rationally, calculating the risks and benefits of performance options and choosing one that, subjectively, appears the most logical. The inevitable conclusion is that organizations must ensure that short- and long-term controls and incentives are consistent and integrated toward the achievement of strategic ends. The organizational environment must be one in which individual rationality and organizational rationality are not at odds but, rather, compatible and coordinated for the successful implementation of strategy. We discuss this integration of incentives in greater detail, but another point must first be stressed.

Short-run Performance: A Critical Ingredient for Strategy Implementation. The second point implied repeatedly throughout this book is that short-run performance need not be looked upon with distrust or disfavor, as some discussions of short- and long-term outlooks and managerial time horizons might imply. Indeed, just the opposite is true. *To achieve rationality in organizations, however limited, long-term objectives and strategies must be* *translated into short-term objectives and plans.* The organization cannot perform otherwise. Managers must transform global, long-term needs or ends into smaller, more local and more manageable pieces to implement strategy successfully. In our opinion, short-term objectives and incentives are absolutely crucial to, not inconsistent with, the achievement of strategic aims, *provided that care is taken to integrate operating-level plans and objectives with longer-term needs.* This is a critical requirement of an effective control system.

Figure 7-3 depicts what we have argued repeatedly. To achieve long-term objectives and plans, the organization must translate global, long-term aims and actions into smaller pieces for operating units and individuals to manage. Few people can operate in the present with only long-term pictures or metaphors to guide them. As March and Simon, Thompson, and others have argued, the reduction of uncertainty and the translation of unclear, indeterminate, global requirements into determinateness and certainty are absolutely essential to organizational performance.[16] In our view, it is the short-term objective that facilitates or aids this translation by providing individuals with a manageable portion of a larger, unmanageable plan. The short time horizon and related short-run performance, then, are clearly supportive of and necessary for long-term control.

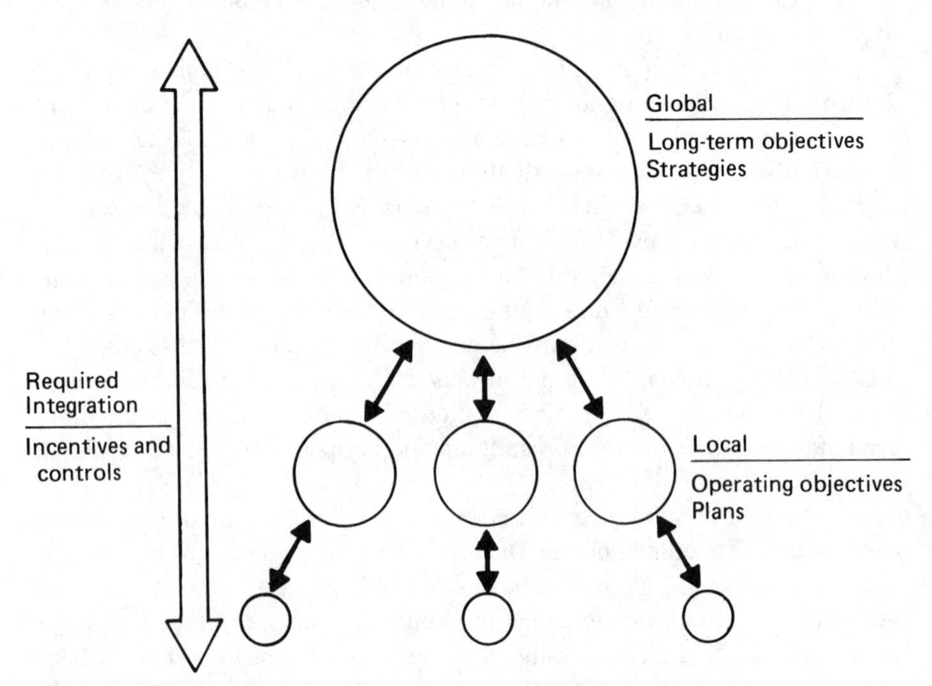

Figure 7-3. Integrating the short and long run in the implementation of strategy.

The critical ingredients or needs for the achievement of this consistency between the short and long run are appropriate incentives and controls, as Figure 7-3 indicates. Attention to the integration of short and long term is essential to guarantee that the former is not treated independently and inappropriately by individuals to the detriment of the latter. Careful, purposeful attention to incentive plans and controls, including performance appraisals and the allocation of rewards, can help to ensure that the requisite integration occurs, thereby helping to achieve consistency between both individual and organizational rationality and short- and long-run performance.

Assessing and Controlling Strategic Contributions to the Organization

To ensure the needed integration between the long and short term, it is necessary *to assess and control both the short-run and strategic contributions of individuals.* We feel that the most logical and viable approaches toward this end demand (1) formal performance appraisal techniques, including provision of appropriate incentives or rewards for strategic contributions, and (2) an emphasis on strategic budgets in the control process.

Appraisal of Strategic Contributions. Most formal performance appraisals and reviews we have encountered focus on the short run and exclude any reference to long-run performance. A much stronger approach would involve a formal evaluation of performance against both short- and long-term plans and objectives. While admittedly such an appraisal can be difficult, the approach helps to increase the salience of strategic contributions to the organization and, consequently, tends to reduce purposeful choices of short-term behavior without regard to the longer term. Such an approach strengthens the strategic control process.

Figure 7-4 depicts a situation of a five-year time frame and assumes a set of strategic objectives and plans. Consistent with the tenets of logic and intended rationality, Figure 7-4 also shows that the five-year objectives and plans have been translated into yearly performance measures for managers to attain. This translation or reduction process is central to the elimination of uncertainty and the determination of clear performance criteria to guide and motivate individual effort.

The usual case of formal appraisal and review assesses managerial performance over a one-year period, as Figure 7-4 indicates for the end of year 3. In our opinion, however, approaching each of the years as separate entities or periods for evaluation does little to focus managerial attention on the totality of the organization's strategic direction. In fact, attaching compensation

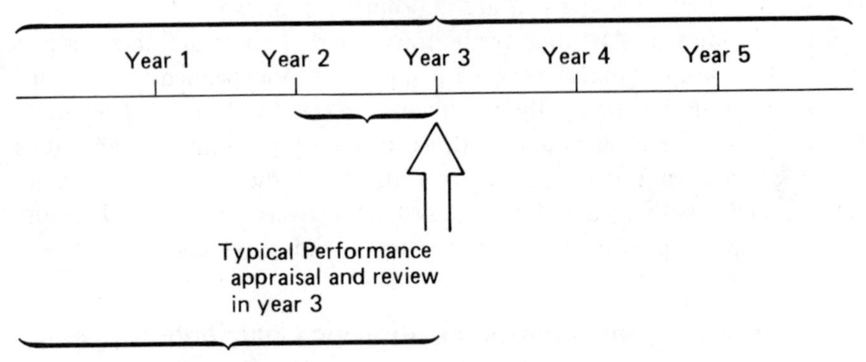

Figure 7-4. Performance appraisal, with assessment of strategic contribution.

increases and other rewards solely to yearly performance reviews reinforces the importance of any given year and detracts from the salience of the effects of interdependence of all the years for the attainment of strategic results.

A better approach is one in which the appraisal in a focal year includes *both* an assessment of that year's performance *and* an evaluation of the total three years' performance in relation to five-year aims and strategies. Adjustments necessary for the successful implementation of strategy can be reflected in the operating objectives for year 4, thereby ensuring that aberrations from strategic plans are noted and that the required integration of short- and long-term needs receives sufficient attention. Under this approach, the importance of any given year derives in large part from its interdependence with other years for the attainment of ends in a longer-term setting. Emphasis is not exclusively on performance in a short time period that is treated as a separate, independent entity for purposes of appraisal and review.

To emphasize further the importance of the evaluation of strategic contributions in the appraisal process, it is necessary to design incentive plans that reinforce long-term thinking and performance needs. Here we are suggesting the use of such incentives as *deferred* bonus or payment plans, under which a portion of compensation earned in a given year is deferred for future payment. Similarly, tying bonuses and other payments over longer periods of time to such indexes as earnings per share, growth in market share, stockprice performance, scale economies, and other measures reflective of strategic aims is consistent with the partial deferral of reinforcement to the long term and the strategic control system.

The details and mechanics of these types of plans are varied and typically are tailored to specific organizations. Suffice it to stress at present that tying compensation in part to future performance or progress against strategic as well as short-term operating objectives is a useful and important way to integrate short- and long-term thinking in a strategic control system. We have argued that reinforcement of desired ends is critical in utilitarian organizations and that individuals will behave logically and rationally in their own interest. Recognizing this, proper attention to long-term aims and plans can be obtained most easily when rewards are based in part on an assessment of strategic contribution.

Strategic Budgets: Controlling Long-Term Performance. Another way to try to ensure long-range as well as short-term thinking is to use and emphasize "strategic budgets" as an integral aspect of the control process.[17] Strategic budgets are employed simultaneously with short-term operating budgets, but the objectives, plans, or programs supported by each vary a great deal. The purpose of the two budgets is to make individuals aware of both the short- and long-term responsibilities of an organizational subunit, for example, a functional department or strategic business unit (SBU). This differentiation in perspective is accomplished primarily by subsuming different activities, tasks, or responsibilities under the strategic and operating portions of allocated budgets and resource allotments.

The first task of strategic control is the differentiation of short-term operational budgets from strategic budgets. The former represent funds or resources that are required for "business as usual," the routine activities that support normal operating procedures; the latter are earmarked for specific strategic programs or activities that are long-term and that result from the strategy formulation process. Resources provided under operating and strategic budgets, then, are intended to support different activities or objectives in the organizational subunits that have both sources of funds.

Figure 7-5, a brief illustration derived from the work of Lorange, provides an example of the different sources of funding and the strategic control questions raised.[18] For the sake of brevity, the example uses just four functional departments to indicate contribution to operating and strategic objectives. The vertical axis in Figure 7-5 indicates the types of objectives and budgets, including those resulting from operational needs and three hypothetical strategic programs.

The figure reveals, predictably, that all functional departments have standard operating procedures, short-term objectives, and concomitant budgets to support routine organizational activities. Figure 7-5 also shows the strategic programs, but it indicates that not all departments are equally involved in

	Market Research	R&D	Engineering	Production
Operational (Budget)	Yes	Yes	Yes	Yes
Strategic (Budget):				
A	No	Yes	Yes	No
B	No	Yes	Yes	No
C	Yes	Yes	Yes	No

Figure 7-5. Sources of funding (budgets) for a sample of functional departments. [Derived from P. Lorange, "Strategic Control: Some Issues in Making It Operationally More Useful," in R. Lamb Warren (ed.), *Latest Advances in Strategic Management* (Englewood Cliffs, N.J.: Prentice-Hall, in press)]

them. Market research, for example, has an operating budget and a separate source of funding because of its contribution to the achievement of one set of the organization's strategic objectives (Program C). In contrast, R&D is involved in all three strategic programs (A, B, C) and, thus, receives funding to support four different sets of tasks or objectives—one short term and three long term. The sources of funding can similarly be determined for engineering and production.

The contribution of such a bifurcation of budgets is simply to make functional managers aware of the departments' short-term and strategic tasks. The existence of separate budgets serves to reinforce the differential salience of operating and strategic needs. The control questions or issues arising from the use of dual budgets are similar to those raised previously when discussing control, but because of the importance of strategic performance, they are worth emphasis at the present time.

The *first* and most obvious issue deals with the monitoring and assessment of performance against strategic objectives. Needs here include (1) deployment of measurable objectives or milestones based on them; (2) development and use of appropriate criteria of strategic task performance and completion; (3) variance analysis of desired and actual performance, including actual versus budgeted expenditures; and (4) evaluation and corrective action, as needed. In essence, the monitoring and assessment of performance against strategic objectives, given the constraints of strategic budgets, are virtually identical to the tracking and evaluation of performance against short-term operating indicators. A difference worth noting is due to the longer time frame involved with strategic objectives and budgets. In the short term, environmental or exogenous variables are relatively fixed compared with external conditions in the longer, strategic time frame. The evaluation of performance against strategic objectives and budgets, then, typically *must include a more careful analysis of external conditions and the assumptions based on them than is usually the case with short-term performance and operating budgets.*

The *second* control issue is to *ensure that resources earmarked for strategic programs are not being used or wasted on short-term needs.* This need is critical, but often problematic, for it creates additional information processing and reporting requirements. Separation of monitoring and evaluation against both short- and long-term performance and cost criteria adds to the complexity of control, as indicated. Nonetheless, such a separation does emphasize the importance of strategic thinking. Monitoring performance against strategic objectives and budgets adds accountability and responsibility reporting that transcends short-run pressures and tasks and increases the salience of the long-term aims and contributions of the subunit. Coupled with the use of performance appraisal methods that incorporate assessments of the strategic contributions of managers, reliance on strategic budgets as an element of control can do much to avoid the myopia of thinking and planning only for the short term.

Summary

Proper understanding of motivation and appropriate use of incentives and controls are central to the successful implementation of strategy. Considerable time spent on the formulation of long-term objectives and elaborate plans for their achievement may, in fact, be wasted if incentives and controls result in behavior that is inconsistent with intended results.

We argue that most strategy formulation and implementation occur in "utilitarian" organizations in which individuals weigh the balance of inducements and contributions when deciding on the appropriateness of competing behaviors. This view of motivation and what others have termed the "employment contract" allow us to develop and use a stimulus-response-reinforcement model when discussing incentives and controls. In essence, individuals interpret and assess the consequences of their behavior and decide on courses of action that they feel will positively affect the perceived ration of rewards to costs. The validity and appropriateness of their perceptions are challenged or reinforced by the organizational control system, whose function it is to examine and evaluate individuals' actions in light of required standards or desired benchmarks of performance.

The control system is especially important to the successful implementation of strategy. We argue that effective controls result in timely and sufficient information to allow for the evaluation of performance and the determination of progress against short-term and strategic objectives. We argue, too, that an effective control system positively affects risk taking and organizational learning, while simultaneously eliminating the deleterious effects of management by "negative exception" and an emphasis of "avoiding error" at all costs.

Control systems and the appraisal and review they indicate must also be concerned with both short- and long-term performance. Incentives and controls that reinforce short-run thinking to the neglect or detriment of long-range objectives and plans are clearly inconsistent with the present strategy implementation model. The need is to integrate the short and long term and ensure that performance against short-run operating objectives facilitates and adds to the achievement of desired strategic outcomes for the organization. This integration is supported, we argue, by appropriate performance appraisal techniques and the use of strategic budgets in the control process. Only when strategic performance becomes salient in the budgeting and formal appraisal process will the requisite integration of short and long run occur.

For all intents and purposes, we have presented the key elements of our model of implementing strategy, beginning with formulation and ending in the present chapter with a treatment of the incentives and controls that support and reinforce strategic aims. There is, however, one remaining critical issue to be discussed: namely, the management or conduct of the strategy implementation process. While our concern thus far has focused on the content of the implementation model, what is still needed is a brief consideration of the adaptation process and the ways in which managers conduct change over time to support strategy implementation. This is the purpose of the next and final chapter.

Notes

1. Chester I. Barnard, *The Functions of the Executive* (Cambridge, Mass.: Harvard University Press, 1938).
2. Amitai Etzioni, *A Comparative Analysis of Complex Organizations* (Glencoe, Ill.: The Free Press, 1961).
3. Barnard, *The Functions of the Executive;* and James G. March and Herbert A. Simon, *Organizations* (New York: John Wiley & Sons, Inc., 1958).
4. Robert A. Dahl, *Modern Political Analysis* (Englewood Cliffs, N.J.: Prentice-Hall, Inc., 1963); Jeffrey Pfeffer and Gerald R. Salancik, "Organizational Decision Making as a Political Process: The Case of a University Budget," *Administrative Science Quarterly,* 19:135–151 (1974); and L. G. Hrebiniak, *Complex Organizations* (St. Paul: West Publishing Company, 1978).
5. William F. Joyce and John W. Slocum, "Climates in Organizations," in S. Kerr, ed., *Organizational Behavior* (Columbus, Ohio: Grid Publishing Company, 1979), pp. 317–333; Hrebiniak, *Complex Organizations;* Robert K. Merton,

"Bureaucratic Structure and Personality," in Robert K. Merton, ed., *Social Theory and Social Structure,* rev. ed. (New York: The Free Press, 1957), pp. 195–206; and Donald N. Michael, *On Learning to Plan—and Planning to Learn* (San Francisco: Jossey-Bass, 1973).

6. Arnold S. Tannenbaum, *Control in Organizations* (New York: McGraw-Hill Book Company, 1968); and Hrebiniak, *Complex Organizations.*
7. Michael, *On Learning to Plan.*
8. Jay R. Galbraith, *Designing Complex Organizations* (Reading, Mass.: Addison-Wesley Publishing Company, 1973); and Stanley Davis and Paul Lawrence, *Matrix* (Reading, Mass.: Addison-Wesley Publishing Company, 1977).
9. Michael, *On Learning to Plan.*
10. Merton, "Bureaucratic Structure and Personality," in *Social Theory and Social Structure.*
11. Michael, *on Learning to Plan.*
12. Ibid.; Hrebiniak, *Complex Organizations;* Tannenbaum, *Control in Organizations;* and Merton, "Bureaucratic Structure and Personality."
13. Michael, *On Learning to Plan,* p. 133.
14. Robert Anthony, *Planning and Control Systems: A Framework for Analysis* (Cambridge, Mass.: Division of Research, Graduate School of Business Administration, Harvard University, 1965); William H. Newman, *Constructive Control: Design and Use of Control Systems* (Englewood Cliffs, N.J.: Prentice-Hall, 1975); E. Gerald Hurst, "Controlling Strategic Plans," in P. Lorange, ed., *Implementation of Strategic Planning* (Englewood Cliffs, N.J.: Prentice-Hall, 1982), pp. 114–123.
15. Hurst, op. cit.
16. March and Simon, *Organizations;* and James D. Thompson, *Organizations in Action* (New York: McGraw-Hill Book Company, 1967).
17. Peter Lorange, *Implementation of Strategic Planning* (Englewood Cliffs, N.J.: Prentice-Hall, Inc., 1982), and "Strategic Control: Some Issues in Making It Operationally More Useful," in R. Lamb Warren, ed., *Latest Advances in Strategic Management* (Englewood Cliffs, N.J.: Prentice-Hall, Inc., in press).
18. Lorange, op. cit.

STRATEGIC CHANGE: MANAGING THE IMPLEMENTATION PROCESS

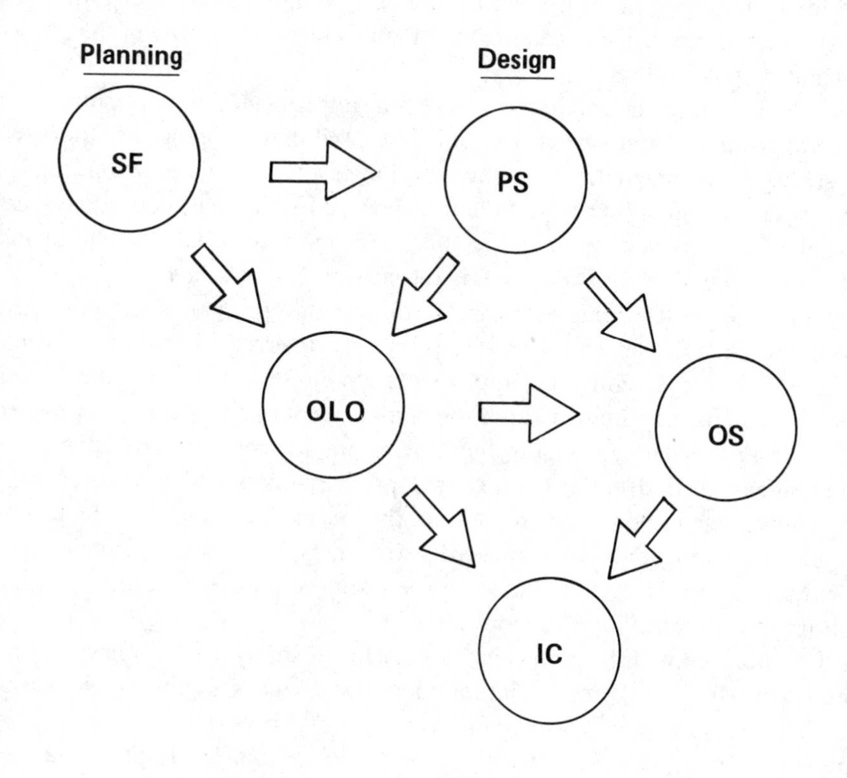

The previous chapters have shown how planning and organizing decisions are related when implementing strategy. The implementation model, in conjunction with what we have called the principles of intended rationality and minimum intervention, indicates what must be done to achieve important strategic objectives and shows the key variables that can be changed to implement strategy. It also provides guidance concerning which of the several possible points of intervention should be attacked first.

These decisions determine the content of an implementation effort; that is, they specify what must be done or changed to successfully implement strategy. When we also consider the timing required for such changes—the implementation horizon—different styles of implementation result, as described briefly in Chapter 1.

These styles can reasonably be thought of as constituting the *design* of an implementation effort, but obviously more decisions remain. Once having decided what to do in implementing strategy, we must also decide how to do it; in other words, we must address the management or *conduct* of the implementation process itself.

A discussion of the conduct or process of implementation is important on several grounds. First, one of the guidelines used in developing this approach to strategy implementation was the criterion of action. This criterion implies that simply knowing what to do is not enough; in the final analysis, success is judged in terms of actual rather than intended results. Choice *and* action determine actual results, and each is incomplete without the other.

Second, experience suggests that a considerable portion of the problems encountered in implementing strategy occur due to errors of omission or commission while managing the implementation process. Until recently, relatively little has been known about the management of change. In the absence of such knowledge, managers faced with implementation problems have approached them from their own perspectives—perspectives often conditioned by their location and role within the larger organization.[1] The consequence has sometimes been uncoordinated and disjunctive implementation, incurring unnecessary and excessive costs and occasionally resulting in the failure of the entire implementation effort.

The purpose of this chapter is to present an integrated approach to the process or conduct of implementation activities. Following the previous discussion, we propose that decisions concerning the content and timing of implementation activities determine the "style" or type of implementation. Implementations may be relatively simple, as in the case of evolutionary or managerial implementation, or complex (e.g., what we have termed sequential or complex implementations). *The conduct of implementation activities depends upon the style of implementation.* Methods appropriate for controlling managerial implementations are different from those appropriate for the management of the more complex, sequenced style. Different styles require different methods in terms of transition mechanisms and change-planning processes, paralleling on a smaller scale the planning and organizing decisions made in designing the content of the implementation itself. Specific recommendations concerning the selection of transition mechanisms and proper planning for change are made contingent upon the type or style of implementation. The chapter concludes with an overview of important decisions in the conduct of implementation activities.

DESIGNING THE IMPLEMENTATION PROGRAM

We have argued that the design or style of an implementation program is determined by decisions concerning the content and timing of change activities. These two factors interact to generate the styles' taxonomy discussed in Chapter 1 and restated in Figure 8-1. Implementations may be relatively "large" or "small," and the time available for them "long" or "short." Combinations of these variables identify the styles or designs of implementation

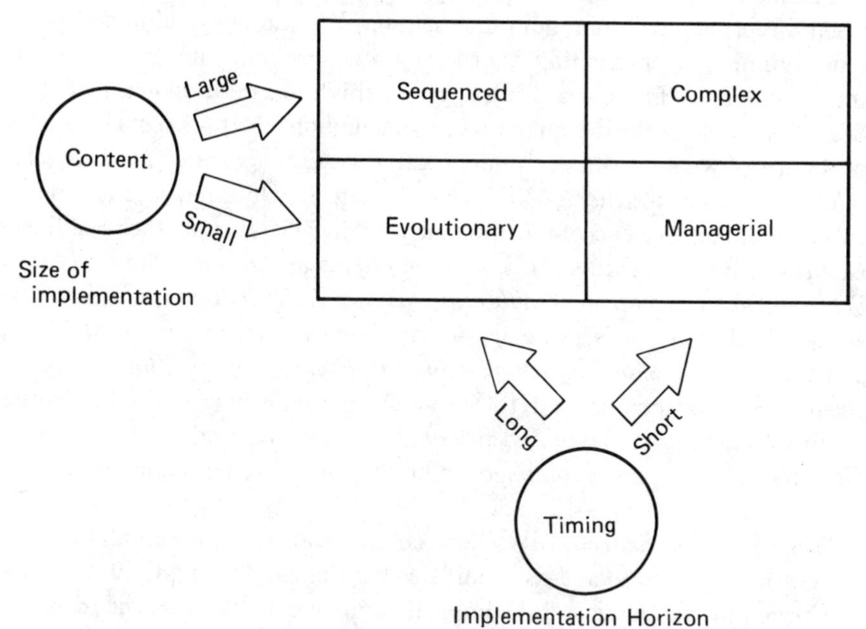

Figure 8-1. Implementation style, content, and timing.

possible, proceeding from relatively small, simple, and inexpensive styles (evolutionary) to large, complex, and expensive implementation efforts (complex). Because the design of an implementation, in turn, determines specific transition mechanisms and planning processes, in this section we present specific models for determining the content and timing of implementation activities and, thus, the consequent style of strategy implementation.

Determining the Content of Implementation Activities

Knowing what to change in implementing strategy is problematic; although a number of points of intervention are possible, all are not equally relevant in specific situations. Choices of what to change determine the content of an implementation. When several components of the implementation model require significant adjustment, as, for example, when a change in operating objectives requires supporting changes in operating structure and reward systems, large implementation problems result that imply significant costs to the organization. Similarly, smaller adjustments in only one component of the implementation model are less costly than larger adjustments. It is important, therefore, to identify the factors that lead an organization to engage such "large" and costly implementation problems.

In Chapter 1 we presented a preliminary discussion of these factors relying upon the principle of minimum intervention. We can now add to and refine our argument by presenting a process for determining the content of an implementation. There are three stages in this process, as shown in Figure 8-2. First, because the design of an implementation effort is itself a consumer of resources, we argue that it is important *to localize the search for acceptable solutions to the implementation problem* (stage I). Once having identified a subset of the components of the implementation model that are the most likely candidates for change in stage I, it is then necessary to *refine the analysis to determine which component within the subset specifically requires adjustment* (stage II). Finally, it is necessary to say when *expansion of the search for acceptable implementation activities is justified and how such further search should be undertaken* (stage III). Subsequent sections refer to these activities as *initial search* (stage I), *consistency analysis* (stage II), and *expansion* (stage III) phases of the process of determining the content of an implementation.

Stage I: Initial Search. All elements of the strategy implementation model are not initially considered as candidates for change. During the first phase of determining the content of the implementation, search is localized, *depend-*

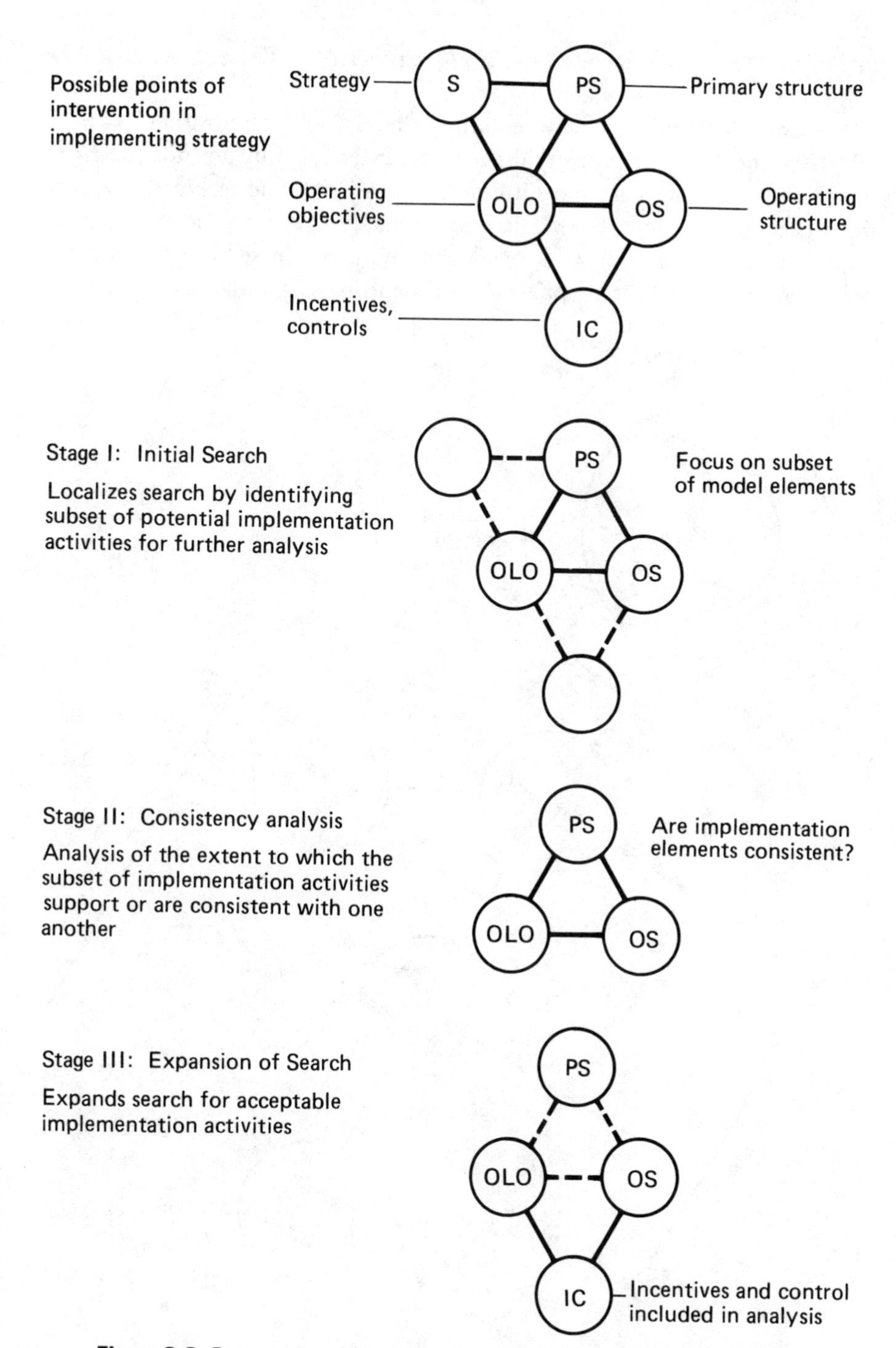

Figure 8-2. Stages of analysis determining the contents of implementation.

ing upon the relative importance of effectiveness or efficiency issues in the strategic problem at hand.

Parsons[2] distinguished between three "levels" of organization, each of which performs a qualitatively distinct, yet essential, function for the firm. These levels are termed the institutional, managerial, and technical levels of the organization (Figure 8-3). The institutional level is concerned with aligning the organization with its environment and is comprised of such individuals or groups as the top management of the firm, long-range strategic plan-

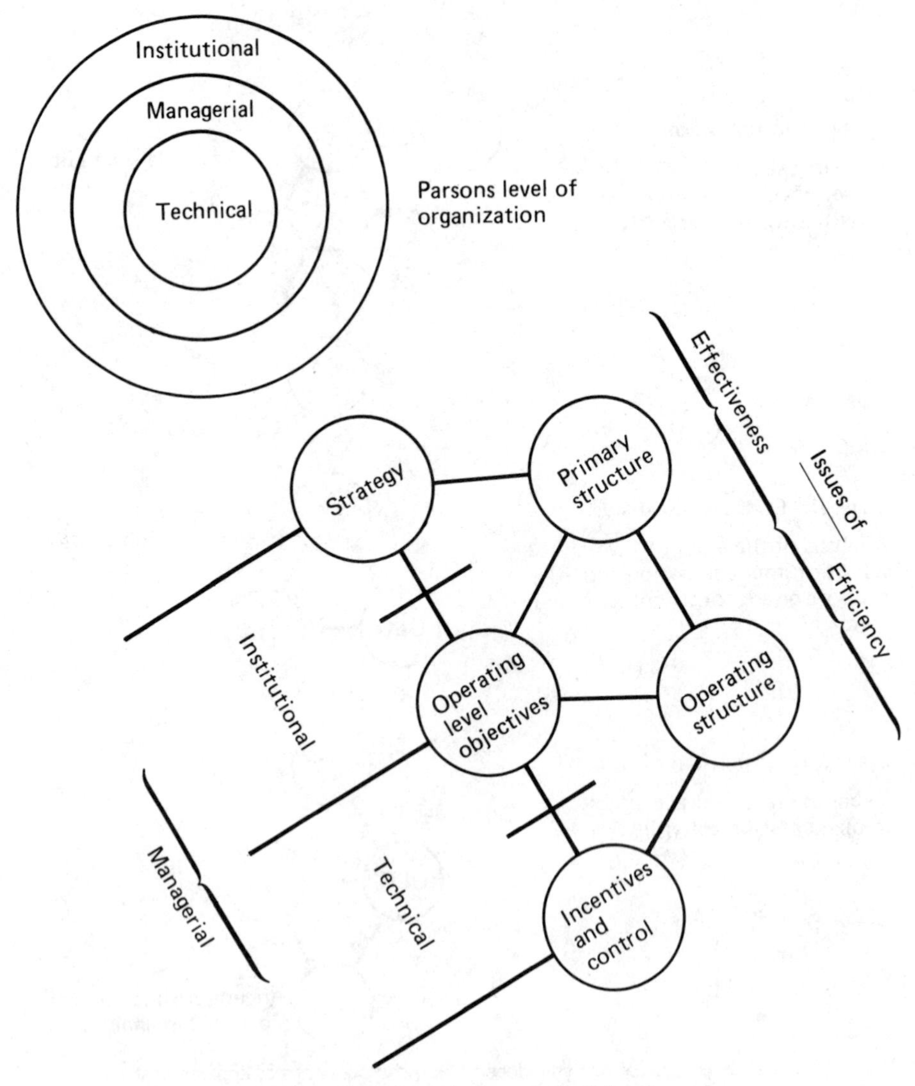

Figure 8-3. Effectiveness and efficiency.

ners, and market researchers. The technical level is concerned with the efficient transformation of inputs into outputs, or maintenance of the input-process-output cycle. The managerial level functions so as to integrate and articulate the activities of the institutional and technical levels—the familiar linking or coordinating function—as well as "buffers" the technical level from the uncertainties of the environment so that technical rationality and efficiency are reasonable goals.

The distinctions between the missions of these levels suggests a rough parallel to what Hofer and Schendel[3] have called issues of effectiveness and efficiency. Effectiveness is defined as "doing the right things," whereas efficiency refers to "doing things right." The institutional level rightly concentrates on issues of effectiveness, whereas the technical level concentrates on problems of efficiency. Because no issue is ever entirely one of either effectiveness or efficiency, the managerial level functions to relate these two complementary objectives of the firm.

The organizational levels discussed by Parsons parallel somewhat the components of the strategy implementation model, as shown in Figure 8-3. The concerns of the institutional level are largely reflected in choices of strategy, primary structure, and operating objectives, whereas the technical core is most concerned with the efficient *accomplishment* of operating objectives through operating structure and control systems. The institutional level focuses on the identification of appropriate strategic and operating objectives (effectiveness), whereas the technical level is most concerned with the successful attainment of those ends (efficiency). Operating objectives represent the point in strategy implementation where effectiveness and efficiency considerations are melded; consequently, the managerial level is the one primarily concerned with the development and administration of these objectives.

It is logical, given these distinctions, to focus on later components of the implementation model when faced with issues of efficiency and earlier components of the model when dealing with problems of effectiveness. Initial search for problems or activities should occur within the lower three components of the implementation model when efficiency issues are at stake and within the upper three components when the problem appears to be primarily one of effectiveness. Of course, it is possible that the real problem is some mixture of these areas; that is, at times managers are really most concerned with "doing the right things *right*." In this case, initial search should focus on the middle three components of the model, or those most closely aligned with the managerial level of the firm.

Once an initial choice of components of the model has been selected for consideration, an analysis of the consistency among these components indicates which will require adjustment. This type of stage II analysis is discussed in the next section. It is also possible that consistency analysis suggests that the initial choice of components was in error, requiring a broadening of search to include adjacent components of the implementation model in an expansion stage (stage III).

Stage II: Consistency Analysis Within Implementation Triads. Identification of the strategic problem as primarily an effectiveness, efficiency, or mixed issue indicates which of the components of the implementation model should be considered as initial candidates for change. As noted, the top, middle, or lower three components of the model should be examined for consistency in the analysis phase (stage II). These three sets of components of the model are conveniently referred to as *implementation triads,* and they form the basis for further analysis to determine which, if any, of them require adjustment in the face of the strategic problems requiring solution or the strategic issues requiring implementation.

Three implementation triads are possible (Figure 8-4), each appropriately identified with issues of efficiency, effectiveness, or both. Figure 8-4 refers to triads 1 and 3 as the upper and lower planning triads because two of their three components are planning components. The middle triad is called the design triad because two of its three components are design components. The upper planning triad focuses mainly on effectiveness, the lower planning triad mainly on efficiency, and the design triad on mixed effectiveness-efficiency issues.

In stage II, analysis takes place within one of the implementation triads to determine which if any of its components are inconsistent with the others. The focus of the analysis is to determine the extent to which components of the implementation model support one another in furthering the strategic aims of the organization. Thus, if we were analyzing the lower planning triad, we would be concerned with the extent to which choices of operating structure and control systems supported the attainment of operating objectives. Inconsistency would be noted, for example, when reward systems were found to reinforce only functional skills within a matrix organization requiring simultaneous commitment to both functional and project goals to achieve operating level objectives.

Chapters 2 through 7 of this book have explored in detail the implications of choices made in each component of the implementation model for relevant other components. We have discussed how primary structure is related to strategy and how operating-level objectives are, in turn, delimited in scope by previous choices of strategy and primary structure. Operating structure was shown to depend upon the decision-making requirements imposed by choices of operating-level objectives and primary structure, and so on. These discus-

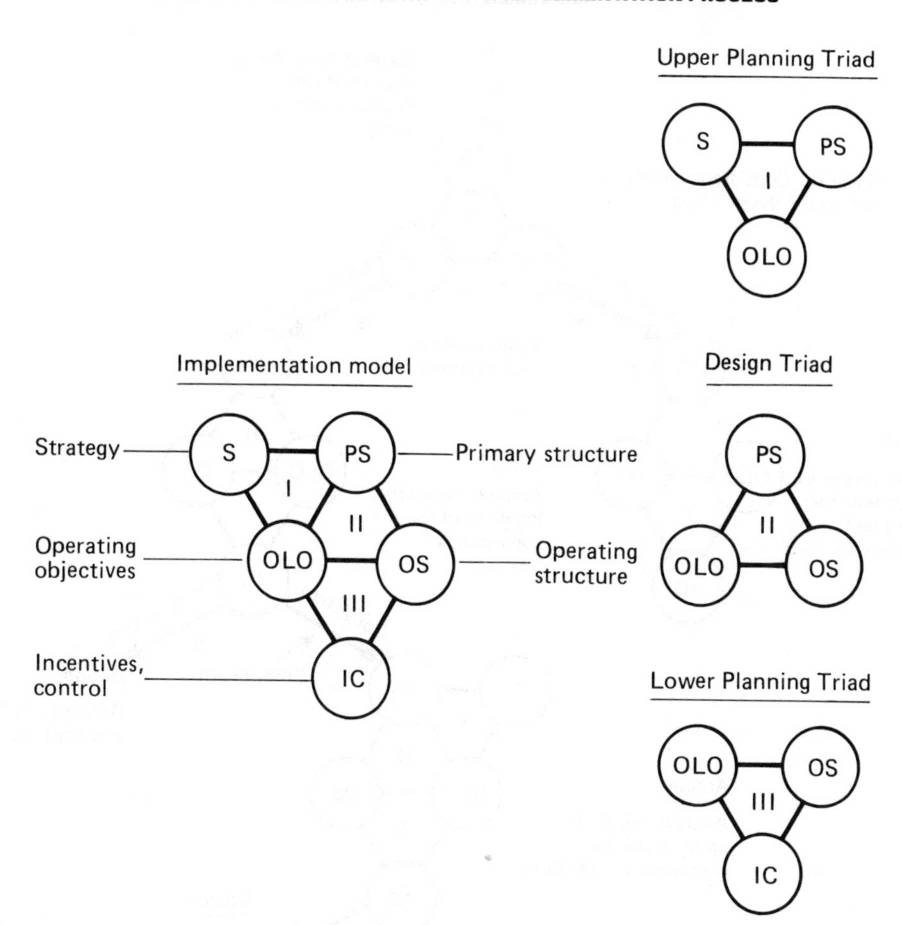

Figure 8-4. Implementation triads.

sions have implicitly focused on the consistency of the components constituting what we are presently calling implementation triads. Consequently, analysis of consistency should proceed in light of the insights or facts derived from previous discussions of the relationships among components of the implementation model.

This analysis will indicate which, if any, of the implementation components are inconsistent with one another and, consequently, where adjustment is required. What is needed is a rationale for determining explicitly how consistency impacts on the content of an implementation effort. Such a rationale is relatively straightforward, although there has been little previous discussion of this critical problem in the management literature.

Figure 8-5 illustrates one of the three possible triads for analysis, the design triad. We have chosen this one because it illustrates the most general case of

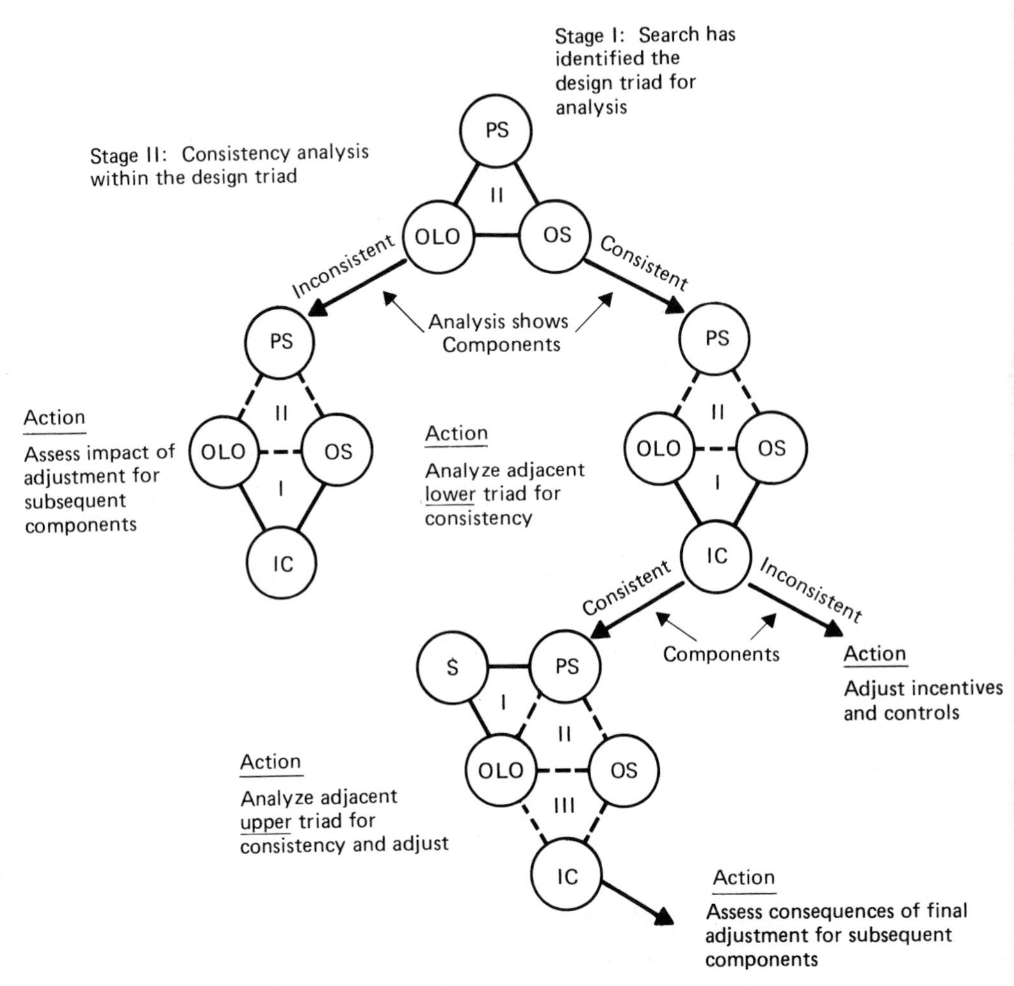

Figure 8-5. Stage III consistency analysis: expansion.

consistency analysis. In this hypothetical analysis, the uppermost two components of the triad, primary structure and operating objectives, are assumed to be correct, and the consistency of the operating structure is evaluated with respect to these two elements of the implementation triad. Both primary structure and operating objectives are treated as constants because they are components of the adjacent upper planning triad, which has been assumed to be consistent as a result of stage I analysis. Should this assumption be incorrect, it will be detected at a later point in the analysis. Correct initial localization of implementation search activity is therefore necessary to minimize the costs of search and analysis.

If an inconsistency is noted, it is brought into alignment in accordance with the theory developed in Chapters 2 through 7. This would occur, for example, if the operating structure were seen to be inadequate to support the information processing and decision-making requirements imposed by primary structure and complex operating objectives. As Chapter 6 indicated, under conditions of complexity brought about by high interdependence across projects or functions, a shortage of scarce resources, and a need to achieve synergy or cross-fertilization, a matrix operating structure may be appropriate. A redesign and introduction of the matrix would represent a change resulting from consistency analysis within the design triad.

If initial selection of the implementation triad were appropriate, consistency analysis would indicate which components of the triad required changing in order to implement strategy, as just shown. However, consistency analysis is sometimes indeterminate, requiring expansion of the search for implementation alternatives consistent with the principle of minimum intervention. Such expansion should occur as described in the next section.

Stage III: Expansion. Expansion of the analysis takes place for two reasons: first, to assess the consequences of a change in model components that is required by stage II analysis and, second, when stage II analysis indicates no inconsistency among components. Both cases of expansion take place in accordance with the principle of minimum intervention.

When analysis indicates that a component of the implementation triad being considered requires changing, it is possible that subsequent or lower components of the model will also then require adjustment to support such changes. In the example developed, if operating structure is changed to be consistent with operating-level objectives, it may then become necessary to alter reward systems as well. When change in a component of either the upper planning or design triad is required, *search and analysis should be expanded to assess the consequences of such changes for subsequent components of the implementation model.* Further adjustment may not be required; reward systems may be flexible enough to support the required changes in operating structure without substantial modification. Change, however, may be warranted to avoid dysfunctional motivational consequences such as those discussed in Chapter 7. The desirability of such change can only be assessed through further search and analysis activities.

The second case in which expansion of search and analysis is warranted occurs when all elements of the implementation triad being considered are consistent with one another. When this occurs, *search and analysis should be expanded to lower adjacent components of the implementation model, consistent with the principle of minimum intervention.* In our example, if all elements of the design triad are consistent with one another, search should first be concentrated on lower components of the implementation model, in this case, on incentives and controls. This amounts to focusing on the adjacent lower implementation triad for further analysis as required by the principle of minimum intervention.

When there are no lower adjacent components (the lower planning triad), or when analysis indicates that such components are consistent, then, and only then, should search be expanded to the next higher component adjacent to the initial implementation triad that was considered. This again amounts to expansion of the analysis to the adjacent implementation triad, but in this case to the higher one. This is the only type of expansion of search and analysis possible when the lower planning triad has been selected for initial search and evaluation. When inconsistency is encountered, the required adjustments should be made as in stage II, along with an assessment of the consequences of such changes for subsequent components of the model, as described.

Considerations of effectiveness and efficiency, consistency, and minimum intervention determine which implementation triads to focus on initially, when search and analysis activities should be expanded, and ultimately which components of the implementation model require adjustment. Such analysis determines the content of the implementation. One or several components may require adjustment leading to what we have called "small" or "large" implementations. The style or design of the implementation is determined by considering its size in the context of the time available to accomplish it, or the implementation horizon, as described briefly in Chapter 1. The next sections present a more complete discussion of the specific factors that determine the implementation horizon, completing the analysis of decisions determining the style of implementation. Following this, specific transition mechanisms and change-planning processes are presented, contingent upon the style or design of the implementation adopted.

Assessing the Implementation Horizon

In Chapter 1 we argued that the implementation horizon is determined as the response to the question, "If my organization stays as it is today, how long will it be in business?" Although useful, this simple idea must be expanded and refined to allow identification of managerial actions that impact on the implementation horizon. This will conclude our discussion of how styles of strategy implementation can be diagnosed and influenced. Decisions in the conduct of an implementation can then be indexed to these styles.

Figure 8-6 summarizes the factors that determine the implementation horizon. The model argues that variations in the nature of the business situation

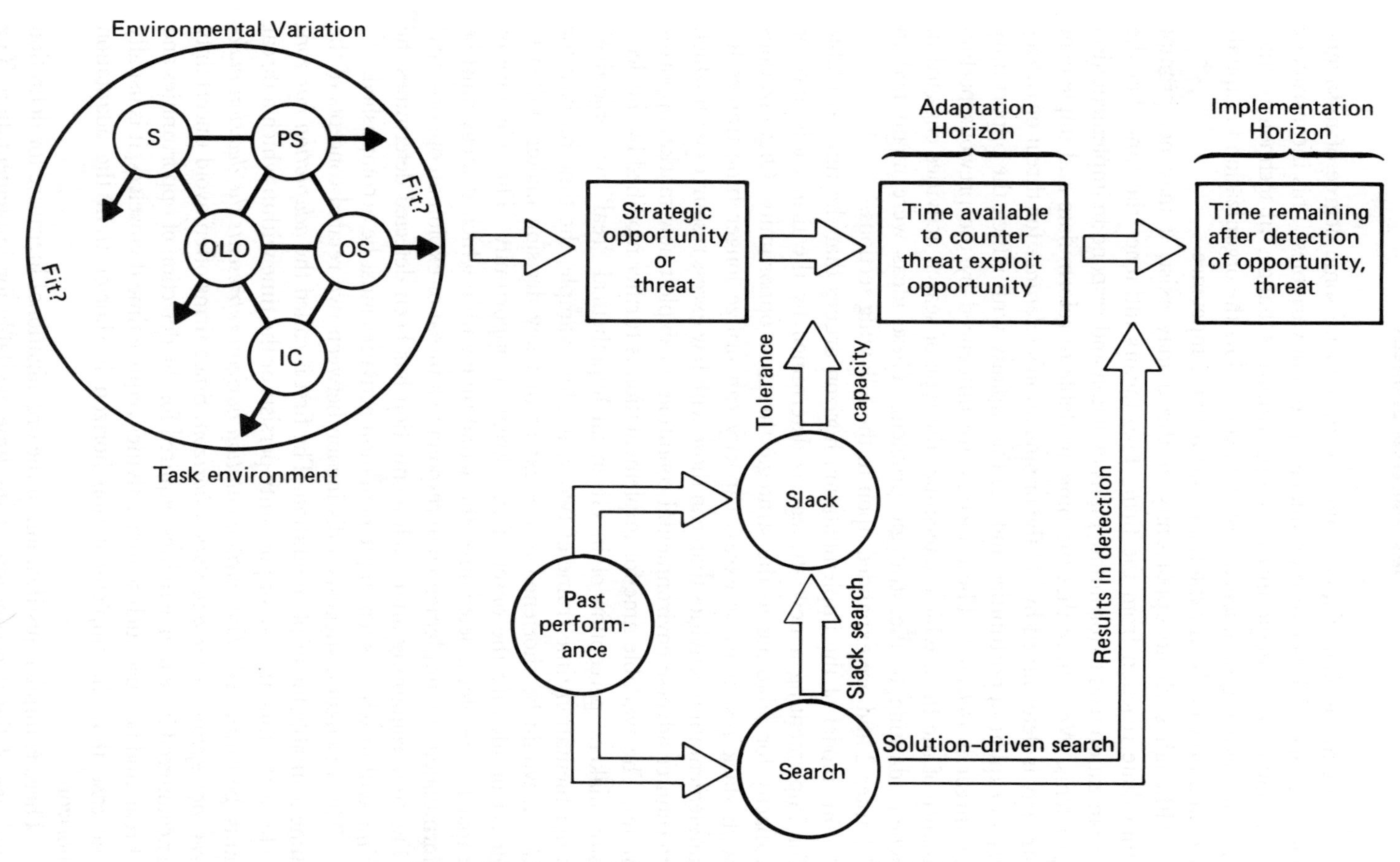

Figure 8-6. Factors influencing the implementation horizon.

or in organizational strategy and structure create some degree of misalignment or lack of fit between or among important variables. This inconsistency poses either a strategic threat or opportunity. Changes in technology may threaten existing products or, alternatively, allow the organization to capitalize on a previously unexploitable distinctive competence.

Although such an opportunity or threat may exist, it may not prompt immediate reaction from the firm. Two factors influence the time that the organization uses to formulate plans of action and respond to implementation problems. We believe that the time available to reformulate and implement strategy is determined by (1) the organization's *tolerance* for threat or *capacity* to exploit opportunities and (2) the rapidity with which the opportunity or threat is *detected.* These factors are influenced by the previous performance of the firm, which determines the type of search activities engaged in when adapting to the strategic problem. These ideas were mentioned in Chapter 2 and are expanded upon in the following sections.

Our model of the implementation horizon argues that the time available for implementing a new strategy is determined by the firm's tolerance or capacity for adapting to the strategic threat or opportunity. Organizations with slack resources or excess capacity can utilize longer time frames for implementation activities than can those with few excess resources with which to counter adverse environmental conditions or exploit new market opportunities. The available time for implementation is further modified by the decision makers' perception of it. Given an hypothetical "real" or "objective" implementation time frame of two years, for example, the time horizon for action would be shortened to the extent that key decision makers failed to detect or identify the onset of the threat or opportunity. The tolerance or capacity, therefore, determines the actual time within which strategy must be formulated and implemented to respond to a threat or exploit an opportunity. The time remaining after such a situation has been detected determines the time within which such implementation activities must be accomplished.

This discussion suggests a distinction between two related concepts of the time available for implementation. The first is called the *adaptation horizon.* This is the time that an opportunity persists or the time within which a threat must be countered. *The implementation horizon represents the decision makers' perception of the adaptation horizon.* Since firms often avoid uncertainty encountered in search activities required for the detection of opportunities and threat, and because such search activities require time themselves, it is usually the case that the implementation horizon is shorter than the adaptation horizon.

There is implicit justification in the organizational literature for definition and use of the two concepts of the time available for implementation. The literature summarized in Chapters 2 and 4 regarding the utilitarian benefits of planning suggest the two distinct time horizons. It is implied in this work, for example, that good planning increases the implementation horizon and allows the organization time to cope with external threats and exigencies before these problems can impact negatively on it. The implication is that the threats, problematic dependencies, or exigencies will surely be felt in some period of time (adaptation horizon) but that planning and environmental surveillance allow for the reduction of threat by increasing the available time for organizational adaptation or response (implementation horizon).

Recent work on the population ecology model provides additional support for the two separate time horizons.[4] This model discusses, among other things, environmental variations or changes that are important for organizations. Over time, critical variations call for or require certain types of organizational adaptation; inappropriate adaptations may result in an organization being "selected out" by the environment. That is, the organization has a finite period of time within which to adapt and develop characteristics that the external environment deems crucial to selection and survival. Organizations that implement appropriate changes within the requisite time frame for adaptation survive; they represent the "fittest" organizations, given environmental variations or demands and an implementation horizon sufficient for required changes.

It is clear from these and other examples that (1) different adaptation and implementation horizons can exist simultaneously for any given organization and (2) the time horizons can be relatively long or short. The former point reflects the fact that the organization faces many different types of threats or dependencies and that it is judged against different measures of performance or effectiveness by various groups or stakeholders. The latter point is related to the importance, primacy, and nature of the demands for adaptation, as the following discussions indicate.

Organizational Performance and the Implementation Horizon

The organization's capacity to tolerate threat and exploit opportunities and the responsiveness with which it detects the onset of such conditions determine the implementation horizon. Both tolerance and capacity and detection are influenced by the firm's previous performance through the types of search activity that are employed.

March[5] has argued that because of the limited information-processing or decision-making capacity of managers, it is impossible for them to have a knowledge of all alternatives, the consequences of such alternatives, and an unambiguous and consistent method for choosing among them. As applied to strategy implementation, this idea of bounded rationality implies that decision makers only have partial knowledge of strategic threats and opportunities and are subjected to conflicting beliefs about objectives and means-end relationships when responding to them (see Chapter 2). In such a situation, managers act consistently with what March calls intended rationality, a concept that we have used to organize the strategy implementation model developed in this book. March[6] points out that "the intelligence of organizational action is seen, not in the capability to know everything in advance, but in the availability to make marginal improvements by monitoring problems and searching for solutions. Thus, theories of limited rationality are *essentially theories of search* or attention." Such search activities directly impact the firm's tolerance and capacity for adaptation as well as on its detection of the need for such adaptation.

March has suggested that the performance of the firm influences the nature of its search activities. When performance is inadequate, firms pursue *solution-driven search*. March notes that "organizations do search for new alternatives in the face of adversity. They discover more efficient refinements in technology; they economize." Such search activities consume slack resources and, thus, reduce the firm's tolerance and capacity for adaptation. However, they also can be expected to shorten the time required for the detection of the need for such adaptation, as shown in Figure 8-7.

When the organization is performing well in relation to its goals, the type of search activity is referred to as *slack search* (see Chapter 2). "Under conditions of success . . . search occurs as part of the slack activities of the organization."[7] Such search contributes to the *slack reservoir* of ideas. The existence of such a reservoir increases the firm's tolerance and capacity for adaptation as shown in Figure 8-7 because "an organization is able to meet brief periods of decline by drawing on discoveries and innovations generated but overlooked during better times."[8] At the same time, however, the successful firm is *less* likely to detect an opportunity or threat early because the effects of success encourage slack search rather than solution-driven search, which is more closely linked to organizational goals.

The interesting point is that organizational performance tends to produce search effects that offset one another somewhat in their impact on the implementation horizon. Successful performance lengthens what we have called the adaptation horizon by leading to search activities that increase the slack reservoir of ideas; however, it may also lead to later detection of the need for adaptation because solution-driven search activities are slighted. The opposite occurs when performance has been poor: a lower tolerance and capacity for

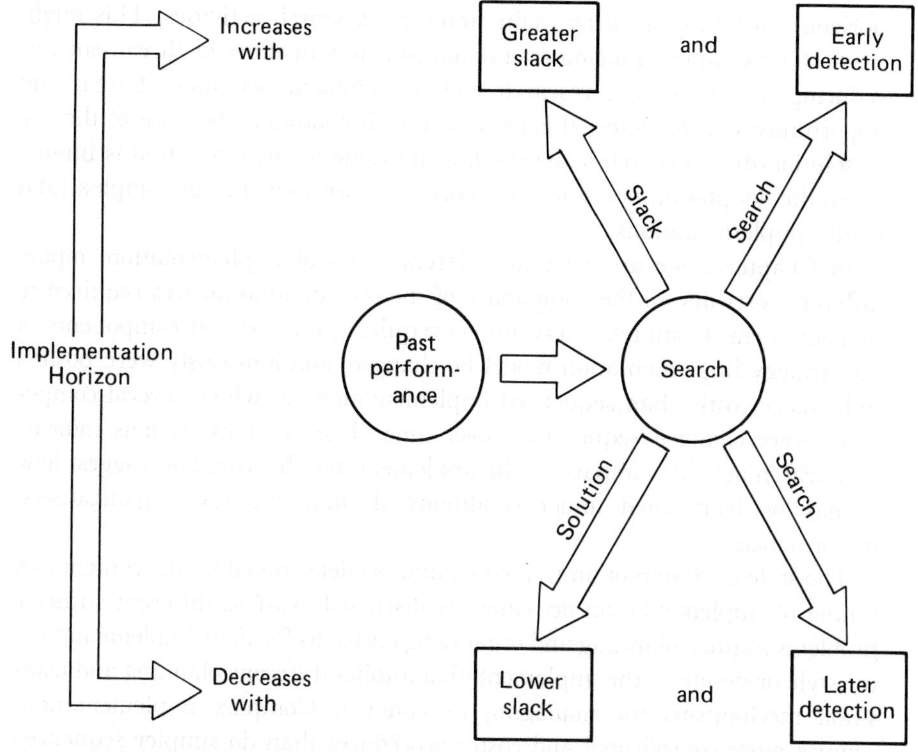

Figure 8-7. The effects of organizational performance on search activities impacting the implementation horizon.

adaptation exists, but the time available for such adaptation is maximized by detection through solution-driven search activities.

Consideration of these conditions suggest that the implementation horizon may be extended by concentrating on different search activities, depending upon the performance of the firm. High-performing firms can increase the implementation horizon through earlier detection of opportunity and threat. Cyert and March[9] noted that slack resources are used only grudgingly and that, in the face of uncertainty, firms typically react rather than forecast. The model presented here argues that such tendencies must be countered by explicit attempts to forecast and anticipate the onset of strategic threat and opportunity through solution-driven search activities. Such activities will complement existing slack search to make the largest portion of the adaptation horizon available for implementation activities.

Similar prescriptions can be offered for the firm that has not been performing well. Our model suggests that, in times of adversity, the implementation horizon can be extended by maintaining slack search activities. This might mean, for example, ignoring traditional practices in times of threat, such as reducing or eliminating research and development activities. Threat and opportunity will be detected early under such conditions because of the use of solution-driven search activities, but the value of such detection is limited when the adaptation horizon is so short as to preclude all but complex (and costly) implementations.

In Chapter 1 we argued that different styles of implementation impose different costs due to the complexity of the coordination devices required to manage them. Complex interventions requiring that several components of the strategy implementation model be changed simultaneously were posited to be more costly than sequenced implementations in which several components were changed sequentially over time. The previous sections indicate how search activities impact on the implementation horizon and suggest how it may be lengthened under conditions of high and low organizational performance.

The style or design of an implementation is determined by the content and timing of implementation activities, as discussed. Just as different strategic problems require planning and organizing decisions for their implementation, the style or design of the implementation implies different planning and transition mechanisms for managing its conduct. Complex implementations require more complicated and costly procedures than do simpler sequenced or managerial implementations. The following sections indicate change processes and transition mechanisms required for the conduct of each of the four major styles of implementation.

THE CONDUCT OF IMPLEMENTATION: TRANSITION MECHANISMS AND CHANGE-PLANNING PROCESSES

Beckhard and Harris[10] have argued that in any significant organizational change there are three states of the organization that must be accommodated. These are (1) the organization as it existed prior to the change, (2) the organization as it will exist following the change, and (3) the transition state that exists as the firm moves from condition 1 (the old organization) to condition 2 (the new organization). This transition state exists as the firm implements strategy and requires planning and organizing decisions for its management, just as the more stable pre- and postimplementation organizations do. The following sections outline the primary planning activities and transition mechanisms necessary for the successful implementation of strategy. As the style of implementation becomes more complex, more sophisticated and costly planning processes and transition mechanisms are required. The section concludes by suggesting specific planning activities and structural mechanisms for each of the primary styles of implementation.

Planning Processes and Transition Mechanisms for Implementing Strategy

Planning Processes. The procedures discussed in earlier parts of this chapter for determining the content and timing of implementation activities and, thus, the style or design of implementation, constitute the essential elements of change-planning activities. The outcome of these processes specifies what will be changed, how, and in what order, to achieve the strategic objectives of the firm. However, further planning actions are necessary to produce the following two outcomes: (1) a formal, written, *implementation plan* and (2) *a communication plan* for (a) informing those affected by the proposed implementation about the contents of the implementation plan and for (b) soliciting participation in the refinement of the plan.

The implementation plan represents a formal written statement that outlines the objectives of the implementation, the changes in the strategy implementation model required to obtain these objectives, and the time frame within which such changes are expected to be accomplished. These decisions are made in accordance with the theory of strategy implementation developed in this book, but they must be formalized so that the intent, content, and timing of the implementation will not be distorted during communication.

The construction of the implementation plan represents more than the simple codification of previous decisions concerning the design of the implementation. It represents an attempt to convey the essential character of the implementation, its rationale, and the commitment of those instituting the change. At the same time, the implementation plan invites the participation of those affected by the changes without creating unrealistic expectations concerning the extent to which they can impact the change or the time frame within which implementation activities will be complete.

These considerations imply a delicate balance between unilateral and participative elements of the implementation and the generality and specificity of the implementation plan. Most research clearly indicates that participation is an important element of successful large-scale organization change. This partially reflects the bounded rationality of managers who cannot possibly foresee all the implications of decisions made in implementing strategy and who, therefore, must encounter unintended, and potentially dysfunctional, consequences. Participation becomes essential in "multiplying" the limited information processing abilities of strategic planners and top managers so as to anticipate and accommodate the possibility of such consequences.

The implementation plan, therefore, must invite participation of a special kind. It must not create the unrealistic and inappropriate expectation that the fundamental design of the implementation can be substantially altered or avoided; rather, it should solicit local refinement of implementation activities and methods, accommodating the critical specialized knowledge of affected groups of workers. The implementation plan thus specifies the style or design of the implementation, but it invites participation concerning the specifics of the change as applied to individuals, jobs, and local work procedures.

The communication plan indicates the individuals who should receive information concerning the implementation. Those involved in an implementation can be categorized roughly into two groups: (1) individuals *directly affected* by the change and (2) individuals *indirectly affected* because they must support or work with those directly affected by the implementation. A change in operating structure, for example, may result in individuals being grouped differently, reporting to different managers, and subjected to new work procedures (directly affected). Others may simply interface with workers from affected areas and may experience only minor effects due to the change (indirectly affected).

Individuals who are directly affected by the implementation should be communicated with on a face-to-face basis, usually in a private meeting with their supervisor. In the meeting, the implementation plan is used to focus the discussion and ensure that a common message is being delivered to all employees. Communication flows from top down within the affected areas of the organization, as shown in Figure 8-8. Top managers communicate with subordinates, who talk to workers reporting to them, and so on, until all directly affected workers have been informed of the content of the implementation plan and have had an opportunity to participate in the local design and application of the plan.

Such a procedure is costly and time consuming and is, therefore, justified only for those directly affected by the change. Individuals indirectly involved in the implementation can be informed using more cost-effective procedures, such as company memoranda, mass meetings, and company newspapers. The final communication plan specifies the targets of communication, the organization of the communication process, and the media of communication for workers who are both directly and indirectly involved in the implementation.

Transition Mechanisms for Implementing Strategy. Because the transition state differs from either the prior organization or the intended new

Content		
Who should be communicated with	Directly Affected	Indirectly Affected
Organization of the communication process	"Cascading" top to bottom 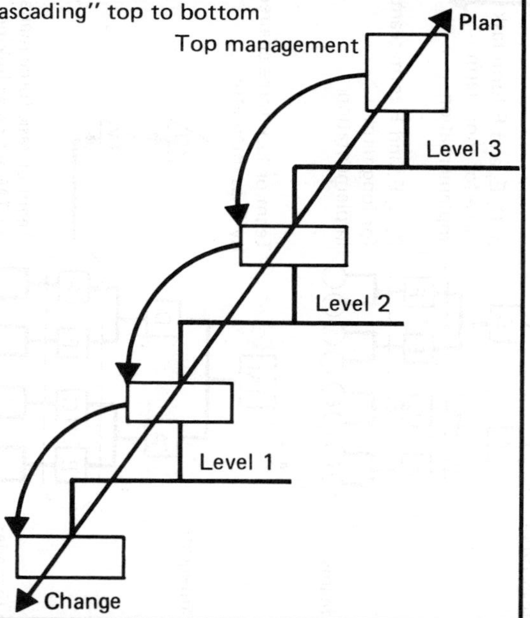 Top management Plan Level 3 Level 2 Level 1 Change	Concurrent "all at once" 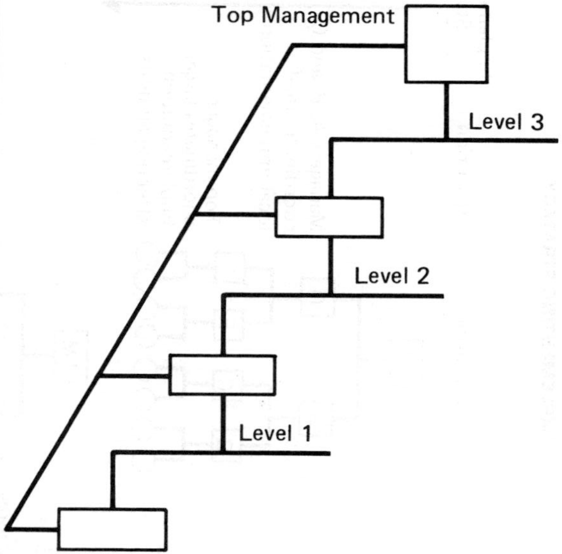 Top Management Level 3 Level 2 Level 1
Medium	Face to face with focus on implementation plan	Mass: Memoranda, company news, group meetings
Quality	Participation concerning local implementation	Informational

Figure 8-8. Communication planning.

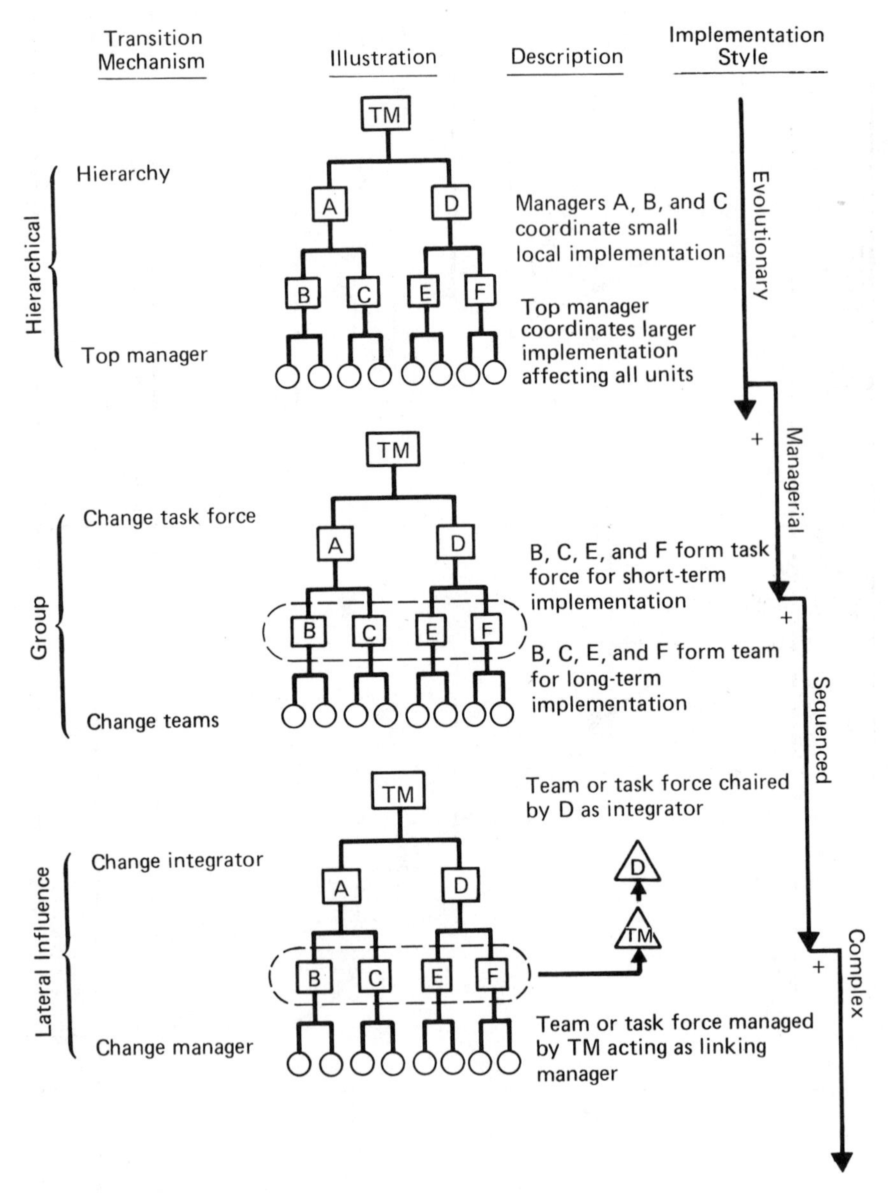

Figure 8-9. Transition mechanisms and implementation styles.

form, transition structures or mechanisms must be designed to manage the firm during the implementation process. Beckhard and Harris[11] argue that "the transition is facilitated in most cases by having a management system for the transition state that is separate, or at least *uniquely identified,* from either the present state of operations or the future state of affairs."

A hierarchy of transition mechanisms can be identified (Figure 8-9). We distinguish among hierarchical, group, and lateral influence varieties of transition mechanism in a manner similar to distinctions made in Chapter 6 between different strategies of lateral relations. As the complexity of the implementation increases (as we move from simple evolutionary styles to complex implementations), more sophisticated mechanisms are necessary to provide the decision-making capacity required to manage the implementation process.

The first two mechanisms, hierarchy and top managers, use the existing organization to manage the transition. Managers take on implementation-related activities in addition to their existing responsibilities. At some point, the top manager assumes primary responsibility for the implementation, delegating responsibility for other normal activities to subordinates.

Just as complex, uncertain, and interdependent tasks pose information processing burdens necessitating group forms of lateral relations, so do the demands of more complex implementation activities. *Change task forces* and *change teams* are established to manage such implementations.

For large implementations involving several components of the implementation model, formal influence may be assigned to managers who chair teams and task forces. Two approaches are possible: use of (1) a *change integrator* who influences the process of implementation or (2) a *change manager* who has formal authority to make choices regarding the content of change when the team is unable to reach agreement. Generally, this person is either the top manager of the firm or a suitable high-ranking alternate.

Choices of change-planning processes and transition mechanisms depend upon the style of the implementation. The conduct of an implementation follows from its design. The next sections relate change-planning activities and transition mechanisms to the four primary styles of strategy implementation.

Relating Planning and Transition Mechanisms Decisions to the Style of Implementation

In Chapter 1 the primary styles of implementation were presented and were distinguished partially in terms of the components of the basic implementation model that were explicitly accounted for in designing the change. *Evolutionary* styles are styles in which changes in components of the model were so slight as to obviate the need for formal planning processes. *Managerial* implementations involve only one component of the model, but since time is of the essence in implementing strategy, formal planning within the affected component is necessary. *Sequenced* implementations by definition involve more than one of the basic model components; formal planning both within and between these components is necessary. Finally, *complex* implementations require that several components of the model be changed concurrently. This necessitates coordination by mutual adjustment and effective management of conflict because planning alone is insufficient to provide the requisite integration. The complexity of change-management activities (change-planning processes and transition mechanisms), therefore, increases as we move from evolutionary to complex implementation. The following sections relate specific choices of implementation plans, communication plans, and transition mechanisms to the major styles of implementation as a function of this increasing complexity.

Evolutionary Implementations. Evolutionary implementations are by definition unplanned implementations. Consequently, formal implementation and communication plans are not developed. The transition mechanism in this case is the implicit use of the formal hierarchy of the organization. Individuals attempt local improvements of organizational practices and procedures without relating such activities tightly to organizational objectives. Formal change objectives do not exist. Evolutionary implementations include some elements or aspects that are related to the idea of slack decisions. March[12] notes that "under conditions of plenty, organizational decisions become more decentralized, more diffuse, less tightly linked to a coordinated organizational strategy." Consequences include the accumulation of local improvements in functioning and the occasional discovery of something of considerable value.

A related possibility concerns what is sometimes termed the "tyranny of small errors." This results when search and decisions over time result in a cumulative course of action that amplifies a misfit between elements of the strategy implementation model with consequent deleterious effects on performance. This possibility also occurs when the well-intended actions of managers result in local improvements in practices and procedures, but which, overall, make the firm more efficient in doing the wrong things. The "tyranny of small errors" is most likely to be found in strategy implementation when the need for a more complex implementation is not detected and adaptation takes place through inappropriate evolutionary adjustment.

Managerial Implementations. Managerial implementations involve only one component of the implementation model. Following the principle of minimum intervention, this implies that most managerial implementations will involve adjustments in incentive and control systems. Other varieties are possible, when previous errors in implementation have been made and require only local correction, as when adjacent components of an affected planning or design triad are sufficiently flexible to accommodate change without further adjustment.

Change-planning processes are required to prepare an implementation and communication plan similar in form and content to those just described. Transition mechanisms are also required for small managerial implementations. In this case the appropriate mechanism is the hierarchy—the managers of affected groups and possibly the top manager of the firm. Larger problems may require the use of a change task force. Such problems would involve larger number of personnel, affect a greater variety of job-related behaviors, or require significant alterations of existing work behavior. A change task force is appropriate to manage the decision making imposed by such complexity. A change team would not be constituted due to the relatively short implementation horizon involved. General rules for the selection of task force members would apply, with the following modifications:[13]

1. Use of primary-line managers to constitute the team.
2. Use of an external consultant selected on the basis of his or her expertise in managing the change process.
3. Use of an internal consultant selected on the basis of his or her expertise in the functioning of the firm.
4. Appropriate representatives of staff groups such as personnel, human resources, or information services.

Sequenced Implementation. A sequenced implementation can be viewed as a *coordinated, overlapping succession of managerial implementations.* Consequently, change-planning activities are sequenced as well. The implementation plan should outline the series of changes anticipated and the relationships among them and be supported by more specific plans developed to implement the *within-component* aspects of the implementation. A hierarchy of implementation plans exists, with (1) the primary implementation plan specifying the required sequence and consistency of changes in the basic implementation model and (2) each of these changes being further elaborated and supported by a specific within-component implementation plan. Communication takes place using a series of efforts directed toward the current aspect of the implementation being addressed. Implementation and communication planning, therefore, would represent a concatenated series of smaller planning efforts that within the available implementation horizon culminate in the desired sequenced implementation.

Because planning is required *between* components of the model as well as within them, and because a sequenced implementation occurs over a long time span (often several years), different transition mechanisms are required to manage them. A transition team is required with flexible membership. A small core of managers may be assigned full time to the team, with other members coming and going as the team manages different aspects of the sequence of implementation activities. The same rules for the selection of team members apply as in the selection of transition task forces with the exception that, as the implementation includes more elements of the upper planning and design implementation triads, expertise in strategic management becomes a more important criterion for the selection of outside consultants. A team member may also be designated to help manage the interdependence between key implementation activities and ensure continuity and consistency of effort across sequenced implementations. This individual, thus, also functions as a change integrator. An internal consultant can often fulfill this role well.

Complex Implementations. Complex implementations occur when two or more of the basic elements of the strategy implementation model require adjustment and the implementation horizon is so short as to preclude the possibility of sequencing the required changes. *Everything must be changed at once, and everything depends upon everything else.* Under such conditions, the benefits of change-planning activities are significantly curtailed; when the implementation horizon becomes extremely short, a situation of crisis management exists, and coordination of implementation activities is accomplished using mutual adjustment.

In less extreme situations, change planning can proceed but requires new transition mechanisms. In the case of sequenced implementations, a primary plan is developed along with supporting within-element implementation plans. Unlike the sequenced style, however, complex implementations require that all within-element plans be prepared *at once* rather than sequentially. To accomplish this, a series of transition task forces is constituted, one for each of the implementation elements being changed and each headed by a transition manager with discretion to determine the control of that aspect of the implementation. These transition managers comprise a transition team that would direct the management of the complex implementation as well as elaborate the primary implementation plan.

Occasionally, even such a sophisticated transition mechanism is inadequate to provide the requisite information processing to manage a complex implementation. In such extreme cases, what Thompson[14] called "synthetic organization" emerges to accomplish critical implementation activities. Resources are disengaged from their normal uses and are dedicated to the implementation, and information begins to circulate concerning the need for such resources. "When knowledge of need and resources coincide at a point in space, the *headquarters* of the synthetic organization has been established. . . . Only occasionally does this power fall to previously designated officers; rather authority to coordinate the use of resources is attributed to—forced upon—the individual or group which by happenstance is at the crossroads of the two kinds of necessary information, resource availability and need." Thompson further suggests that what distinguishes this type of organization from normal organizations is significant consensus about objectives and great freedom to utilize resources as necessary.

The implementation situation can therefore be characterized as one in which problems are looking for solutions and solutions are looking for problems, or what March and Olsen called the "garbage can model of decision making."[15] When solutions in the form of uncommitted resources coincide with the need for such resources, an ad hoc command structure emerges to accomplish the implementation task.

Little is known about the management of synthetic organization, but two general managerial actions are important to ensure that they develop quickly and are as effective as possible. First, information concerning change objectives and activities, as well as available resources, must be circulated as quickly as possible to ensure the emergence of the "headquarters" of change; second, the objectives of the implementation must be communicated as quickly as possible to facilitate obtaining consensus around such objectives. Consensus about implementation objectives serves to mobilize action and acts as a powerful tool for conflict resolution. When such consensus exists in the form of a superordinate goal, disagreements about alternative courses of action can often be resolved by appealing to such objectives.

Synthetic organizations are instrumentally rational; they accomplish what they set out to accomplish. However, they are extremely costly because resources are not employed efficiently and often are used in conflicting ways. Thompson suggests that this occurs because "Under conditions of great uncertainty, it [the organization] must learn the nature and extent of the overall problem [and] *At the same time it must assemble and interrelate the components*" (emphasis added). As we progress from simple evolutionary implementations to more difficult complex implementations, the costs of changing increase significantly.

Summary

The conduct of implementation activities depends upon the design or style of implementation. This design results from the interaction of the two basic parameters of implementation: the content or size of the change and the time available to accomplish implementation activities.

Consistency analysis is used to determine the content of implementation activities. This process contains three stages termed initial search (stage I), actual consistency analysis (stage II), and expansion (stage III). The purpose of initial search is to identify for further analysis the appropriate subset of implementation activities or, what we have termed, the proper implementation triad. Consistency analysis employs the material developed in Chapters 1 through 7 of this book to determine the extent to which the implementation activities or variables within the triads support or are consistent with one another. Expansion of search occurs when consistency analysis reveals no major problems within the chosen implementation triad or when changes in a triad can be expected to affect other implementation activities. The result of these stages of analysis is an adequate definition of the content of the implementation effort.

The time available to implement strategy is the implementation horizon, which is defined as decision makers' perceptions of the time that an opportunity will persist or within which a threat must be countered. The implementation horizon is influenced by the firm's previous performance through the nature of search activities undertaken. Good performance lengthens the adaptation horizon by positively affecting slack search and the slack reservoir of ideas, but it can also result in a shorter implementation horizon because solution-driven search is less salient. When performance is poor, in contrast, the perceived time for implementation is maximized by early detection resulting from solution-driven search activities.

Depending upon the content and timing of implementation activities, four styles or designs of implementation result that require more managerial attention as we move from simple evolutionary styles, through managerial and sequenced styles, to more difficult complex interventions. Particular change-planning processes and transition mechanisms are appropriate for each of the distinct styles of implementation. The latter parts of this chapter paid detailed attention to the planning processes and communication mechanisms needed when the intervention or style of implementation is evolutionary, managerial, sequenced, or complex.

Notes

1. D. C. Dearborn and H. A. Simon, "Selective Perception: A Note on the Departmental Identification of Executives," *Sociometry,* 21:140–144 (1958).
2. Talcott Parsons, *The Structure of Social Action* (New York: The Free Press, 1946).

3. C. Hofer and Daniel Schendel, *Strategy Formulation: Analytical Concepts* (St. Paul: West Publishing Company, 1978).
4. M. T. Hannan and J. Freeman, "Obstacles to Comparative Studies," in P. S. Goodman, J. M. Pennings, and associates, eds., *New Perspectives on Organizational Effectiveness* (San Francisco: Jossey-Bass, 1977).
5. James G. March, "Decisions in Organizations and Theories of Choice," in Andrew H. Van de Ven and William F. Joyce, eds., *Perspectives on Organizational Design and Behavior* (New York: Wiley-Interscience, 1981), p. 212.
6. Ibid, p. 212
7. Ibid, p. 214
8. Ibid, p. 214
9. R. M. Cyert and J. G. March, *A Behavioral Theory of the Firm* (Englewood Cliffs, N.J.: Prentice-Hall, Inc., 1963).
10. Richard Beckhard and Reuben Harris, *Organizational Transitions* (Reading, Mass.: Addison-Wesley Publishing Company, 1977).
11. Ibid, p. 49
12. March, "Decisions in Organizations and Theories of Choice," in *Perspectives on Organizational Design and Behavior*. p. 214
13. Jerome Franklin, "Characteristics of Successful and Unsuccessful Organization Development." *Journal of Applied Behavioral Science,* 12:471–491 (1977).
14. James D. Thompson, *Organizations in Action* (New York: McGraw-Hill Book Company, 1967), p. 52.
15. J. G. March and J. Olsen, *Ambiguity and Choice in Organizations* (Oslow: Universitetsforlaget, 1976).
16. James D. Thompson, *Organizations in Action* (New York: McGraw-Hill Book Company, 1967). p. 53

INDEX